Religious Imagination and the Body

Religious Imagination and the Body

A Feminist Analysis

PAULA M. COOEY

New York   Oxford
OXFORD UNIVERSITY PRESS
1994

Oxford University Press

Oxford   New York   Toronto
Delhi   Bombay   Calcutta   Madras   Karachi
Kuala Lumpur   Singapore   Hong Kong   Toyko
Nairobi   Dar es Salaam   Cape Town
Melbourne   Auckland   Madrid

and associated companies in
Berlin   Ibadan

Published by Oxford University Press, Inc.
200 Madison Avenue, New York, New York 10016

Oxford is a registered trademark of Oxford University Press, Inc.

Library of Congress Cataloging-in-Publication Data
Cooey, Paula M., 1945–
Religious imagination and the body : a feminist analysis / Paula M. Cooey.
p. cm.   Includes bibliographical references and indexes.
ISBN 0–19–508735–6
1. Body, Human—Religious aspects.
2. Imagination—Religious aspects.
3. Woman (Theology).
4. Feminist theory.
5. Partnoy, Alicia, 1955–
6. Morrison, Toni.
7. Kahlo, Frida.
8. Philosophical theology.
I. Title.
BL604.B64C66   1994   291.2'2—dc20   93–30807

9 8 7 6 5 4 3 2 1

Printed in the United States of America
on acid-free paper

For Philip C. Nichols, Jr.

Preface

This book is a work of philosophical theology. In the preface to *Religion within the Limits of Reason Alone* Immanuel Kant coined the phrase "philosophical theology," which he proposed as a science directly related to what he called "biblical theology." He defined the concerns of biblical theologians as the care of the soul, the establishment of right teaching (therefore, censorship), and, if the theologians were scholars as well as clergy, the prevention of theological interference in the cultivation of the other sciences (self-critique). Although a philosophical theologian might draw upon some of the same materials available to the biblical theologian, the distinguishing purpose of philosophical theology was critical, constructive, and theoretical rather than doctrinal, and the chief criterion of accountability, human reason, rather than ecclesial or biblical authority. The philosophical theologian thus had responsibility for rendering such concerns for the care of the soul, right doctrine, and theological self-critique accountable to reason. Exploring theoretical assumptions within limits set by reason meant for Kant focusing especially on theological assumptions about the relation between human nature and religion. He even recommended further that academic instruction in biblical theology be concluded each term with a series of lectures on what he called a "purely *philosophical* theory of religion."[1] Kant submitted the second section or "book" of *Religion within the Limits*, his treatment of good and evil as conflicting principles within human nature, in 1792. This critical analysis was ironically denied permission for publication by the state's theological censors on the grounds that it controverted biblical teaching. Nevertheless, the volume in its entirety was finally published in 1793, though the controversy over Kant's right as a scholar (rather than a cleric) to publish the work continued beyond its publication.

Two hundred years later, we have lost much of the anti-establishment and democratizing power of reason. Reason, far more narrowly and less morally defined than Kant would have intended, has itself taken on connotations of the censorial. Reason in the Western present, not unlike revelation in the Western past, has become a domain of elite interpreters, now primarily academicians, whose knowledge is so specialized and esoteric that intelligent lay people have little or no access to knowledge. Defined even more narrowly in a positivistic, scientific context as technological ratiocination (again in striking contrast to Kant's view), and abstracted from any historical context, the exercise of reason has often masked authoritarian ideological concerns, such that one necessarily comes to regard appeals to reason as suspicious and to view the authority vested in both reason and science as troubling and problematic.

Healthy suspicion and skepticism notwithstanding, if one is honest, these very qualities themselves depend upon the ability to analyze critically and to articulate publicly to another, in short the ability to reason. Reason, historicized and understood more generously, is not only potentially available to almost everyone; it is indispensable to historical agency, however socially constructed, just as it is necessary to change for the better—both individual and social betterment. Though Kant's own assumptions are now as subject to questioning as those he challenged, his point was, among other objectives, to legitimate questioning as a supreme value in its own right and as an empowering activity.

In a context of questioning, the phrase "philosophical theology" continues to be a useful way to describe analysis and critique of systematic and dogmatic theology in regard to their underlying presuppositions concerning the relation between religious phenomena and behavior, on the one hand, and what it means to be human, on the other hand. Furthermore, in this post-modern era, critical analysis extends to the underlying assumptions involved in the development of theories of religion as well. And most importantly, because philosophical theology addresses a relation between religion and the human, what it means to be human itself, particularly the significance of gender, is subject to scrutiny. In short, nothing escapes critical analysis, or what is now more fashionably called deconstruction. Philosophical theology, understood to include all these tasks, thus becomes cultural critique and construction. It remains philosophical *theology*, nevertheless, insofar as it reflects an approach to culture in general and religious symbol systems in particular centered by theological concerns. In contrast to the relation between doctrinal theology and its theological author, philosophical theology does not depend for its validity upon whether the philosophical theologian, or more recently, thealogian, is theistic or atheistic, idealist or materialist, part of a religious community or solely an academic scholar (still a member of a community).[2] On the contrary, the task of the philosophical theologian partly depends on challenging these very dualisms and their conceptual content, to begin with.

This book is a work of philosophical theology as I have defined it here. As such, it is concerned with various presuppositions of religious symbol systems, religious beliefs, and narratives of transformational experience. I focus not only upon the authority with which we invest beliefs and experience, but also upon the theoretical assumptions held by theologians, thealogians, artists, and scholars concerning what constitutes experiencing human selves, the worlds in which they live, and the deities they worship (though less attention is given explicitly to deities). What distinguishes this book from other books to date that share similar concerns lies in my approach to these issues. Taking my cues from Elaine Scarry, who writes in a different academic field, I approach these issues by raising over and over again the question of the relation between religious imagination and the body, most especially, though not exclusively, the "gendered" female body.[3] This approach has been fruitful in my opinion not so much in terms of finding definitive answers, as in clarifying and re-casting old questions and forcing new ones.

Ambitious as the scope of this project and its approach may seem, I have nevertheless limited myself to public (or quasi-public), explicitly religious contexts. I deal with a range of experience, defined at one end of the spectrum by narrative and visual imagery, expressed in religious symbolism, testifying to physical suffering and political violence, and by narrative positively describing spiritual transformation in explicitly thealogical and theological terms, at the other end. Though I allude to other forms of pain and violence briefly, I do not explicitly address their significance insofar as they may occur in religious contexts. Scarry herself has done an excellent treatment of the ritual substantiation of reality through the male human body in contexts of war and torture. In addition, though there are scholars in religious studies who may disagree with Mary Daly's approach and conclusions, I consider her work on religious sadomasochism as it affects women's bodies to be ground breaking.[4] Yet neither these two works nor mine addresses one of the most violent arenas of human life in this country, an arena often shrouded in religious mystification, the family home. At least as dangerous to women, children, and sometimes men as the battlefield, the concentration camp, and the streets, violence in the family home, by virtue of the complexity of relations among family members, differs significantly from other forms of violence. Given the legal and religious distinctions we make between the public and private realms, how kinship is established through blood lines, and what we consider normative relations of love among family members, such phenomena as incest and physical assault force a different consideration of power, different from power in the public realm. These differences in context and form may produce significant differences in the relations between imagination and the body. One difference lies, I think, in the horrible ambiguity of what Toni Morrison in *The Bluest Eye* calls "bad love."[5]

In addition to this omission, I have also not explicitly addressed the interrelations among human religious imagination, human sentience, and a wider ecological context. Clearly the epistemology I am here proposing has fruitful implications for an ecologically focused philosophical theology. Nevertheless, this task remains for the future.

I bring these omissions to the reader's attention simply to clarify the limitations of this work.

I wrote this book, the research for which was begun in 1987, in the context of a small liberal arts institution, rather than a seminary or a research institution. There are some very important advantages to working in such an environment, worth noting at this time. First of all I am grateful to Trinity University for granting me two academic leaves of one semester each, respectively, the spring of 1988 and the fall of 1992. I am further grateful to William O. Walker, Jr., dean of Humanities and the Arts, and Francisco O. Garcia-Treto, chair of the Department of Religion, for funding travel to Mexico City to study firsthand many of Frida Kahlo's paintings, as well as her home in Coyacán, filled with *retablos* and other Mexican religious artifacts. In addition, three people from the Department of Religion staff merit special mention: John Mendoza, one of our majors and work-study assistants who motivated me to begin learning Spanish, proofread early drafts of the first four chapters, and did bibliographical research for me; Andrea Kanten, also a major and work-study assistant, who diligently and carefully proofread and checked all quotations and citations, and who claims to have saved me much embarrassment; and Margaret Miksch, one of the secretaries to the department, who typed the bibliography and proofread the manuscript in its entirety. Chris Nolan, assistant professor appointed as liaison to the Department of Religion in the Elizabeth Coates Maddux Library, also provided bibliographical assistance.

I am most grateful for the extraordinary resources afforded me by easy access on a daily basis to a small, excellent faculty in a variety of relevant disciplines, including my own. Dean Walker, Frank Garcia, Doug Brackenridge, and Randy Nadeau, all members of my department, as well as John Martin from the History Department (though more or less adopted by my department), read and commented on various stages of my initial proposal. Also from my department, Mary Ellen Ross read and commented on Chapter 5, and Mackenzie Brown read and commented on the last chapter. Mackenzie determinedly overcame my stubborn antipathy to word processing and painstakingly taught me XYWRITE during weekly sessions for a semester. I also appreciate several walks taken with him, along the Trinity jogging track, during which we argued, in the best sense of the word, opposing positions on the epistemological status of religious experience, especially mystical experience.

John Hutton and Lisa Reitzes from the Department of Art History, Harry Haines from Communication, Nanette Le Coat from Modern Languages and Literature, Paula Hertel from Psychology, Rob Baker-White from Speech and Drama, and Meredith McGuire from Sociology helped me think through various parts of my argument. John and Lisa read the chapter focused on visual representation (Chapter 5) and gave me excellent comments; John also provided me with an annotated bibliography of Kahlo scholarship. Meredith, whose research is on sociology of the body, met with me often for lunch to exchange ideas and to discuss chapters, continually sent me notices of new books or classics in the field through the campus mail, and wrote recommendations for funding proposals. John, Harry, Nanette, Rob, Frank Garcia, and I constituted the "Bakhtin Group" that met almost weekly throughout the summer to discuss modern and post-modern theory, thus providing me numerous opportunities tó try out ideas. Paula Hertel, a cognitive psychologist, not only suggested the literature on cognition and affection to me and walked me through some of the more difficult parts, but read chapters, talked ideas, and was always there to keep my confidence up when it seemed on occasion that I would never get through the project; she is an excellent thinker and a patient listener.

The one serious disadvantage in terms of scholarship for a teacher/scholar at a small liberal arts institution lies in lack of colleagues in one's immediate area of scholarly expertise. I am very fortunate in lieu of this to be part of several overlapping networks of scholars crisscrossing the country. Some of the scholars who make up these networks deserve special mention. I continue to be indebted to Linell

Cady for reading drafts of the manuscript. Together with Linell, Sheila Davaney serves, usually by phone and often at national conferences and professional meetings of one kind or another, as a major resource for the preservation of my sanity, good humor, and will to keep on keeping on; may the three of us always be the "Terrible Trinity." I thank Dick Niebuhr, who with Gregor Goethals, to whom I am also greatly indebted, first taught me to cherish visual images and to relate them to understanding theology and religious symbol systems. Dick never ceases to be a major source of intellectual and emotional support, whether writing recommendations for funding or participating in thoughtful extensive conversation by phone. During one extended phone conversation in particular, he helped me think through the concept "mapping," developed in Chapters 5 and 6. Like Dick, Gordon Kaufman has also supported my work in a variety of different ways. Since I received my doctorate from Harvard in 1981, Gordon has read and commented extensively in writing on virtually everything I have written, including the entire manuscript for this book. He is my toughest theological critic. There are also those whose influence and support loom more subtly in the background of my thinking. Among them are Emily Culpepper, Eugene V. Gallagher, Naomi Goldenberg, Beverly Harrison, Mary Hunt, Barbara Kotowski, Jay McDaniel, Rita Nakashima Brock, Judith Plaskow, Rosemary Radford Ruether, and present and former students Valerie Bridgeman Davis, Cathy Kotowski, Elizabeth Schexnailder, and Karen Marie Schutt Yust. Emily's person and her work in particular inspire me to courage.

That this book went to press has depended upon reviewers as well as a host of people who work for Oxford University Press. Their anonymity notwithstanding, I am grateful for their work. I am especially grateful to Cynthia Read for her initial interest and ongoing support, to Peter Ohlin for his timely responses to all queries, and to Ruth Sandweiss and Ellen Fuchs who patiently walked me through the various stages from copy editing to final results.

The support of all these colleagues makes my work an occasion for enduring joy. However, the ongoing encouragement of a closely knit family, characterized by "good love," provides me the most extraordinary and unexpected gift of all. Our son, Benjamin, has grown into a young adult whose conversations on Kant, postmodernism, and Thomas Pynchon I cherish; I dedicate this book to Phil, his father. It has been over twenty-five years since Phil and I first committed ourselves to a lifetime with each other as lovers and companions. Phil took the slides and photographs of Kahlo's paintings in Mexico City, so indispensable to my research. When I found out that Kahlo's house, the *casa azul*, was closed for renovation, he proposed that I talk, bluff, and beg my way in, something I would never have thought of. Broken Spanish notwithstanding, I did it; it worked; and I was treated to a grand tour, accompanied by an extensive lecture from a friendly guide, who verbally caressed artifact after artifact throughout the house and courtyard. Together Phil and I walked miles and miles for days and days, whether from Kahlo's house to Trotsky's house in Coyacán, or from museum to museum in Mexico City—Phil with his camera always ready to use, where permitted, so that I would have the widest possible selection of images of paintings and other artifacts to choose from when I settled in to write. I look forward to many more such adventures with Phil; he knows me best and loves me anyway.

San Antonio   P. M. C.
August 1993

Acknowledgments

Permission from various people and institutions to use certain material in this book is hereby gratefully acknowledged:

ILLUSTRATIONS   Carolyn Farb for use of "The Little Deer" by Frida Kahlo; Raquel Partnoy for use of three of her drawings in her book *The Little School: Tales of Disappearance and Survival in Argentina;* Isidore Ducasse Fine Arts, New York, for use of the painting "Tree of Hope" by Frida Kahlo; DKL Art for use of "My Birth" by Frida Kahlo (Private Collection, USA); The National Institution of Fine Arts (Instituto Nacional de Bellas Artes), Mexico, for use of the paintings "Naturaleze Muerta con Sandia," "The Little Deer," "The Tree of Hope" and "A Few Small Nips" by Frida Kahlo.

TEXT   Cleis Press for excerpts from *The Little School* by Alicia Partnoy; Putnam Publishing Group for excerpts from *Praisesong for the Widow* by Paule Marshall (© 1983 by Paule Marshall, reprinted by permission of The Putnam Publishing Group); Beacon Press for excerpts from *The Journey Is Home* by Nelle Morton (© 1985 by Nelle Morton, reprinted by permission of Beacon Press); *The Journal of Buddhist-Christian Studies* for "The Tension between Religion and Culture" by Paula M. Cooey, which appeared there in a slightly different form in volume 11, 1991; *Anima,* for "*Woman* and Women: The Relation between a Concept and Actuality" by Paula M. Cooey, which appeared there in a slightly different form in volume 17, 1990; *Harvard Theological Review* for "Experience, Body, and Authority" by Paula M. Cooey, which originally appeared there in volume 82, 1989 (© 1989 by the President and Fellows of Harvard College. Reprinted with permission); Toni Morrison for excerpts from *Sula* and *Song of Solomon* (© 1973, 1977 by Toni Morrison. Reprinted by permission of Toni Morrison).

Contents

Religious Imagination and the Body

ONE

Introduction

On January 12, 1977, Alicia Partnoy disappeared. An Argentine citizen, poet, university student, and mother of a small child, she was detained by army personnel and incarcerated, along with other activists, in a concentration camp known as la Escuelita, the Little School. The Argentine military held her without charge and without the knowledge of her family for six months, after which, for reasons she never discovered, she "re-appeared," only to remain imprisoned for an additional two and one-half years, at which point she went into exile.[1] On reading her poetry and an account of her experiences, I was struck by her focus upon the body as the battleground over which she and her torturers struggled to lay claim to her agency or subjectivity. She expresses this struggle in religious imagery, specifically Jewish and Christian biblical imagery. For example, in "Bread" she writes:

> Bread is . . . a means of communicating, a way of telling the person next to me: "I'm here. I care for you. I want to share the only possession I have." Sometimes it is easy to convey the message. . . . Sometimes it is more difficult; but when hunger hits, the brain becomes sharper. The blanket on the top bed [of a bunk bed] is made into a kind of stage curtain that covers the wall, and behind the curtain, pieces of bread go up and down at the will of stomachs and hearts.
>
> When tedium mixes with hunger, and four claws of anxiety pierce the pits of our stomachs, eating a piece of bread, very slowly, fiber by fiber, is our great relief. When we feel our isolation growing, the world we seek vanishing in the shadows, to give a brother some bread is a reminder that true values are still alive. (84–85)

This particular passage conjures up images of both seder and communion, re-invested with revolutionary meaning in that the passing of bread from person to person defies attempts to efface the prisoners. It is typical in its focus upon the concrete as revelatory of wider meaning and value. Poems titled "Form of Address" and "Nativity," like "Bread," are obvious in their dependence upon a religious history; such poems as "The One-Flower Slippers," "My Nose," "The Small Box of Matches," and "The Denim Jacket," although less overtly dependent upon religious imagery, nevertheless convey a sensibility attuned to the power of biblical parable to surprise and transvalue through the revelation of the extraordinary found in and through the common, the ordinary—in Partnoy's case, body parts or objects directly associated with the body. The most humbling of all ironies lies in her disclosure that brutality and cruelty, rather than aberrations, constitute the norms for daily life in la Escuelita.

These images take on further irony, given that Partnoy insists that she is atheistic, a cultural Jew rather than an observing one. Though at the time of her disappearance she worked closely with Christians from base communities, non-violently protesting the military junta of the mid-1970s, she bitterly opposed the priests and rabbis, representative of Argentine establishment religious institutions, who blessed the weapons of the military (63). Her poetry reflects a tension between her anti-religious convictions and her use of religious imagery as prophetic. Hence she concludes her prose-poem "Bread" with a defiant parody of the "Lord's Prayer" in which she speaks of eating bread as a reminder that present incarceration and torture result from fighting for justice "so that bread, our daily bread, the very same bread that has been taken away from our people, will be given back because it is our right, no pleas to God needed, forever and ever. Amen" (86).

Partnoy now lives in the United States, where she works for Amnesty International, raises her two daughters, pursues her education, and continues to write her poetry. When she visited Trinity University as a guest speaker in 1988, she requested to be taken to Esperanza House, a local refugee shelter, so that she might take early morning communion with the staff and current residents, some of whom were friends of hers. Her atheism notwithstanding, religious symbolism clearly centers her life as well as her work.

Alicia Partnoy's life and work illustrate a clear-cut instance, I think, of religious imagination at work making up and making real a self and its world, directly out of the pain and, even in the context of imprisonment, the pleasure of the very bodies of the victims of disappearance. By "imagination" I mean what Elaine Scarry calls an intentional state "that is wholly its objects," the only evidence for which is that "imaginary objects appear in the mind."[2] Because the activity of imagining and the objects imagined depend on pre-existing social and material conditions, and because the objects are further shareable with others through visual, verbal, and audial symbol systems, imagination, both as activity and as condition, is necessarily social, however individually exercised. By "religious imagination" I mean imagination whose creativity is governed by and expressed through religious imagery; a person who exercises religious imagination may or may not be conventionally pious in relation to religious institutions.

In this particular instance, Partnoy bears witness not only as a victim of torture, but also as an agent of revelation and memory, as one who will neither let us remain ignorant nor let us forget. Her poetry serves as an extreme exemplification of an altogether too frequent conflict between human creativity and destructiveness, waged over and through the human body, itself understood as a disclosure of subjectivity.

Scholarship that focuses on the body as a central category of analysis and cultural critique has proliferated over the last two decades in virtually all fields in the study of religion, in literary and social theory, and not surprisingly in women's studies and gender studies.[3] It is not at all unusual to find whole issues of academic journals devoted exclusively to the body as a general category or, more specifically, to the female body.[4]

The results of this scholarship, whether directed toward practical or theoretical issues, have only widened and extended what were already highly complex epistemological problems for students of religious phenomena. Nevertheless, one benefit of this endeavor, in spite of growing complexity, has been to render impossible the disassociation of questions of value and power from questions of knowing. The body as central category has reinforced critique of assumptions taken as normative since the Enlightenment, especially assumptions regarding universal claims about the nature of reality and the human condition, and claims regarding certainty and objectivity in respect to knowledge. The more we understand about the body and the role it plays as object of and vehicle for the social construction of reality, the clearer the inseparability of knowledge, value, and power becomes. This inseparability makes inescapable the perspectival character of all claims to knowledge; it intimately links knower and known to the particular historical, material context in which the knowing relation occurs. This inseparability forces us to reexamine old questions in new ways and to raise new questions as well.

For example, what is the significance of the human body for religious imagination? From the perspective of the sociology of knowledge "body" is a social construct that provides the framework for the way we experience physicality. Any claims to a knowledge gained directly through sentience or experience in ways that circumvent culture or society arise from misunderstanding not only the inseparability of our experience from the social context in which it occurs, but also the dominance of social or cultural symbol in the relation between experience and historical context.[5] So, in the case of Partnoy, we see clearly that she voices her pain not only through language, but through a symbol system laden with religious meaning, meaning she appropriates even as she challenges it. One could rightly say that her imagination, informed by Jewish and Christian biblical tonalities and nuances as well as images, in turn construes her pain, a process at once social and individual.

Nevertheless, Partnoy's particular context is anomalous, the very antithesis of what we normally mean by "context," in that the aim of her imprisoners is to deny her both physical and imaginative access not only to the world as she knows it, but to any world whatsoever beyond the destructive assertion of power within the confines of la Escuelita.[6] Through a macabre mimicry of educational processes, she is being taught at the time of her incarceration that there is no order outside the arbitrary exercise of her captors to break her down. The primary pedagogical resource is her body, turned as weapon upon her. She writes of her treatment:

> When it rained, the water streamed into the rooms and soaked us. When the temperature fell below zero, we were covered with only dirty blankets; when the heat was unbearable, we were obligated to blanket even our heads. We were forced to remain silent and prone, often immobile or face down for many hours, our eyes blindfolded and our wrists tightly bound. . . .
>
> We were constantly hungry. . . . Added to the meager food, the lack of sugar or fruits, was the constant state of stress that made our bodies consume calories rapidly. We ate our meals blindfolded, sitting on the bed, plate in lap. When we had soup or watery stew, the blows were constant because the guards insisted that we keep our plates straight. When we were thirsty, we asked for water, receiving only threats or blows in response. . . . The atmosphere of violence was constant. The guards put guns to our heads or mouths and pretended to pull the trigger. (14–15)

From the rest of the book it is clear that Partnoy's pain provides not simply an occasion, but arguably a cause for challenging the limits of culture, especially the limits of language. That her experience is negative because it occurs against her will (as opposed to experiencing rituals of self-flagellation or fasting, for example) forces scholars of religious traditions to ask anew what epistemological role the body plays when experience occurs at the boundaries of what counts as normative for a society.

The contextual character of the knowing relation thus raises new questions. For example, in interpreting the significance of the human body for religious faith and practices, why do we, whether we are scholars or adherents, seem to need vehemently either to invest the body with epistemological authority or to de-authorize the body as an epistemological resource? This conflict over the epistemological status of the body is interesting in its own right, and manifests itself in at least two different though related ways: as embedded in the conflict over the epistemological authority of religious experience, particularly religious feeling, and, more explicitly as an ongoing debate among feminist theorists over the significance of gender difference and the status of the female body as an alternative to culturally accepted modes of knowing. These controversies warrant critical examination no less for the implicit assumptions concerning power and value held by various theorists than for the explicit claims they make regarding the nature of knowing itself. One ultimately has to ask what practical difference it makes to people in extreme circumstances, unchosen or chosen, whether they think the body provides an alternative to cultural norms.

The ambiguous status of the body as both location and artifact of human imagination, as well as human ambivalence toward the body, given its potential as weapon against subjectivity, forces the central question organizing this discussion: *In the context of religious symbol systems what is the relation between the ''bodied'' imagining subject and the body as cultural artifact?* As I hope to demonstrate shortly, the relation involves a reciprocal socionatural process of introjection, projection, and resistance best understood as mapping. This process is always embedded in a context of value, which in turn reflects power arrangements that often stand in dissonant relation to the experiencing subject. One significance of religious phenomena for this process lies in the double role religious symbols can play, both to enforce and to disrupt the continuity of the cultures in which they take hold or from which they emerge.

In the case of Alicia Partnoy we see religious people who ostensibly share the "same" symbol system lined up in opposition to one another while appealing to their shared symbols as authoritative. Priests and rabbis bless military governments and their weaponry, as students challenge the power of the same government in part by appealing to the very symbols that authorize the clerics in their office. Obviously this conflict arises out of differing interpretations, based in part on a power struggle. Nevertheless several questions remain: Why do the opponents, many of whom on both sides come from privileged classes, interpret so differently? What roles do conflicts in interpretation play in the making of culture? What roles do bodies play in the substantiation of new values? What role does the body imagined play in the attribution or denial of subjectivity to a human being, an attribution which, if it is withheld, permits, even demands the devaluation, degradation, or destruction of the one from whom it is withheld?

With respect to disappearance in Argentina, the "students" of la Escuelita spend most of their waking hours with their eyes blindfolded, yet they clearly "see through" their captors' attempts to destroy the prisoners' senses of identity and agency, while they, the captors, maintain their own anonymity. The prisoners rebel in a variety of small ways; Partnoy herself learns to see by arranging her blindfold in such a way that what she describes as her rather large nose forces an opening through which she can view her world without her captors' knowledge. She uses her nose to see in order to warn the others as the occasion demands.

Partnoy's mother, an artist, depicts this situation with irony in a series of illustrations in which the prisoners are shown with eyes superimposed on their blindfolds. Partnoy's own image appears from the neck up at the beginning of each prose poem, represented face front, her hands arranging (loosening?) her blindfold over her distinctive nose. These images are defiant in their insistence on maintaining the agency of the captives even in their extreme victimization. Visual and verbal bodily imagery work together to force the reader's attribution of subjectivity to the "disappeared." The intensity of the visual images in particular forces one to consider a revolution of vision and its connection to voice; they teach the viewer to recognize and to attribute subjectivity in the least likely of places—a concentration camp.

This attribution of subjectivity carries a moral burden to testify in behalf of victims of terror, and indeed, Partnoy testified to this abuse of human rights before the United Nations, the Organization of American States, Amnesty International, and human rights groups in Argentina. She continues to bear witness by speaking publicly wherever she is invited. She speaks carefully and haltingly out of concern lest the testimony romanticize and mystify the situation. It is as if she were not quite prepared to speak. But then, how appropriate to the situation, even for a poet![7] Thus the questions become, What language credibly communicates terrorism to those who do not suffer it, indeed those who unknowingly benefit from it in indirect fashion, those upon whose ignorance its perpetuation absolutely depends? How does one persuade another to hear?

Touch. Smell. See. Hear. Speak. What then is the significance of the human body, both imagining and imagined, for understanding religious phenomena in general and for constructive theological or philosophical work in relation to a specific religious tradition? Even in a culture as secularized as contemporary Anglo-European culture human bodies, visually and verbally represented in religious and quasi-religious contexts, bear witness to processes of creativity and destruction that generate and sustain personal and social identity. Focusing upon relations between body as artifact and an imagining subject allows us to grasp not only a better sense of how the body represented bears witness to a complex religious ethos, but also a better sense of how representing the body itself bears witness as well. As we shall see, this has methodological ramifications both for theory of religion and for theology.

This book addresses these questions. The pages that follow explore various epistemological relations between the human subject as embodied imagining subject or agent and the human body as cultural artifact in the context of religious life and practice. I argue that religious traditions provide a pedagogical context for the sociocultural transfiguration of human pain and pleasure in ways that continually recreate and destroy human subjectivity, the world within which it emerges, and the transcendent realities with which the subject seeks relation. I propose that we think of the body lived in relation to the body imagined as a testing ground or crucible, indeed in some cases a battleground, for mapping human values, as these are informed by relations of and struggles for power. I suggest that it is precisely the body's role as resource for and object of value and power that elicits the contrary responses of attributing and denying epistemological status to the body lived. As I hope to show, nowhere does this become more strikingly clear than in regard to the cultural attribution of gender difference.

The book consists of an Introduction followed by five chapters. The next chapter addresses critically the role played by the female body as metaphor for alternative knowledge, that is, knowledge that escapes cultural determination. The issue of gender difference and its epistemological significance relates directly to the controversy surrounding the body as source or means for attaining religious wisdom. In this chapter I challenge both theories that tend to reduce gender difference to the body and theories that tend to claim that the body itself is so socially construed that it is irrelevant to theories of knowledge. The third chapter examines the relation between human experience and culture in a religious context by focusing upon the relation between the body as site for pain and pleasure, on the one hand, and religious imagination, on the other hand. Within this discussion I address the controversy surrounding the issue of the authority of religious experience in relation to the culture within which it occurs, by using feminist claims to alternative knowledge grounded in religious experience as a case in point. In this chapter I propose my own hypothesis for relating religious imagination and the body as an alternative to the theories challenged in the previous chapter. The fourth chapter makes explicit the implications of my hypothesis for subjectivity in a religious context. It addresses relations among sentience, sensuality, and female subjectivity as textually represented, by examining the work of Toni Morrison, a contemporary African-American writer. Morrison's fiction, which is heavily informed by a theological perspective, illustrates how, using the body as sign, an author employs the physically grotesque to force the reader (as well as other fictional characters) to attribute or to deny subjectivity to a particular character. The fifth chapter relates the body as site to the body as sign, and both in turn to religious imagination, by exploring the role of visual representation of the female body. In this chapter I examine the paintings of Frida Kahlo, who was occupied with reconstruing the female body's cultural significance, who used physically grotesque visual imagery as a technique of representation. The sixth and final chapter pulls together textual and visual representation by examining the status of the body in the processes of making and unmaking (as always in a religious context) with reference to religious conceptions of the human. Here I suggest how serious consideration of the ambiguity of the body challenges both current conceptions of religion and current views of theological discourse.

Approach and Underlying Assumptions

This discussion depends in its approach upon the recent work of Elaine Scarry[8] and Michael Taussig.[9] Each of these thinkers, albeit from different disciplinary perspectives and by means of different methods, argues that the processes of violence and terror mimic the processes of creativity; both draw upon the testimony of others, including perpetrators, observers, and victims. Scarry focuses upon the human body in the contexts of torture, war, the Jewish and Christian bibles, and *Das Kapital,* as in some sense source for, as well as substantiation of, the reality we call "world," though she describes rather than develops the epistemological relation between the two. Like Scarry, Taussig focuses upon the making of culture out of the material of the human body, in his case colonial society in Colombia, constructed out of the exploitation of Indian labor. Taussig's psychology of terrorization, unlike Scarry's, assumes the sociology of knowledge as fundamental to his project. Like Scarry he argues that cultures of terror, far from anomalous, are quite ordinary; unlike Scarry, he demonstrates persuasively the interdependent relation between such cultures and what Western society considers to be normative, desirable, and ideal. Both thinkers challenge the dissociation of value from knowledge as epistemologically problematic; both concur that this dissociation is itself politically ideological in its intentions in some cases and always in its effects. Neither scholar addresses sufficiently to my mind the equally pernicious effects of a thoroughgoing and cynical cultural and moral relativism, though neither assumes such a relativism.

This discussion augments their work by bringing it more explicitly into the context of religious symbol systems, as these shape human social and individual identity, and by focusing directly upon the issue of gender difference as this has been culturally construed. Gender analysis, an issue addressed by neither thinker, is central to understanding the significance of the human body as artifact and its relation to religious imagination. As far as we know, "human body" apart from sexual difference as this is socially construed according to gender distinctions simply does not exist.[10] Although all humans share sentience that has morphological and physiological commonalities, sexual difference has appeared to dominate the structuring as well as the artifacts of human society and culture. Apparent biological difference, not commonality, appears to have struck those who have shaped human history as the more salient feature of human existence. Thus, for example, even though human rights are abused irrespective of gender, gender is not incidental to the form abuse will take. Furthermore abuse occurs specifically in response to gender insofar as females are regarded as less "human" than males, or differing in the quality of their humanity from males.[11] Religious institutions and traditions often collaborate to justify abuse; they likewise serve alternatively to challenge it.

This double role played by religious symbol systems raises a further methodological issue regarding the ambiguous position of religious life in relation to the rest of culture.[12] A concern to clarify this issue underlies the central epistemological questions this book raises. Though consideration of this concern occurs throughout this text, my assumptions and intentions require brief attention at the onset. Consider, if you will, the appointment of Archbishop Jose Cardoso Sobrinho to replace Dom Helder Camara in Recife and Olinda, Brazil, as reported several years ago in *The New York Times*.[13]

The article focuses on the striking contrast between the attitudes and practices of the two archbishops in response to the material concerns of the poor. According to the article, Dom Helder, who lived a simple life in rooms behind a parish church, on one occasion invited a poor man who sought audience with him to sit upon the archbishop's throne. He is a strong proponent of liberation theology and a supporter of Christian base communities, aspects of a Christian biblically grounded movement for social justice. This liberation movement characteristically challenges exploitive governmental systems and, insofar as the Christian churches are aligned or identified with them, the churches as well. By contrast, the article reports that Dom Jose responded to peasants seeking audience with him by calling upon police to expel them. He justified his action in the name of restoring the Roman Catholic church in Brazil to order and to its true spirituality, one marked more properly by ceremony than by concerns for hunger, unemployment, and human rights. The reporter goes on to add that both those who agree with his appointment and those who disagree see it as an overall pattern of the Vatican to disempower the Christian liberation movement.

The reporter, James Brooke, notes further that this spirituality is not without its political alliances with the state, alliances that seek the mutual preservation of institutional control of an elite few at the expense of the majority of the population. Whereas Brazilian religious conservatives view the appointment of Dom Jose as a triumph over destabilizing political forces within Brazil and a necessary response in the face of a rapidly growing Protestant fundamentalist movement, proponents of the Christian liberation movement point out that it marks a return to the Roman Catholic church's traditional complicity with repressive political regimes.

This event captures well the inadequacy of drawing hard and fast lines between the religious and the secular, whether for reasons of confrontation or of combination. Let us, for the purpose of an experiment, analyze the event from each of two perspectives. For the sake of discussion, I shall present these perspectives in their most exaggerated forms as the limits of a range of possible responses. The responses have in common that they are held by adherents to a religious tradition.

The position that there is a religious or spiritual order separate from a secular order presupposes a concept of religion that in theory, if not in actuality, is in some meaningful sense free of culture.[14] This understanding often depends upon a view that through proper discipline humans can cultivate non-linguistically and non-culturally bound states of awareness of reality at its most profound depths. According to this perspective ultimate reality transcends human reason, language, and culture, all of which at best mediate this reality and at worst serve as obstacles to our access to it; hence, access to what is real lies in cultivating states and emotions receptive to its disclosure. These states or emotions manifest what in Christian or Greek terms is understood as the human soul, and they lie at the heart of human piety and moral character. Furthermore the reality they disclose is absolutely trustworthy, true, from the perspective of the adherent. The disciplines and rituals that cultivate these emotions or states constitute what is referred to as "spirituality" in Christian traditions; there are functional parallels in other religious traditions as well. Such a view of spirituality may or may not include the additional claim that the human soul is in some sense immortal.

Those who adhere to this view of religious life and practice tend to define their view of secularity set in opposition to religion in terms of materialistic self-interest, as this is buttressed by a denial of any reality beyond the phenomenal order. They characterize the present age or the modern world as manifested by culture in terms of scientism, technocracy, and an egocentric craving for political power won by the few through the exploitation of both the rest of humanity and the natural environment. In short, secularity from this perspective represents the worst of culture, and religion is defined ideally as separate from culture.

There are several benefits to be gained from this perspective. I shall mention only the one that I consider to be the greatest and most relevant to this discussion. First of all, provided that the disciplines involved are not ridiculously elaborate and obsessive, spirituality or the cultivation of piety can have a democratizing effect by ultimately shifting authority for the adherent from institutions and their representatives directly to his or her right relations with what is understood to be ultimately real. This shift can potentially de-authorize oppressive power structures in ways that may free the adherent to seek actively to transform them. There are, however, no guarantees. Indeed there is much evidence to support that the cultivation of spirituality in opposition to secularity often serves as an illusory escape from and denial of the world rather than a vivification and energizing of a human will to struggle with the pressing problems that threaten its future existence.

Escape from this-worldly reality is not the least of the problems, however. Such a view can lead to a denial of the relevance of sentience to lived existence in ways that reinforce oppressive systems of power—I have specifically in mind here, for example, the refusal by religious authorities across several traditions to acknowledge women's rights to control reproductive choices. Furthermore, the claims of a separation from culture often depend upon selecting and comparing the desirable aspects of the religious tradition practiced with undesirable characteristics designated by the definition "culture." Even when selectivity can be defended on rational grounds, the claim to separate religious traditions from culture may result in unacknowledged parasitic dependence upon institutions and systems of power characteristic of the secularity the proponents of this view seek to oppose. In short, it becomes difficult within this oppositional perspective to be self-critical with respect to the religious symbol systems and institutions that inform it and to challenge their complicity in the exploitation of human and other sentient life.

The defensiveness of Dom Jose's response to the peasants and his call for more ceremony serve as a case in point. The *Times* article reports that Orlando C. Neves, a conservative law professor at Catholic University in this country, greeted the new appointment as a return to the church's primary goal, namely the saving of souls. Neves affirmed that after all, "Christ said, 'My Kingdom is not of this world.'" An underlying assumption, that religious life should be concerned only with the spirit to the exclusion of this-worldly concerns for justice, characterizes both the acts of the new archbishop and the law professor's response to his appointment. Meanwhile the actual material conditions as these impinge upon the wholeness of life for the peasants remain totally neglected. This assumption not only devalues the wholeness of historical existence, it is also a necessary concomitant to the self-preservation of religious institutions, for it keeps them secure in relation to secular governmental and military institutions.

Those who turn to hermeneutical theory, socioeconomic theory, and anthropological theory as authoritative for understanding religious traditions presuppose a very different concept of religion from their counterparts, namely that religious symbol systems are themselves human artifacts, manifestations of culture. As products of human making religious symbol systems are governed by principles characteristic of human making. As religious human beings, adherents project an ultimate reality; thus central symbols reflect and further shape what is at the core thoroughly human from beginning to end. These symbols govern or organize not only human social and individual identity, but also human institutions representing vast networks of power. The various disciplines of spirituality socialize the adherents of religious traditions either to accept or in rare instances to challenge these networks of power. For example, for Durkheim, when humans become aware that humans construct reality, this awareness renders them incapable of continuing to do so and threatens both social and psychological anomie. For Feuerbach, in contrast, consciousness of human responsibility for the construction of reality challenges humans to do a better job.[15]

The chief value of this perspective lies in its effectiveness and adequacy as an interpretation of human power in ways that potentially free human imagination to be critical of religious symbol systems in addition to other symbol systems. For example, this perspective unmasks the political implications of a spirituality withdrawn from or set in opposition to secularity. It can likewise challenge the claims of scientific authorities to objectivity and neutrality in regard to valuation, though it seldom does so.

Nevertheless, pushed to an extreme it can provide little in the way of criteria by which to validate choosing just, over oppressive, treatment of human beings, not to mention other forms of life. If the religious despisers of culture err in the direction of a presumption to absolutism, this second perspective errs in the directions of moral relativism and nihilism. If we agree that the purpose of understanding the world is to change it, what are our resources for discerning "ought" from "is" or even "better" from "worse"? The conceptualization of religion as cultural artifact in and of itself provides us with little beyond analyses of power and the much-needed critique of the corruption of our traditions. Although this critique is necessary, it is insufficient.

In the case of our example, we can explain the differences in terms of a power struggle in Brazil between the "haves" and the "have-nots" with reference to the way both groups depend upon their respectively contrasting interpretations of the same tradition. We can point to how an ideology of opposing the religious and the secular actually serves to mask an alliance of the religious with the secular, to a greater degree in the case of Dom Jose than in the case of Dom Helder. Nevertheless, we are provided no criteria for establishing whether or why one response is religiously, morally, or politically preferable to the other.

I suggest that religious traditions as challenged by the secular order still provide their adherents with a constructive starting point. Whatever their origin and status with respect to claims of the nature of ultimate reality, religious traditions in very distinctive ways have concerned themselves directly with the condition of suffering. Christians, for example, live and work, albeit at a distance, within sight of a crucified God. Buddhists are called by wisdom to compassion—quite literally a "suffering with" the other. The transfiguration of suffering manifested in creaturely or sentient existence lies at the heart of each symbol system. This recognition of the heart of the matter presupposes a model of religion different from the previous two, though derived to some extent from the second perspective. I can only suggest some of its features at this time; I shall address this issue at length elsewhere.[16]

Briefly, this third perspective not only depends upon so-called secular skills and principles in conjunction with the internal principles of various traditions. It not only draws on secular resources for self-critique. In addition, precisely because the transfiguration of suffering lies at its heart, this perspective provides a position from which to evaluate critically and to choose, on spiritual and moral grounds, action for a better future. The transfiguration of suffering understood as focused on *this* world allows adherents to challenge the egregious exercise of human power in its exploitation of others, including the rest of sentient existence, at every point. This means within religious traditions as well as beyond them.

Thus adherents are in a position to re-form religious claims not only through mutual understanding and transformation, but in light of other criteria. They are likewise in a position to challenge the validity of those other criteria as well. A focus on the transfiguration of suffering in relation to the abuse of human power further provides a coherence by which to view the world that ideally inhibits tendencies to reify either central symbols or the principles external to the traditions. Although it provides no easy single system or program to follow, the transfiguration of the suffering of sentient or creaturely existence, as mediated by very different symbol systems, provides a place to start that transcends both a dualism of religion and secularity and a too-easy identification of one with the other.

So, in regard to the example from the *Times*, Dom Helder's this-worldly concern for justice for the poor is truer to the Christian tradition's focus upon the transfiguration of suffering. His concern has allowed him to challenge both political and religious institutions that depend for their perpetuation upon the exploitation of the Brazilian peasants. This does not exempt him or the Christian liberation movement from self-critique any more than in the case of Dom Jose; rather it permits Christians in either case religiously mediated grounds for self-understanding.

So far my analysis of the relation between religious symbol systems and the rest of culture has been from within a given tradition. This kind of self-understanding is not unique to Christians, nor is it restricted to events from within one's own tradition, whatever this tradition may be. For example, magazine photographs of Buddhist martyrs' self-immolation in the streets of Saigon in the sixties played a central role in persuading many United States citizens to oppose the war in Viet Nam. In 1989, in El Salvador, the murders of the Jesuit university professors, their housekeeper, and her daughter forced Buddhists and Protestant Christians, as well as Catholic Christians, once again to oppose United States involvement in "peace efforts" in Central America, and further to oppose the involvement of fundamentalist churches in evangelizing Latin Americans in ways that diffuse legitimate political critique of brutal right-wing governments. More recently, at local Muslim services where Imam Shakir prayed for Iraqi and Kuwaiti refugees, I observed the prone bodies of Muslims of all races, facing east in an appeal for peace. Their prayers elicited my further resistance to national euphoria with U.S. "success" in its war with Iraq, a victory gained through massive carpet bombing and fire bombing of Iraqi civilians and military alike, a victory gained by displacing thousands of refugees, and motivated by national economic self-interest, cloaked in a thinly disguised rhetoric of fighting for the freedom and self-determination of a monarchy that is equally as oppressive as its invader.

In all cases, those who calmly risk their lives by identifying with the victims of *this* world's political, economic, and spiritual oppression; who see themselves, whether atheist, Buddhist, Christian, or Muslim, simply as one among many; and who see the victims with whom they cast their lot as likewise agents, rather than objects of pity, challenge the religious of whatever persuasion to seek a transformation of *this* world to a just and lasting peace. In short, the transfiguration of the suffering of sentient existence renders a this-worldly prophetic and iconoclastic tension between religious practice and the rest of culture imperative; nevertheless, it also requires their relation. The focus on *this* world further requires critical knowledge of and engagement with both social and natural scientific theory, as well as hermeneutics, as a necessary condition.

The relation between religious tradition and the rest of culture is not simply a matter of concern for the religious, however. The concept "religion," insofar as it designates an object of study, is a highly dubious one. Though its historical roots are earlier, the concept is largely a modern one, laden like any other social construct with political significance; as such, the concept lacks even basic, agreed upon definition among scholars. Furthermore, the study of religion, understood as an academic discipline, is fraught with methodological inconsistencies, contradictions, and disorder. Where there is systematic theoretical consideration taking place, the theories themselves reflect a range of assumptions regarding the relation between religious symbol systems and the rest of culture similar to that of the religious themselves. Resulting theories are further subject to criticism on various grounds ranging from gender and racial bias and ethnocentrism, to a post-modern critique of the absurdity of theorizing at all.

For purposes of discussion here, I am obviously assuming an anthropological definition of religion as symbol system, which I seek to augment and, ideally, to enrich in the chapters that follow.[17] Nevertheless, I would be hard pressed (and in the classroom, often am) to articulate what distinguishes a religious symbol system from any other symbol system. Myth, ritual, sacred text, holy days, pilgrimage, a sense of the holy, a distinction between the sacred and the profane, and all the other usual elements marshaled to distinguish a symbol system as religious occur to some degree in various other symbol systems as well—political and scientific, for example. There being no essentialist definition available that does not at some point break down, it seems artificial to designate the Zen Buddhist tradition a religious tradition and Marxism a political movement. Hence, many of the examples upon which I focus in the pages that follow transgress conventionally drawn distinctions between the religious and the political realms. Scholars of religion thus live caught between the knowledge that "religion" is a reification that distorts the very reality we seek to study, on the one hand, and, on the other hand, the compelling nature of the phenomena themselves and their significance in the making of human life, for better or for worse. A reconsideration of this tension and its implications for theological and philosophical discourse therefore necessarily concludes this book.

TWO

The Body and Gender

Issues of gender remain implicit throughout Alicia Partnoy's account of her incarceration and torture in *The Little School;* however, gender itself is not incidental. At the time Partnoy is a mother separated from her very young daughter, as well as a wife separated from her husband. The stress of imprisonment, bad diet, and constant fear causes the female prisoners' bodies to cease to menstruate. The possibility of rape, a violation that could result in pregnancy when perpetrated upon a female, preys upon the minds of the women. The guards amuse themselves by watching prisoners engage in sexual behavior. One female prisoner actually delivers a child; the mother never reappears, and the fate of the child remains unknown to this day. Such phenomena are typical violations of human rights; indeed, though hard to imagine, they could actually have been worse. Acts of violation themselves especially illustrate that human bodies are never simply bodies in some general sense; rather they are marked by gender as the interpretation of their sexual and reproductive significance.[1] These marks, according to gender difference, elicit different scenarios of terror. Worse still, in some contexts, though not in Partnoy's, being female itself is the sole or primary criterion for violation.[2] Whatever else "body" may mean, and its meanings are multiple, acknowledgment of gender must lie at the center of its definition. Once gender is introduced, gender difference must be accounted for.

Issues of sexual and gender difference,[3] entailed in the concept "woman," have produced two conflicting intellectual tendencies in feminist theory: essentialism and cultural determinism. Essentialist arguments tend to claim that "woman" stands in some sense outside cultural construction, a status produced by sexual difference as somehow inherent in the human species. This status as "other" in relation to culture determines women's experience as distinctly different according to gender, a difference that generates alternative knowledge or wisdom, contrasted with knowledge recognized and validated by culture. By contrast, cultural determinist arguments claim in their most extreme form that "woman" is, strictly speaking, entirely a social construct upon which patriarchy necessarily depends for its self-perpetuation. Whatever differences exist that are gender defined are themselves due to socialization as "other" rather than some quality or qualities of alterity inherently female. Gender defined experience is itself a consequence of culture; therefore, in theory women enjoy no privileged knowledge that circumvents culture.

Essentialism and cultural determinism as two opposing schools of thought are not unique to feminist theory; rather they frame virtually all discussion of the significance of gender and sexual difference. Thus understanding the concept "woman" requires critically analyzing these two tendencies in terms of their commonalities as well as their differences. The purpose of understanding, however, is to move beyond the debate itself. Analysis of each position indicates that debate concerning the status of difference depends as a whole upon an irresolvable dualism that is itself patriarchal in its roots, namely, the nature/culture dualism. A more fruitful approach to the question of woman entails a shift in focus from dualistic thinking to a context that assumes the unity in reciprocity of nature and culture, body and language as it is used, namely, discourse.[4] Religion potentially provides this unity. As will shortly become clear, in order to grasp the relation between the concept "woman" and actual women's sense of identity as women, we need not ask whether nature or culture plays the more primary role in its formation. Instead we must ask what and how women value (positively and negatively) and to what extent this valuing participates in the creation, perpetuation, and destruction of culture.[5]

The Primacy of Nature

One way to grasp a typical essentialist response to the question of "woman" is to begin with the concept "woman" as a universal. To ask what is "woman" in this sense of the term is to ask what belongs to the meaning of the concept irrespective of historical, geographical, cultural, and individual differences among actual women. Cultural/historical relativists and philosophers of language might argue that the question is misguided and reflects a misunderstanding of both cultural pluralism and the function of language. Such criticism notwithstanding, feminists who find the question meaningful in this context point to biology and the division of tasks along gender lines across cultures. Women are recognized to be women by virtue of manifesting a female reproductive system or female sexuality, as distinguished from male biology. Furthermore, all cultures, regardless of their relative differences, divide social tasks along gender lines; that is, they socialize males and females according to a masculine/feminine polarity of characteristics that reinforces certain roles ostensibly necessary for the perpetuation of the society. From the perspective of many feminist theorists who ask the question in a collective sense, the socialization of roles according to gender indicates that gender itself ties directly to sexuality or embodiment. Hence, feminine characteristics, although not the exclusive possession of females, nevertheless relate in some sense, usually hormonal, to female physicality. Within this theoretical framework sexual difference, that is, psychobiological differences between males and females, provides the key to understanding what it means to be an actual woman in terms of both oppression and liberation.

The various forms of argumentation for this position depend heavily upon the interaction of body, discourse, and value as mediated by a masculine/feminine polarity. In Western culture, this polarity has taken the form of identifying the concept "woman" along with the concepts "body" and "nature," as feminine, in contrast to "man," "language," and "culture," identified as masculine. The premise is that woman's identity *necessarily* stands more directly related to her physicality as female because of her generalized sexuality and her prolonged role in reproduction, in contrast to man's identity, which is tied more closely to language and culture because of his comparatively more localized sexuality and more restricted role in reproduction. These differences produce femininity as that involves passivity, receptiveness, irrationality, and carnality as opposed to masculinity manifested by activity, aggressiveness, rationality, and spirituality.[6]

Feminist theorists on both sides of the Atlantic have developed accounts of woman's identity as woman that presuppose an essential connection, implicit or explicit, between female biology and a gender polarity.[7] French feminists have, however, provided the most extended and hotly debated discussion of *féminité* as a celebration of female eros. Although the proponents of *féminité* disagree seriously among themselves, there are certain common tendencies that allow for characterizing their work as in some sense a school of thought, namely, a critique and rejection of patriarchy as *phallogocentric* and an espousal of *jouissance* as a constructive alternative.[8]

Phallogocentrism refers to symbolizing male power, especially the power of language, and therefore culture, by the *phallus,* itself an image of the penis. It is a somewhat more graphic image for focusing on the significance of sexual difference and its relation to power than the cognates of *androcentrism* more frequently used by many North American feminists. Though the phallus is itself an image that distinguishes male from female anatomy, it signifies, by virtue of its identification with language and patriarchal culture, the denial or denigration of nature and incarnation, more specifically woman's body and woman's pleasure in her own body, considered apart from serving male sexual needs. *Phallogocentrism,* then, connotes the extent to which woman's body, her sexuality, her language, and her subjectivity (i.e., her identity in her own right) are defined, denied, or treated as a means of exchange in patriarchal culture.[9]

Given the nature of *phallogocentrism,* for woman consciously to separate herself from man, by rejecting his language and culture, and to explore sexually her own body, alone or in intimacy with other women, is for woman to discover *jouissance:* orgasmic pleasure or delight.[10] *Jouissance* liberates; it gives rise to woman's identity and language as it simultaneously dismantles patriarchy in its dependence on sexual control over woman to assure patrimony so that power continues to pass from father to son. *Jouissance* thus threatens a property-based economy where property both actually and symbolically includes women and children as well.

For example, as chief characteristic of a positive experience of female physicality, *jouissance* presupposes touch at its most fundamental level, namely, the ongoing friction between the *labia.* Touch, thereby, becomes a primary and inescapable mode of self-knowledge. By inference it also becomes an essential mode of power in bringing about a revolution in values that begins with a rejection of *phallogocentrism.* As Luce Irigaray writes, ''But *woman has sex organs just about everywhere.* She experiences pleasure just about everywhere . . . [t]he geography of her pleasure is much more diversified, more multiple in its differences, more complex, more subtle than is imagined.''[11] Autoeroticism experienced as *jouissance* expresses a celebration of *féminité,* the feminine, that is tantamount to guerrilla warfare.

Jouissance, experienced through touch, has this power, for it raises the subconscious to the surface. Release of what was once repressed liberates consciousness from all repression, but most notably from the bondage of reason and the logic of language. Women (and in some cases, men) speak and write instead in a language of the subconscious, a language of mood, disposition, or feeling analogous to music and chanting, rather than a language of rational analysis.[12] *Jouissance* thus connects woman's body and language, by rendering audible and visible the underbelly of consciousness as a different language, one that reflects emotional, visionary, and fragmentary aspects of existence. The language of subconsciousness, akin to music on the one hand and madness on the other, further reflects a reversal in value, for the character traits associated with *féminité*, such as carnality, receptivity, and emotionality, insofar as they challenge their patriarchal correlates, assume a status of superiority.

Jouissance dismantles patriarchal institutions in that defying sexual repression disrupts control over women as the means of reproduction and perpetuation of patrimonially transferred power. As the identity of the mother is self-evident in contrast to the uncertainty involved in identifying the father, control over woman's body is necessary to ensure the continuance and identification of a male line. This control manifests itself in a variety of forms, not the least of which is the definition of "woman" as dependent upon "man" for sexual gratification, economic sustenance, and physical support. Hence *woman, body,* and *property* become inextricably related as objects of male possession and manipulation. *Body,* the symbolic connection between *woman* and *property,* once experienced by woman as a source of *her* pleasure, apart from male need, undergoes a transvaluation that challenges the very notions of ownership and control of whatever or whoever is "other," characteristic of patriarchy. (It is important to note that such a transvaluation has tremendous positive potential to liberate men from patriarchy as well.)

Jouissance, while it does signify erotic delight or pleasure, thus takes on additional metaphorical meaning. The concepts upon which it depends ("body," "woman," "man," and so forth) become metaphors, indeed, symbols themselves. One of the greatest sources of possible misunderstanding of an essentialist position arises from interpreting essentialist theory in too crudely literal a fashion. Adamant in their insistence that sexual difference transcends socialization and cultural construction, essentialists are, nevertheless, not reducing everything to biology. On the contrary, they are ironically elevating biology as a source for metaphors that have enormous social and political implications. *Jouissance,* as a celebration of *féminité,* opens up an avenue to transcendence: not only a transcendence of ordinary patriarchal institutions, but of phallogocentric constructions of subjectivity and spirituality as well.[13]

This response to the question of "woman" merits serious consideration for a number of reasons. Its emphasis on "woman" as a universal form bonds all women in theory; thus, it precludes easy exclusion of particular women, regardless of serious intellectual and political differences, even conflicts. It further provides a positive re-evaluation or transvaluation of woman as "other" exemplified in and through the "feminine." This emphasis on sexual difference not only allows a positive self-evaluation for actual women as women, but additionally creates a stance for women that recognizes needed psychological, and in many cases social, distance from men as a highly creative vantage point from which to understand and challenge patriarchal structures. What makes this response most compelling, however, lies in the seriousness with which it takes female physicality and the sense of touch as manifested in an adamant refusal to relinquish woman's erotic pleasure or sexual joy *in herself*.

Control over woman's sexuality as that involves everything from orgasm to reproduction is essential to the perpetuation of patriarchy. *Jouissance* threatens patriarchy at its most fundamental level by refusing to relinquish control over women's sexuality as manifested in patriarchal constructions of woman's desire and desirability, always and everywhere in terms of man's own need. *Jouissance*, by way of contrast, is positive rather than privative; it insists on woman's power to define her sexuality in terms of her own pleasure as it may or may not include man's participation. This power lies not only in the actual experience of erotic joy, but in the voice this joy releases, the new language to which it gives birth, and the creative energy to use this language (creative in both an aesthetic and an ethical sense) to dismantle oppression in any form. *Jouissance* thus provides a positive resistance and alternative to patriarchy.[14]

Such a response to the question of "woman" would be altogether persuasive, were it not that its greatest strengths taken in excess generate its greatest weaknesses. "Woman" understood in a universal sense, although it may in theory bond all women, can, and often does, blur significant differences among woman—both substantive differences with respect to point of view, and differences of race, class, creed, and sexual preference that might seriously challenge the meaning of the concept "woman" itself. The differentiation or individuality of an actual, given woman gets lost as well. In short, use of the universal sense of "woman" often overly systematizes women, resulting in the loss of the texture of actual women's lives and faces. The fine balance between individual subject and community loses out to an arid and vacuous universality. Bereft of plurality, "woman" loses meaning altogether.

The emphasis given sexual difference is also riddled with both theoretical and practical difficulties. Sexual difference taken as a starting point, although it has certain advantages, largely overlooks the extent to which existing men and women simply do not fit the categories delineated by a masculine/feminine polarity, most especially the alleged identification of language with masculinity. While attaching this significance to sexual difference transvalues "woman" as "other" by celebrating *féminité,* it also reinforces the reduction of women to sexuality and reproduction. Attaching this significance to sexual or gender difference further does not relate reproduction and economic production and does not explicitly acknowledge the need for man to take seriously his own physicality, particularly as symbolic of limitation and finitude. The glorification of the female body through *jouissance,* worst of all, underestimates the extent to which women experience their bodies as battlegrounds for domestic violence, rape, forced sterilization, forced pregnancy, and economic deprivation. In short, beginning with sexual difference as a fundamental premise precludes raising what may be some of the most significant questions of all regarding the concept "woman": To what extent is sexual difference itself culturally constructed? Might the very idea of sexual difference itself, placed in the context of patriarchal culture, be one of the chief means by which women remain subordinated to the men of their class and race, with whom they are affiliated as daughters and wives? Can sexual difference ever escape patriarchal construction? Should we not respond best to the question of "woman" by challenging dualisms such as culture and nature, masculine and feminine, subject and object, self and other, all of which show a consistent and remarkable parallelism in supporting a hierarchy of value and power that subordinates women to men?

The Primacy of Culture

These questions typify a second major response to the question of "woman," that of cultural determinism. Feminists who raise these questions share the fundamental premise that the concepts "woman" and "man" and the associated gender polarity of feminine and masculine character traits are constructed by culture or society. This premise rests in turn on the sociology of knowledge, the chief claim of which is that all human reality is socially constructed and mediated through symbols, especially through verbal and written language; indeed language, or more accurately discourse, almost exclusively structures individual and corporate identity and experience. Within this framework, meaning and value are not only *logocentric*, but inseparable from actual political and economic arrangements. Concepts like "woman" and "man" that attempt to interpret the significance of biological difference, in fact, serve a more primary purpose of differentiating a division of labor through the creation of gender and gender-defined roles, ostensibly to ensure the perpetuation of a particular culture or society, in short to maintain hegemony of existing power structures. The significance of sexual difference never occurs apart from cultural mediation, and therefore power arrangements reflected in and perpetuated by language itself, specifically as discourse.[15]

In the context of patriarchy concepts such as "woman" and "man" and their associated pairs "feminine" and "masculine," "nature" and "culture," "body" and "spirit," and "other" and "self" constitute, broadly speaking, an ideology authorized as "natural," "scientific," or "revealed by God," depending upon the interests, aims, and particular community of those in power. This ideology, internalized by whole cultures, becomes a self-fulfilling prophecy and therefore self-perpetuating. For example, successfully socialized to be feminine, one acts feminine and therefore assumes being woman means that being feminine is "natural." Gender difference, so constructed, forms the bedrock of patriarchy. The chief beneficiaries of patriarchal arrangements, male and female alike, use sexual difference to preserve them. The conceptual distinction between "woman" and "man," and therefore sexuality itself, is cultural. Rather than reflecting an interaction of biological and psychological structures and needs, "woman" is a myth in the most pejorative sense of the word, and woman's identity is the product of a social relation, reflecting male economic need and political power. The first task of feminism becomes, as Monique Wittig points out, "to dissociate 'women' (the class within which we fight) and 'woman,' the myth. For 'woman' does not exist for us; it is only an imaginary formation, while 'women' is the product of a social relationship."[16]

What is socially constructed can be deconstructed and reconstructed through the deconstruction and reconstruction of language itself. Liberation from patriarchal society requires at the theoretical level seizing the power of the word and turning it on all oppressive concepts and dualisms, especially those involved in establishing and maintaining gender difference. Theory that assumes or claims difference to be decisively significant in the formation of identity, even if it is committedly feminist, only reinforces patriarchy in the long run.[17] As theory always serves praxis, whether consciously or unconsciously, feminist theory according to this perspective must consciously serve a revolution in value that dismantles patriarchal societies by challenging the ideology of sexual difference and the politicoeconomic arrangements it supports in whatever form the ideology manifests itself.

Feminists who hold this position may differ widely among themselves with respect to their politics. They may or may not be separatist; they may be liberals or socialists. A revolution in value from this perspective can begin with any number of possibilities. Although sociopolitical and economic arrangements provide a central focus, cultural determinists, nevertheless, approach the issue of sexuality with reference to language in what can appear to be conflicting, even contradictory ways. For example, Wittig retains the concept "woman" (and its correlative "man"); however, she redefines each as a class. By contrast, Carolyn Heilbrun and Susan Suleiman argue, though in different ways, for the reconstruction of the concept *androgyny* as a way of sustaining a sexual pluralism that simultaneously enriches and transcends sexual difference by overcoming the logical opposition between the two terms.[18]

Compared to an essentialist response to the issue, cultural determinist theory tends to focus more explicitly and specifically on action. It is on the whole more sociologically and less psychologically informed than its essentialist counterpart. At least suspicious of, if not overtly hostile to, concerns with the female body as manifested in *féminité*, cultural determinists tend to emphasize underlying historical and social structures as having primacy over, indeed producing, psychological structures.[19]

The greatest strength of cultural determinist theory lies in its awareness of the role played by culture in the construction of human reality, particularly with respect to sexual difference. The emphasis placed on language, now much more clearly understood as discourse, allows proponents of this view to focus directly upon actual historical conditions and ways to change them. It further acknowledges the significance of cultural, creedal, racial, and class diversity in a way that at least in theory tends more explicitly to support pluralism within a community as well as across communities.

There are, nevertheless, serious problems with this position, whether expressed in liberal or Marxist terms. Among liberals there is a tendency to assume that both the symbolic order and the material conditions it mediates are more subject to conscious manipulation than is actually the case. If one could simply purge the offending symbol system and construct a better alternative, then a better economic and political order would soon follow; in other words, ideas make things be the way they are. Were this assumption even accurate, this tendency, when excessive, produces a philosophical idealism that is both gnostic and elitist, for power by default belongs to the social engineer "in the know." A variation on this same problem can occur among Marxists as well. Although much more focused on actual material conditions in a social sense than their liberal counterparts, Marxist feminists, suspicious of an ideology of sexual difference, can fail to take seriously enough the interaction of biology and psychology that produces human beings in general and human individuality in particular, albeit always in a socially or culturally determined context.[20]

Liberal and Marxist denials of the roles played by psychology and biology in the formation of identity have a common failure. Both fail to take seriously the extent to which the social construction of reality constructs what is genuinely real. For example, if we assume that gender difference is socially constructed, it is no less real for being a social habit than it would be if it were "natural." On the contrary, it is so powerful a habit as to have thoroughly permeated all presently known cultures regardless of the differences in how it manifests itself across cultures. At least one of the reasons for its powerful hold upon the human imagination lies in its *apparent* foundation in biological differences.

In short, cultural determinists of whatever kind can ironically neglect the most fundamental of all material conditions in human society, namely, sentience itself. Whereas essentialist thought focuses on the female body as metaphor for the subconscious, the land of emotions, to the neglect of culture's role in fostering mood and emotion characteristic of subconsciousness, cultural determinists focus on the cultural construction of identity without sufficient attention to the psychic and somatic qualities of the material constructed. This latter neglect produces an oversimplification of the interaction of body, discourse, and value that yields individual and social identity, by reducing reality to being a function of language. The oversimplification lies in a lack of sufficient awareness of possible relations between discourse consciously employed as specific discourse and human subconsciousness. Oversimplification furthermore lies in assuming monolithic structures of dominance as primarily, or even exclusively, responsible for social construction. Whereas essentialists err on the side of reducing identity to sexual difference, cultural determinists err by reducing identity to an oversimplification of cultural construction. For the cultural determinist this can lead to a naive optimism with respect to political solutions—naive in its excessive voluntarism that ultimately contradicts its claims to linguistic determinism.

The question thus remains: Quite literally *how* do we recognize which human beings to classify as women? (Is it not precisely on the basis of biology, especially reproduction, in which case embodiment and its significance remain issues?) If language as discourse is so all-pervasively deterministic, how does it become a weapon against itself? How does an individual human being, never mind a whole society, move from assuming a crude philosophical realism, whether ordained by "Nature" or by "God," to recognizing the human construction of, and therefore responsibility for, human value? What, speaking practically, prevents a cultural narcissism (at its worst totalitarian) within this theoretical framework? Have we not simply added one set of patriarchal conceptual tools, those of sexual difference and dualistic thinking, for another—the ultimate exemplification of *phallogocentrism*, an overestimation that approaches the worship of cultural processes and culture?

Essentialist and cultural determinist responses to the question of "woman," taken together, pose a dilemma that is at once social and logical. The two responses ironically confront us with choosing between gender difference grounded in nature and gender difference constructed by culture, in short, the old nature/culture dualism decked out in different garb. This dualism, itself patriarchal through and through, presents no choice at all. On the one hand, to turn to nature as an authoritative symbol for woman by focusing on female biology and gender difference is to perpetuate the dualism and the patriarchy. On the other hand, to insist that nature, sexual difference, and the nature/culture dualism are "simply" cultural constructs further perpetuates a problematic hierarchy of value, which subordinates the worth of the material order and all associated with it to the life of the mind in a way reminiscent of phallogocentrism, even as theorists insist that they are manipulating discourse and the reality they claim it creates more justly than their patriarchal predecessors. It would appear that posing the question of "woman" gets us more than we bargained for, for raising the question not only challenges patriarchy, but challenges feminist theory as well.

For the concept "woman" to have constructive significance for actual women's lives, feminist theorists need explicitly to reject all tendencies to set nature and culture in opposition to one another in favor of an emphasis on the inseparability of nature and culture. This shift in emphasis requires a focus on lived existence, however symbolically mediated. Lived existence, characterized chiefly by change, dissolves tendencies toward dualistic thinking.

Identity and Transformation

To be adequate, an understanding of woman's identity as woman must draw upon the fundamental strengths of each major theoretical response to the question of "woman." For example, the essentialist emphasis on woman's body as metaphor for the land of emotions allows emotion, both anger and joy, to generate new discourse that becomes a major force in liberating women from oppression. However, unless this insight is grounded in a keen awareness that emotion itself is subject to symbolic structuring, and therefore cultural qualification, *jouissance* and *féminité* degenerate into mystification and narcissism. Social analysis provided by a cultural determinist position, especially a Marxist one, though not without problems itself, goes a long way in prohibiting such degeneration by stressing the roles played by economic and political systems in shaping sexual identity.

Nevertheless, a contrived synthesis between the two positions is not desirable, not only because they are mutually exclusive with respect to the significance of difference, but because neither takes seriously enough the dramatic role played by change, both individual and social, in creating woman's identity as woman in the plurality of its manifestations. Stated positively, a feminist theory of woman's identity must cultivate a high tolerance, indeed outright appreciation, for complexity, plurality, variability, multi-vocity, and ambiguity in meaning. Focused on identifiable faces in community in the midst of life, and therefore change, such theory reveals woman's identity by capturing the concreteness of women's lives, by portraying their convincingness. Empirical in the broad sense, such theory remains true to the fundamental insight that the process of communicating and reflecting upon women's experiences of oppression and liberation provides the starting point for personal and social change.[21]

This process provides a starting point precisely because of its focus upon emotion as the mediatrix between body and discourse, nature and culture, that inextricably connects personal and communal identity by moving one to constructive action in concert with others.[22] Focus on this process captures the intersection of what otherwise appears to reason to be dualisms of body and spirit, self and other, nature and culture, and so forth. Only a theory that begins with the ordinary women telling their own stories to one another and becoming transformed by this experience can do justice to the dialectical tension between the individual in community, on the one hand, and the conflicts (between women and men, and among women) that generate and legitimate a feminist struggle against patriarchy, on the other hand.

Most feminist theory, regardless of differences among feminists, shares a practical commitment to challenge patriarchal and androcentric structures. Whether essentialist or cultural determinist in its presuppositions, theory focuses on what is perceived to be the interaction of actual conditions with hopes for changing them. Theory that addresses woman's identity in terms of an interaction of biology with psychology provides important insight into the structures of individual transformation possible through the body's mediation between the realms of consciousness and subconsciousness and through assumption of conscious responsibility for extending culture in new directions through re-imagining or re-mapping the body. Theory concerned with social relations, by emphasizing the cultural construction of identity, accounts for the logic of actual conditions of oppression for women as a class or group and in so doing provides grounds for bonding and direction for needed change. Yet, because each position rests ultimately on a dualism of nature and culture, neither can account sufficiently for the interaction of personal with social change.

Change, for better or for worse, characterizes lived existence. Social and personal transformation, understood as a relatively discrete, symbolic structuring of change, thus provides a crucible for exploring the formation of social and personal identity. Whether consciously committed to social action or not, personal transformation, whether gradual or abrupt, always has social implications. A study of how personal and social dynamics interact in the process of transformation as it in turn restructures identity, in this case woman's identity as woman, contributes a crucial, but so far missing element to feminist theory as a whole, for it discloses the connection between individual persons and social change.[23]

Attention to the interaction between personal and social change or transformation requires serious consideration of religious life. It does so for a variety of reasons, not the least of which is that religious symbols play a major role in the formation of identity even in a culture as ostensibly secular as that of the United States. Religion, understood as a symbol system that provides both models *of* and models *for* reality, creates, sustains, and challenges cultural values through the cultivation of certain moods and dispositions in individual persons that qualify their characteristic activity.[24] These moods and dispositions, fundamental to the development of character, itself the chief expression of identity, emerge in most cultures in response to a complex interaction of myth, ritual, and discipline organized around central symbols that can come to define identity, often in terms of vocation. Said another way, we are what we value, for by giving us worth, what we value gives us recognizable shape. Identity in this sense is a dynamic, psychosomatic pattern of value mediated by sociocultural symbols. Religious life, centered on such symbols, serves as one primary locus for value-in-the-making as it creates persons in their solitude and in community.[25] Furthermore, religious life exemplifies an instance of the intersection of particular or micro-concerns with cosmic (if not entirely universal) or macro-concerns, for it provides a context for connecting one's own personal story or narrative with open-ended grand narratives that lie at the heart of the various traditions. In short religious life reveals the extent to which religious symbol systems serve pedagogical purposes by providing what Foucault referred to as technologies for the care of the self, where "self" is understood as a socially produced phenomenon.[26]

Precisely because of religious traditions' pedagogical role, negative critique of religious symbol systems from within and without not only is valid and necessary, but should be ongoing. Such critique notwithstanding, analysis of women's narrative suggests that religious symbol systems play positive and creative roles in strengthening women's sense of agency, as well as negative roles. Women's appropriation of myth, participation in ritual and discipline, and self-definition in relation to vocation support the hypothesis that women's value-in-the-making in a religious context provides an alternative avenue for understanding the relation between the concept "woman" and women's actual existence, preferable both to essentialist and to cultural determinist theories.

For example, through the appropriation of myth, individual women have not only come to discover an individual voice, but also to acknowledge the dependence of individual voices on being heard by others, "heard into speech."[27] Maxine Hong Kingston's *The Woman Warrior: Memoirs of a Girlhood among Ghosts* illustrates how this reciprocity of hearing and speaking allows one a strong sense of identity, characterized by a radical openness to others.[28] The text begins with Kingston's recounting of a family story of an unnamed aunt who dies in shame by her own hand after killing her infant born out of wedlock. The narrative proceeds, through the telling of memories, fantasies, and myths, to develop how the author comes to a sense of her own voice in relation to her mother, the legacy of traditional Confucianism, and the mores of the new U.S. culture into which Kingston was born a first-generation Chinese-American. The governing theme that generates Kingston's ultimately positive sense of identity is the myth of Fa Mu Lan, the woman warrior. The apparatus by which Kingston makes this myth her own is talk-story, an instrument, so to speak, given by her mother which she in turn refines in a way that allows her to direct her own historical particularity toward a community. The process, as Kingston describes it, is one in which her mother through talk-story "wrote" Kingston's beginning, but she, Kingston, must write her own ending. In other words, Kingston through appropriating the qualities of Fa Mu Lan, made available to her through her mother's talk-story, herself becomes a participant in the ongoing talk-story of the generations of her family. She not only develops character, she becomes a character, whose special mission it is to share these talk-stories with a wider audience—the barbarians, the ghosts, namely assimilated Chinese and non-Chinese Americans. Assuming and performing this responsibility required not only that she heard her mother well and not only that her mother finally listened likewise, but also that we, the readers, hear her, metaphorically speaking.

Woman Warrior very clearly reflects the extent to which culture and identity are socially constructed and sustained by the transmission of myth in oral or written form from generation to generation. The text further reflects how living at the intersection of two conflicting cultures can generate new interpretations and serious modifications of already existing symbols such that new values are generated. It is equally clear, however, that female physicality generates a sense of being on the periphery of culture in ways that drive the conflicts of Kingston's life, ways amenable to essentialist concerns.

Kingston interprets the acts of infanticide and suicide by the unwed nameless aunt to be acts of spite, of revenge. She connects this story to the mystery of her own sexuality, her first menses, and her capacity to bear life. Revenge in connection with sexuality pervades the narrative such that it finally becomes clear that the narrative itself is an act of revenge against sexual oppression of the traditional Chinese culture she inherits. Her sense of her own physicality, negatively experienced in adolescence, becomes in the form of her tongue her chief weapon against the oppressiveness of sexism. Tongue and female body nevertheless become revolutionary weapons not because they are unconstrued, "raw material," so to speak, but because they are unavoidable and *must* be construed. Hence neither a cultural determinist analysis nor an essentialist interpretation alone is sufficient. Instead one must look to the unifying power of the symbol itself, in this instance the woman warrior Fa Mu Lan, and to the quality of the relation between Kingston and the symbol, namely talk-story, understood as a process. Symbol and relation, taken together, presupposes the inseparability of nature and culture, an irreducible inseparability, a unity that generates value.

Praisesong for the Widow, a novel by Paule Marshall, demonstrates this same process at work, this time in the context of ritual.[29] Marshall portrays Avey Johnson, the central character, as a sixty-four-year-old black woman, recently widowed and upper-middle class, virtually assimilated into white culture. While vacationing on a Caribbean cruise, she jumps ship for reasons unclear even to her. The story unfolds through a series of events, memories recollected, and dreams, all of which force Avey to confront her blackness and the cost of its denial. The narrative represents Avey's retrieval of her own history and its relation to the wider history of an enslaved people.

Though race and its significance are at the forefront throughout the novel, Marshall never divorces race from the issues of gender and sex. The reader gains the full impact of Avey's assimilation in terms of the presence of erotic power that positively defines Avey's relation to her husband, Jay. This power is lost in the subsequent deterioration of their relationship as they become committed to upward mobility and begin to reap the rewards of material success. What French feminists call *jouissance* plays a central role in Avey's transformation. It not only characterizes what Marshall calls the "small rituals" (137) of Avey's and Jay's sexuality. Its absence not only bespeaks a loss of integrity, an unauthentic identity. Its recurrence, this time in a ritual bathing, signals Avey's healing and rebirth.

Through a strange configuration of events Avey finds herself seasick, helpless, and in the hands of strangers. Weak from vomiting, diarrhea, and loss of consciousness, Avey awakens in the home of a stranger, Rosalie Parvay, who with an attendant, bathes and massages Avey. The bathing prefigures Avey's reincorporation into an African-American community through celebration of its heritage, a celebration marked by ritual dancing. Avey's response to being bathed registers an awakening to her sensuality:

Under the vigorous kneading and pummeling, Avey Johnson became aware of a faint stinging as happens in a limb that's fallen asleep once it's roused, and a warmth could be felt as if the blood there had been at a standstill, but was now tentatively getting under way again. And this warmth and the faint stinging reached up the entire length of her thighs. . . . Then, slowly, they radiated out into her loins: When was the last time she had felt even the slightest stirring there? . . . The warmth, the stinging sensation that was both pleasure and pain passed up through the emptiness at her center. Until finally they reached her heart. And as they encircled her heart and it responded, there was the sense of a chord being struck. All the tendons, nerves and muscles which strung her together had struck a powerful chord, and the reverberation could be heard in the remotest corners of her body. (223–224)

This chord, once struck, continues to reverberate as Avey later dances the Carriacou Tramp at the close of the narrative. In a ritual dance to commemorate the ancestors, the steps retell black capture and transportation from Africa to the Americas, black endurance and resistance to slavery and later to white racism, in short, African-American history. Ritualized bathing and dancing serve as the occasion for Avey to acknowledge the full implications of her identity and to accept her calling as a seer and teller of her people's story. Further, her retrieval of a positive sense of identity as an African-American woman and her acceptance of her vocation depend in no small way on the element of sensuality that pervades both rituals. It is the touch of another, in this case a complete stranger, that awakens Avey to new life. It is the movement traveling from head to foot that moves her back into community and arms her with alternative values to those of the dominant culture.

The narrative as a whole bears powerful testimony to the recourse provided by the body, bodily movement, and bodily contact for effecting and reflecting a change in values. That the narrative is fictional is beside the point.[30] However, to give a solely essentialist account here is to fail to do justice to the cultural forces at work in conjunction with sensuality.

It is in the context of another culture that Avey is able to shed assimilation, not in the absence of culture itself. The central issue in Avey's transformation is power, its loss, and its redefinition, not an opposition between nature and culture. To interpret Avey's adventure as one of having stepped outside culture into a force field of raw sensuality is to overlook that African-American culture is indeed a culture and, furthermore, to miss the full significance that Avey's calling, not unlike Kingston's, is to speak, to tell the story of her people, as a way of challenging a dominant culture's claims to domination. Once again the dynamic relation between person and symbol, reflected formally this time in ritual, a relation that yields sociopersonal identity in ways that create new value, cannot be reduced either to body or to discourse. Rather, the process or interaction has an integrity of its own that provides a starting point in its own right to understanding the relation between the concept "woman" and actual women.

Ritual and myth represent relatively isolable instances, elements, or patterns of change. The role played by discipline, itself a complex interaction of myth, ritual, ethical practice, diet, and possibly dress code, is somewhat more difficult to analyze in a relatively brief fashion. Nevertheless, there are certain features that, although not constituting a comprehensive view of the role of discipline, bear identification and discussion regarding the relation between the concept "woman" and women's actual existence. Anne C. Klein in "Finding a Self: Buddhist and Feminist Perspectives" argues for the compatibility of the feminist search for a strong, woman-centered identity with what Mahayana Buddhists call the realization of emptiness (*sunyata*).[31] Although her argument is persuasive and the finer points of realization of emptiness are fascinating, I will focus here on the implications of even making such an argument rather than analyze in full the argument itself. Nevertheless, some background is in order.

Emptiness is one of the symbols central to Mahayana Buddhism. Its realization is quite literally one of making the symbol itself real as the centering force for the adherent. Realization requires the leading of a disciplined life. Though living such a life means entering monastic orders for some adherents, it is accessible to lay people as well.

Although the meaning of emptiness is subject to a variety of interpretations and articulations (the fate of any central symbol), it minimally involves apprehending that change and the correlative interdependence of each distinguishable existent on every other existent form the essential character of reality. In other words, emptiness as symbol captures the fluidity of existence. Making emptiness central to one's life requires the cultivation of certain virtues focused on sensitizing one's awareness of reality including oneself, the practice of certain behaviors organized around non-violence toward all living creatures, and a close and enduring relation with a trustworthy teacher. Instruction in discipline and interpretation of experience occur often through story or myth. Meditation not only structures and relates all other aspects of discipline, but provides the chief context for direct realization of emptiness. Realization of emptiness not only releases the adherent from suffering in some sense, but also releases him or her for wisdom and compassion toward the rest of sentient existence.[32]

Klein argues that life centered by realization of emptiness is like the identity-in-relation that feminist theorists seek to claim as central to what it means to be a woman. Neither the lonely autonomous individual (stereotypically male), nor the other-directed and often fused identity (stereotypically associated with females), nor finally the dissolved identity of the post-modern nihilist, a life centered by emptiness, represents internal integrity simultaneous with relatedness to others without the illusion of completion. In short, making flux itself central to who one is frees one to be a distinct participant in an ongoing process. In the context of feminism, this means that the concept "woman" is itself never finally determined, in the sense of completion, any more than the identities of women.

The practice of meditation, the primary occasion that relates person to symbol in this instance, focuses on breathing. The practice, subjected to analysis, discloses yet another instance of the fundamental interrelatedness of body with discourse, nature with culture. For the realization of emptiness through meditation presupposes both physicality at its most fundamental level and a religious community, present through a specific history, to transmit the connection between breath and symbol. Practiced breathing becomes an occasion for interpretation, appropriation, and interrelation.

Precisely because Klein does not intend to proselytize, her argument implies that feminism itself presupposes a discipline at some level, though Klein herself never explicitly suggests this. What I am inferring finds functional parallels and further support in early accounts of consciousness raising and in presently existing women's religious communities, be they Jewish, Christian, or Wiccan. Such efforts not only provide contexts for personal and social change, but serve as vehicles for perpetuating change. They accomplish these purposes in part because they represent occasions that relate persons to symbols that presuppose the unity of nature and culture through the human activity of recognizing and creating value.

There are obviously other loci for value, other possible symbol systems, and therefore other kinds of transformation. Nationalism, political and economic ideologies, humanism (in its various philosophical manifestations), and naturalism (expressed through the various sciences) provide additional contexts for attending to change. Any one of these systems can serve as an interesting and fruitful starting point. Furthermore, religion, in its various positive, historical forms, often, if not always, combines with these loci for better or worse. Nevertheless, religious symbol systems, to the extent that they are compelling, compel because the symbols hold in tension what would otherwise be conflicting, if not altogether contradictory, impulses in ways that these other systems cannot or do not. It is precisely for this reason that religious symbol systems can seriously damage people as well as positively sustain them.

Value, centered symbolically and lived as a practiced response in terms of such central symbols, not only shapes personal identity and integrates person with community. Life itself also becomes a life of value-in-the-making only insofar as central symbols communicate credibly a relationship between self and other, spirit and flesh, culture and nature—the very concepts that constitute the patriarchal dualisms confronting reason. Experience, especially the experience of transformation, tests the credibility of the symbols themselves. Thus religious transformation provides a superlative context for capturing all the elements that characterize personal and social change.

To understand "woman" in relation to women, then, requires a focus on transformation as a substantive starting point, for, patriarchal inscription notwithstanding, "woman" is finally what, how, and whom actual women value. The relations between person and religious symbols, interpreted as value-in-the-making, suggest that the relation between the concept "woman" and actual women is less one of body or of discourse than one of value itself, a condition potentially shared by all members of the human species though manifested in highly diverse, particular ways. In short, women are constituted and self-constituting subjects, though the public status of full subjectivity has been denied them in some measure, in terms of political, economic, religious, verbal, and visual representation by virtually all known literate cultures.

In summary, the cultural identification of "woman" with "body" requires that any discussion of the relation between imagination and the body acknowledge the necessity for analysis and critique on the basis of gender difference. Theoretical accounts of the significance of gender difference demonstrate a conflict concerning the role played by the female body that presupposes confusion over the body as a site or location or medium for the production of knowledge with the body as culturally generated artifact or sign. Because religious practices provide contexts that integrate, by means of feeling or emotion, particular with cosmic concerns and, further, serve as a pedagogical resource in the production of selves (including and especially egoless selves), religious life illustrates that persons and the communities from which they emerge are what they value. Religious life further exemplifies subjectivity as value by disclosing how social and personal value is generated, sustained, altered, and destroyed.

Issues entailed in the representation of female subjectivity provide the central concern for much of the remaining discussion; however, a prior concern remains. Subjectivity means among other things that one is the subject of or is subject to one's experience. The focus here on religious experience raises questions about the epistemological status of experience itself. Just as theorists have attributed privileged knowledge to women by asserting their position as outside culture, so theorists of religion have attributed protected status to the subjects of religious experience by asserting that such experiences are in some respect outside culture. Likewise, opponents to such claims have insisted that religious symbol systems, like gender difference, are artifacts of culture. Given these opposing claims, on what grounds, if any, do experiences of transformation serve as authoritative, either for the subjects of such experiences or for others who have not had them? Specifically, *how* do religious symbol systems hold nature and culture, body and imagination, in tension? In short, what role does the body play in the imagination's appropriation, and in rare instances, generation, of religious symbols and images?

THREE

The Body as Site for
Religious Imagination

Not solely a victim, Alicia Partnoy is also a witness. She has testified to human rights abuses in Argentina before the United Nations, the Organization of American States, Amnesty International, and human rights organizations in Argentina. Of her poetry, which also bears witness, she writes:

> The voices of my friends at the Little School grew stronger in my memory. By publishing these stories I feel those voices will not pass unheard. . . . Today, while sharing this part of my experience, I pay tribute to a generation of Argentines lost in an attempt to bring social change and justice. I also pay tribute to the victims of repression in Latin America. I knew just one Little School, but throughout our continent there are many "schools" whose professors use the lessons of torture and humiliation to teach us to lose the memories of ourselves.[1]

Sworn testimony, in contrast to poetry, depends heavily for its credibility upon rationality. The circumstances of Partnoy's experience which occasion her testimony nevertheless stand in antithesis to anything remotely resembling rationality. How then can she find the words? What discourse will compel another to hear them as truth? What will make her account of her experience real to one who has not suffered it? To what extent does even her own sense of the reality of her experience depend upon her voicing her own pain and the pain of others that she has witnessed? To what extent might her poetry, by the nature of the genre and by virtue of her skill, provide an avenue that communicates more genuinely than a straightforward rational account? To what extent does the effectiveness of her communication depend in either case upon emotion, evoked by her imagery, as well as predisposed within her hearers?

What is the epistemological status of experience, experience often epitomized in both philosophical discussion and in religious contexts by feeling? The body metaphorically understood as a land of emotions suggests an ambiguity of the body as both site for and artifact of human imagination, as well as human ambivalence toward the body, an ambivalence that saturates religious symbolism. This ambiguity forces the question of the relation between the imagining, "bodied" subject and the body imagined. A history of controversy among theorists of religion and theologians over the epistemological status of emotion or feeling provides a framework for exploring this relation. The human body, as the site of feeling, lies at the heart of this controversy; the body's role as resource for and object of value and power elicits contrary responses of attributing and denying authority to the body as an alternative source of knowledge as distinguished from knowledge formally recognized as such by culture.

Articulating the relation between religious imagination and the body therefore requires focusing first on the significance of emotion. Understanding the role played by emotion in relation to culture and nature is relevant both to theories of religious life and practice and to issues of theological method. The extent to which one grants emotion independence from other psychological processes, designated as cognition and perception, may well determine whether one views religious experience as an avenue available to free a subject from culture, or simply as the product of culture. In theories of religion the role played by emotion may determine both the integrity granted the subject's account of her or his experience and the appropriate methods for interpreting the general significance of the account. In regard to theological methodology, the role played by emotion will likely indicate whether experience is viewed as a relative consequence of construction and critique or the authoritative starting point for construction and critique.

Feminist scholarship provides an excellent case in point. Feminists have claimed women's experience as authoritative for theoretical critique and construction. In addition, in making this claim, feminists have often looked more specifically to the body as it has been identified with the concept "woman" as a positive resource for theoretical thinking.

For several reasons it is important to analyze what is at stake in claiming the authority of experience. For one thing these claims have elicited critical responses from within feminist scholarship. Furthermore, such claims share both a historical and a substantive relationship with nineteenth- and twentieth-century theories of religious experience which are themselves subject to conceptual problems. In addition, much confusion reigns among the claimants and opponents alike concerning the meanings of *experience* and of *body*, a confusion that, as we have just seen, permeates debate over the significance of gender difference. Moreover, the relation between experience and concept or symbol is of general relevance to anyone engaged in critical and theoretical endeavor in the academic study of religion or theological studies. Perhaps most importantly, however, appeals to experience as authoritative in the face of cultural norms and institutions, regardless of the claimant's gender, race, ethnicity, religious affiliation, or politics, challenge cultural hegemony, including academic hegemony, thus rendering intellectual controversies surrounding such claims political in both their implications and their effects.

I do not intend to develop a theory of experience, religious or otherwise, nor do I propose to speak for all feminist theorists who claim experience as authoritative for theory. I do want to suggest where some of the confusion lies and to propose both contexts and limitations for making such claims. I intend to argue that the symbolic construal of pain and pleasure lies properly at the center of claims that religious experience is theologically authoritative; further, the symbolic construal of pain and pleasure accomplishes important but different tasks in regard to human survival and enhancement. Viewed as symbolic construal, religious symbolism and practice provide a pedagogical context that transfigures pain and pleasure in ways that continually recreate and destroy human subjectivity, the world within which it emerges, and the transcendent realities with which the subject seeks relation. Within this framework the body lived becomes a crucible, even a weapon, for both sustaining and changing human values, as these are informed by relations of power.

In order to accomplish these tasks, I shall first critically examine recent general theories of religious experience in relation to recent theories of emotion in the field of cognitive psychology. I shall then turn to an analysis of feminist theory and the critique it has elicited from within. Here I intend to suggest that the proponents of experience as authoritative starting point mean by *experience* something both more and less than their critics attend to. I shall conclude this chapter by suggesting what I hope to be a fruitful direction for further discussion—both at the general level of theory of religion and with respect to theological critique and construction.

The Role of Religious Experience

Feminists of the second wave early on appealed to experience as authoritative starting point for social theory, particularly theology.[2] For those concerned with the academic study of religion and with theological studies, the conceptual link in Western thought between woman and nature through the female body has provided a major focus for critically and constructively articulating experiences of sexual discrimination and oppression as well as glimpses of liberation. As we have just seen in regard to the status and significance of the concept "woman," debate continues among theorists across disciplines over the relation between nature and culture in the construction of reality. Nevertheless, a direct challenge from a feminist perspective to the authority of women's experience, particularly women's religious experience, for theology has emerged only fairly recently.[3] In order to assess critically both the appeals to this authority and the challenge to such appeals, it is helpful first to analyze feminist claims in relation to general theories of religious experience that hold feeling to be in some sense central. It is further important to examine the role (as distinguished from substance) of such claims. I shall than turn to an examination of the issue of religious experience in relation to psychological theory of emotion.

Theories of Religious Experience

The idea of conceptually distinguishing "religion" as a feature of lived existence among other different features has a rich but comparatively short history. "Religion" is a modern concept that emerges with a loss in Western society of the economic centrality and political authority of what we now call religious traditions. The designating of some aspects of life as religious in contrast to other aspects designated as secular thrives especially where religious pluralism occurs in conjunction with the separation of church and state. Whether it is appropriate to make such designations is still subject to scholarly debate.[4] The more consumed one is by the piety and practices of a tradition, the less sense it seems to make, at least from the point of view of the adherent, to draw a line between religious and non-religious or secular experience. All experience occurs in relation to the symbols and institutions of the community in which the adherent participates. Nevertheless, not only scholars but adherents now make such distinctions, however complex and problematic the concept religion may be.

If religion as a concept is difficult to define, the concept "experience" is virtually impossible. We live with the legacy of Kant, even when taking a direct stand against him. He held the view that experience is sensation of stimuli conditioned by time and space and structured by the categories of the understanding as these presuppose reason's empty but regulative ideas of self, world, and deity.[5] Although this view requires modification with respect to the specific role played by historical conditioning, and although philosophers of process thought have seriously challenged Kant precisely on this issue,[6] this view of experience remains to this day the default assumption for many scientists and humanists alike. When designated "religious," especially where the focus is upon what is regarded as the extraordinary or numinal with respect to sensation, time, and space, experience becomes one of the most problematic of all our concepts.

Like experience, the authority granted to experience by the subject is historically and culturally determined. The justifications for granting authority to an experience are explanatory and therefore tied to a subject's concepts and beliefs.[7] Authority derives from claims to *noesis;* that is, from the subject's perspective experience becomes authoritative because it yields insight, illumination, or revelation. Yet *noesis* logically presupposes specific historical and cultural traditions, concepts, and beliefs. It is important to add, however, that the insight or knowledge gained has at least two compelling features for the subject. Namely, it is, for the subject, "how things really are," and it is knowledge that is salutary or salvific for the knower. Whatever prior concepts, symbols, and beliefs religious experience may presuppose, and irrespective of the further speculation to which it may lead, the authority of the experience for the subject is ontological, epistemic, and practical.[8] The authority lies not merely in being insight, but insight that has value for and gives value to the subject. The experience thus generates a norm or norms, in light of which past and future experience is evaluated.

Feminists owe a debt of mixed gratitude to theorists of religion who claim religious experience to be authoritative, in the sense of being exempt from critical reduction from the outside.[9] The protected status granted religious experience has allowed it on occasion to play democratizing and anti-authoritarian roles in relation to social institutions from family to government.[10] Religious experience provides an authority that challenges other cultural authorities, including other religious authorities, particularly hierarchical ones. Moreover, this authority is accessible irrespective of gender, race, class, or education. Feminists who look to consciousness raising and women's support groups as participants in a woman-church, a coven, or a separatist community stand in a venerable tradition illustrated by groups as disparate as the Montanists, the Puritan revivalists, and the Pentecostals of the turn of this century.[11] The tradition is one of appealing to one's own or one's communal experience to challenge the powers that be.

When we turn from a functional analysis to a substantive one, however, the issue becomes more complicated. Theorists have argued for the irreducibility of religious experience by locating it in emotion or feeling. They have further understood feeling to be unqualified by language, or even if qualified by language, to bear certain essential features that distinguish piety from other kinds of experience and other human endeavors such as knowing or moral activity. So Schleiermacher describes the sense and taste for the infinite found in and through the finite; so he later construes the feeling of absolute dependence upon the whence of our existence.[12] Emotion, thus conceived, works to reinforce the privatization, domestication, and mystification of religious practices. This understanding often promotes a kind of individualism isolated from community. Given the often evocative rhetoric of theoretical discourse on this issue, another effect can be to cultivate uncritical acceptance of views of passivity particularly dangerous to the politically disenfranchised, whatever their class, race, or gender.[13]

These difficulties presuppose two logically prior problems with respect to the nature of religious experience as well as theoretical claims made about it. The first involves what properly constitutes emotion in relation to sensation and language, and the second has to do with the status of religious experience in light of historical relativity.

Emotion and Language

Wayne Proudfoot's *Religious Experience* addresses the nature, role, and status of emotion as central to religious experience.[14] He critically assesses the general claim that religious experience is authoritative for the subject, focusing discussion on attempts to delineate religious experience as emotion or feeling, as this occurs logically prior to and unstructured by discourse, or language. He argues that the move to locate piety or religious experience in emotion, so defined, is basically a protective strategy—protective in at least two ways. First, if religious experience is rooted in feeling or emotion as somehow unstructured by language, then the subject's account, once articulated, can be scrutinized only by those who have themselves undergone such experiences. Second, any attempt to explain such experiences coming from those who have not undergone them and who appeal to extra-religious authorities is reductionist in the negative sense—that is, inappropriate. So, for example, Sigmund Freud's reduction of religious life and practice to illusion and Karl Marx's claim that they are a political opiate would be unacceptable because of their having explained religious experience in discourse alien to the experiencing subject.

Proudfoot argues very persuasively that feeling or emotion is interpretive of sensation in response to environmental stimuli, rather than raw data more akin to sensation. In other words, feelings, especially complex feelings such as piety, are linguistically structured interpretations of physiological and external socionatural change. We are taught to feel in response to the events of our lives. Thus, complex emotions such as praise, gratitude, sorrow, and joy become religious feelings because they are cultivated in the context of specific religious symbols and practices. It follows that theories of religious life and practice that claim the centrality of feeling do not simply explain by describing in some neutral sense. Rather they actually determine the experience to some extent by prescribing what counts as "religious."

Proudfoot's best examples occur in his discussion of theories of mysticism.[15] What pass as descriptive features of mystical experience, namely, that it is ineffable and noetic, are in fact cultivated qualities prescribed logically, if not always chronologically, in advance. They operate to determine the experience to be mystical rather than some other mode of experience. In particular, those symbols which communicate ineffability—such symbols as *Nirvana, Sunyata, Tao,* and God as Wholly Other—serve as "place holders," symbols or concepts that set rather than simply acknowledge the limits of discourse. Proudfoot supports his argument by pointing to the role of religious practices and religious teachers in fostering and identifying certain kinds of experience as religious. He goes on to point out that theories of religious experience are themselves often written evocatively, that is, with the aim of eliciting such experiences in the reader.

Having effectively criticized theories of religion that depend on granting religious experience privileged status (beyond culture), Proudfoot proceeds to develop his own alternative view. He distinguishes between description and explanation and argues that the subject's description or account of her or his experience must be granted initial integrity; that is, it cannot be distorted or misrepresented by the analyst. Such distortion he calls "descriptive reductionism''; it involves misplacing the description, logically speaking. Nevertheless, the account, once made, enjoys no privileged status. It becomes public property, so to speak, in that any analytical explanation can be given provided it is adequate to the event. The issue will be adequacy, not whether the explanation is sympathetic to or empathetic with religious experience as such.

By stressing the interpretive nature of feeling or emotion as this arises out of the interaction of physiology with culture, Proudfoot validates feminist insistence that language can and must be changed, given its determinative influence as interpretation. He thereby lays the groundwork for understanding the thoroughly social character of even the most personal experience. He furthermore acknowledges (though not sufficiently, to my mind) the role of physiology or sensation and thereby escapes the problems of extreme philosophical idealism often characteristic of cultural determinism. In accomplishing this task, however, it is important to be clear about what gets lost in the process. Assuming that his view is adequate, the privileged status of religious experience (that is, the claim that it somehow transcends culture) cannot be maintained. This loss has important implications for the authority attributed to any kind of experience as a basis for any kind of theorizing.

Proudfoot's arguments notwithstanding, much controversy still surrounds the nature, role, and status of emotion or feeling in the field of psychology. The issue is not culture versus nature so much as determining the precise interaction between the two. On the whole, psychologists tend to agree that feeling, at least complex feeling, is interpretive, rather than "raw" data from which interpretation is subsequently constructed.

Proudfoot's argument depends heavily upon empirical studies of the nature of emotion, conducted in the field of cognitive psychology, specifically in attribution theory.[16] Since the time of the studies done in social psychology cited by Proudfoot, debate has arisen over the nature of emotion or feeling in the field of cognitive psychology.[17] The debate does not seriously conflict with the claim that language plays a formative role in structuring complex feelings. Nevertheless it does qualify Proudfoot's claims in ways that generate important questions about the relation between religious experience and thealogical or theological authority that Proudfoot does not address. For this reason, the debate is worth brief examination.

In 1980 R. B. Zajonc argued that whereas thought does not always accompany feeling, feeling always accompanies thought. On the basis of experimental studies, he concluded that "the form of experience that we came to call feeling accompanies all cognitions, that it arises early in the process of registration and retrieval, albeit weakly and vaguely, and that it derives from a parallel, separate, and partly independent system in the organism" (154). He nevertheless granted that arousing feeling requires minimal cognizing of objects.

The article generated both refutation and defense, the most notable refutation coming from Richard S. Lazarus. Lazarus pointed out that Zajonc's interpretation of his data depended upon Zajonc's somewhat narrow definition of thought and a model for mind which Lazarus found questionable. He further emphasized that if by "thought" one meant a highly developed, precise concept, then, of course, not all feelings were accompanied by thoughts. The absence of a thought in the presence of a feeling did not, according to Lazarus, allow one to conclude that the feeling was unconditioned or undetermined by cognition. He went on to point out that Zajonc had granted the necessity for cognition of an object in order to arouse a feeling. In short, the claims that emotions are learned and that the learning process is culturally constrained remained intact.

Much of the debate appears to have arisen out of semantic differences. The more narrowly one defines cognition and the more one restricts it to highly complex conceptualization, the more likely one is to grant independent status to emotion. The more widely one defines cognition to include all the workings of mind, the less independence one is likely to grant feeling. Nevertheless, there do appear to be feelings that are inherent, albeit very few, and, on the whole, it would appear that most feelings, particularly those of increasing complexity, are learned.[18]

This debate still leaves important questions unanswered, however. First, what is the significance of Zajonc's observation that all thoughts are accompanied by emotion? In the ensuing debate no one refuted this claim. Zajonc's distinction between "hot" and "cold" cognitions (the significance of a cognition in terms of the strength and intensity of an accompanying affect) bears a striking resemblance to William James's discussion of how consciousness changes in regard to "hot" spots in *The Varieties of Religious Experience*.[19] It further performs functions parallel to those of Jonathan Edwards's distinction between mere understanding and saving knowledge in his religious epistemology.[20] That affect, or feeling, always accompanies thought should surely have implications worth pursuing concerning how and why evocative discourse elicits (or fails to elicit) change. Furthermore, that affect accompanies thought indicates a reciprocal relation between feeling and language, irrespective of cognition's logical priority.

Second, is it possible that feelings characteristic of piety, albeit that they are cultivated rather than self-generating inner states, contribute to human survival, with reference to both individuals and the human species as a whole? Clifford Geertz's discussion of mood and motivation in the contexts of suffering and the problem of evil indicates that this is certainly the case for individual believers and communities.[21] Once we extrapolate to a global level the answer becomes far less clear, especially given the role played by religious symbol systems in national and international conflict.[22] More recently Nico Frijda has argued that emotions are lawful phenomena; he has further formulated twelve specific laws governing the emergence, endurance, and fading of emotion.[23] The law of situational meaning, the law of concern, and the law of care for consequence in particular presuppose the necessary role played by culture in eliciting and sustaining emotion. The laws of change and of hedonic asymmetry suggest limits to the determinative role played by culture, limits set by the body for the purpose of survival.

The law of change specifies that emotions *''are elicited not so much by the presence of favorable or unfavorable conditions, but by actual or expected changes in favorable or unfavorable conditions.''*[24] Reference to "expected" change again presupposes a culture; however, actual change would include not only change in the socionatural environment but in the body as well. Thus hormonal changes associated with gestation, disease, or aging and chemical change associated with jogging or sexual intercourse—though none escape cultural inscription—impose themselves upon consciousness to be addressed. They represent the body forcing its way onto the cultural agenda, so to speak.

The body does so as a matter of survival. The law of hedonic asymmetry posits an asymmetrical adaptation to pleasure or pain in that *''[p]leasure is always contingent upon change and disappears with continuous satisfaction. Pain may persist under persisting adverse conditions.''*[25] Frijda concludes from this law that emotions exist for signaling events and states of consciousness that require a response in order to survive. Again the body imposes itself, and the emotions elicited especially in response to pain, however culturally structured, perdure indefinitely through memory unless overwritten repetitively by other emotions according to the law of conservation or emotional momentum.[26] Hence, the staying power of the trauma of physical and sexual abuse, and the resistance of grief in the face of loss, contrast strongly with the transitoriness of euphoria and infatuation. Such extreme conditions and the determinative role they can play in the formation of identity suggest emotion deserves central attention precisely because it represents the integration of language and body, culture and nature. Although emotion may not generate non-culturally informed knowledge, it does make real for the subject symbols, concepts, and values. In order to address this issue, however, we must first raise briefly the issue of historical relativity. Only then can we turn to the role played by the body in experience.

The role played by language in the form of discourse in structuring feeling provides the central point of agreement between feminists who appeal to women's experience as authoritative and feminists who challenge such authority. Proponent and critic alike insist that language, indeed entire verbal and visual symbol systems, must change in order for egalitarian communities or societies to emerge. Whereas proponents base their insistence upon the experiences of sexual oppression and liberation, critics base their insistence upon the nature of language itself as it interacts as discourse with a will to power, conditioned by historical circumstances.[27] Linell Cady suggests, for example, that feminists tend to assume a cultural-linguistic model for experience in critically challenging the sexism of the traditions while assuming a model more like Schleiermacher's when claiming authority for experience in theological and thealogical construction.[28] The first model makes clear the historical relativity of experience; the second invests experience with an absoluteness that transcends culture and thereby history.

It is this historical relativization of religious experience (or any kind of experience for that matter) that comprises the second, related problem regarding claims to its authority. It would at least appear on the face of it that, given the cultural structuring of emotion, feelings do not provide access to reality beyond what culture validates as real. There is thus no escape route from culture itself such that one can posit experience as a culture-free, religious, or moral authority for challenging culture. History, viewed from this perspective, becomes a record of an ongoing struggle among competing forces seeking to substantiate a will to power. In and of itself religious experience provides no trans-historical absolute against which all else becomes relative. Nevertheless, Frijda's understanding of emotion's role in survival does grant experience serious authority within the context of culture itself, an authority provided by the body.

Sensation and Imagination

The authority attributed to women's experiences of oppression and liberation depends in part upon attention to the body, particularly woman's body. The connection between experience and body is hardly accidental. From a feminist perspective woman's body becomes a resource for authorizing women's voices for at least two related reasons I wish to explore at length. The first generates much of the confusion regarding the logical relation between experience and explanation; the second related reason provides a way out of this confusion.

The first reason consists in the identification made between "woman" and "body" in Western symbol systems and the attitudes this identification cultivates. If you recall from discussion in the previous chapter, for feminist secular and religious theorists alike, sentience or physicality and its relation to the construction of gender have posed a serious conceptual dilemma. In many, if not most symbol systems, the concepts "woman," "passivity," and "body," or "nature," often become identified and set in opposition to "man," "activity," and "mind" or "spirit." This polarity is valorized such that the former is subordinated in value, public power, and status to the latter. This construction of a gender dichotomy dependent on hierarchical relations forms the bedrock of patriarchal societies, whether they are patriarchal de jure or de facto, and androcentric attitudes, whether consciously or unconsciously held. As we have seen, for feminist theorists the question has been one of where to locate the conceptual source of the problems entailed in sexism: Is the polarity (or the act of polarizing) itself the problem? (In which case the nature versus culture debate itself reinforces oppression.) Or does the polarity reflect genuine sexual differences, however they may have been misconstrued and unequally valued? (In which case a possible solution would be to transvalue the devalued end of the polarity and allow for more complex variation to occur within the framework it sets up.)

In seeking to understand sexual or gender difference as a material condition for sexual oppression, theorists have turned again and again to the role played by female physicality in women's experience. So, for example, in *Becoming Woman* Penelope Washbourn, using ritual, has related psychological development to biological cycles women undergo. Carol Christ in "Why Women Need the Goddess" has explored the relation between the formation of identity and a symbol system centered on the Goddess explicitly in terms of woman's body as well as woman's will. Mary Daly has developed at length the link between religious symbol systems and the physical brutalization of women's bodies in *Gyn/ecology*. In *"Stabat Mater,"* Julia Kristeva has explored the role played by woman as symbol for life-giving in male attitudes toward the final moments of dying. More recently, Margaret Miles proposed a carnal knowing as characteristic of women's subjectivity in *Carnal Knowing: Female Nakedness and Religious Meaning in the Christian West*. These few examples reflect a genre that continues to flourish in which feminist attitudes focused on the body range from viewing biological sex or reproduction as a burden to women requiring surgical amputation, as suggested by Shulamith Firestone, to celebrating female biology as a source of mystical and revolutionary power through autoeroticism, as proposed by Luce Irigaray, among others.[29]

Regardless of the specific nature of the debates surrounding these issues, theorists have tended to argue from some feature of physicality to a feeling generated in response to a critical or constructive explanation or action. This developmental or chronological progression can lead and has led to misplacing or confusing causes and effects. Two examples will suffice, one that claims to be an experience of pure joy— namely, the experience of *jouissance*—and one that entails ambiguity—Nelle Morton's description of "imaging out of experience."

As noted in the previous chapter, French feminists, particularly those heavily influenced by Jacques Lacan and Roland Barthes, have focused upon and continue to discuss *jouissance* as it relates to women's experience of liberation through self-induced orgasm.[30] If you recall, *jouissance,* virtually untranslatable in its fullest sense, is sexual joy experienced in orgasm, in this case, joy taken in oneself as this accompanies autoeroticism. One could argue, and some feminists have, that the liberating power this feeling generates lies in its irreducibility, its escape beyond culture, specifically discourse. This escape from culture confers a revolutionary power upon *jouissance* analogous to that of a Buddhist's attainment of enlightenment. Those who have undergone the experience are the ones best equipped to understand it, and their explanations have authority lacking in all other possible explanations (particularly men's explanations).

In a similar fashion, in *The Journey Is Home* Nelle Morton describes her experience of Emily Culpepper's film *Period Piece* as an instance of "imaging out of experience":

> I knew what to expect. I knew what the film contained. I knew that it had been shown the previous year in this same setting—the

American Academy of Religion—and that then half the viewers walked out.

When Emily's vulva was flashed on the living room screen all my Southern primness surfaced. She could have used a picture from a book on physiology! I guess that is what Emily thought too. She too is Southern. It wasn't a picture of some unknown woman she had to deal with. It was herself. By the time the first "pure red blood" dropped from her vagina I was in tears. In one brief moment she had shattered the deep internalized patriarchal image within me, and I knew, not from my head but from the pit of my stomach, what Judy Chicago, Adrienne Rich, and Emily Culpepper were saying to me. I also had the title of my essay— "Beloved Image"! I knew that if ever I laughed at a "dirty" joke or condoned pornography in any way I would be laughing at myself and making my sacred images more distorted.[31]

"[Imaging . . . out of experience,]" Morton adds, "is something one experiences, consciously or out of the personal or collective unconscious. All our lives we have been warned not to trust experience and never begin with one's own self. But the private self . . . is the only source of authentic experience and this experience can be stated and understood only by public image. . . . *Deep in the experience itself is the source of new imaging.*"[32] She identifies them as experiences of the sacred, illustrated in her later essays by her own experiences of the Goddess. Of her first such experience she writes:

In 1972 at Grailville the second national conference on women exploring theology was held. One morning its sixty-five or so women delegates gathered for worship sitting informally in semicircular fashion on the floor of the oratory. A space indicated by cushions on the floor set aside was marked off as sacred. A bouquet of wildflowers on the low table in front of the screen added to the informality. The women faced one another.

Most of us did not understand at the beginning what was taking place. I was aware early, however, that something new and different was happening to me—something far more than the caring I experienced in the presence of an all-woman community. The climax came near the end when the leader said, "now, SHE is a new creation." It was not something I heard with my ears, or something I reasoned, or something I was being told. Everything seemed to coalesce and I felt hit in the pit of my stomach. It was as if the leader had said, "You are now coming into your full humanity. That which has been programmed out is authentically yours—essentially you." It was as if intimate, infinite, and transcending power had enfolded me, as if great wings had spread themselves around the seated women and gathered us into a oneness. There were no ifs or buts. I was not hearing a masculine word from a male priest, a male rabbi, or a male minister. I was sensing something direct and powerful—not filtered by the necessity to transfer or translate from male experience and mentality into a female experience and then apply to myself. The words used in the service were exclusively female words. . . .

That is the first time I *experienced* a female deity. I had conceptualized one before, but I had not experienced one directly. It was also the first time I realized how deeply I had internalized the maleness of the patriarchal god and that in so doing I had evoked cosmic support of male rulership of the earth and had reneged on my own woman identity. Not until that moment did I realize that women had no cosmic advocate in any of the five major patriarchal religions of the world. I knew that I had much unfinished business, which I have been working on now for ten years.[33]

Both examples, *jouissance* and Morton's narrative, contain virtually all the elements necessary to support the claims of both proponents of the authority of women's experience and their critics alike. In addition, Morton's narrative in particular provides clues to suggest a third approach to the issue of authority.

On the one hand, one may explain such experiences as authoritative alternatives to an oppressive culture. The force of both Morton's experience of Culpepper's film and her experience of the Goddess depends upon the depths of her feelings. In response to the image of Culpepper's vulva Morton's feelings move from reserve to tears. The felt-experience yields knowledge that is much more authoritative for Morton than analytically gained knowledge; as she describes it: "I *knew*, not from my head but from the pit of my stomach." Likewise, in response to the Goddess, Morton contrasts insight gained from hearing, reasoning, and being told with a feeling of being "hit in the pit of my stomach." This latter experience occurs in a state of trance. In addition, ordinary words cannot do justice to either experience; rather, the experiences generate "new" language (e.g., "Beloved Image"). Likewise in the case of *jouissance*, words cannot do it justice; indeed words, because they are phallogocentric, are the problem. Nevertheless, the experience of *jouissance* is revelatory. In short, both *jouissance* and Morton's experiences as she describes them contain elements of *noesis* and ineffability characteristic of mystical experiences as analyzed by James. Furthermore, by selecting *noesis* and ineffability as analytical categories for understanding and explaining these experiences, the idea that the experiences are alternatives to culture is reinforced. Morton's own explanation tends in this direction when she refers to a private self and to experience as the source of new imaging. Zajonc's theory of the relation between affect and thought lends further support to this view.

In both examples, the value of viewing such experiences of the female genitals and the significance of paying attention to one's bodily or visceral response lies in the challenge they present. Set in opposition to patriarchal culture, such experiences challenge culturally inscribed restrictions upon the female body, the devaluation of human sentience by culture, and the demeaning effects such restrictions and devaluations have upon a woman's sense of identity as a female person. This view of experience, however valuable, nevertheless overlooks other significant qualities of the experiences themselves.

Therefore, on the other hand, feminist critics of appeals to such experiences have been quick to point out the extent to which the experiences are historically, conceptually, and linguistically informed.[34] Rather than a movement from a private feeling to public concept, such experiences presuppose public concepts as a necessary condition to having the experience. For example, ineffability and *noesis* notwithstanding, both the French feminists and Morton describe their experiences in cognitive terms of liberation. What gives *jouissance* its liberating power lies in part in its deliberate defiance of male attempts to exert control over female sexuality. In Morton's narrative, what gives the image of the vulva its power is that, in the context in which it is presented, it shatters taboos; it liberates the one who beholds it. Morton describes knowing in advance the subject of "Period Piece" as well as knowing the negative response its earlier showing elicited. She further refers to similar work by Judy Chicago and Adrienne Rich with which she is already familiar. Likewise, in her account of her experience of a female deity, she writes, "I had conceptualized one before, but I had not experienced one directly."

From a critic's perspective, the implications are several. Such experiences render concepts and symbols real for the subject rather than generating them ex nihilo. They presuppose a specific end that is prescribed, not just described, in the subject's account. Furthermore, even as they challenge the dominant culture, they reflect an already existing counter-culture that comprises social networks, the members of which have at least minimal access to discourse and symbolic systems representative of their particular groups. These experiences logically presuppose already emergent conceptual work among subjects predisposed by these concepts to defy existing taboos and conventions. The theorists who argue from the authority of such experiences have not so much escaped cultural structuring through experience; rather, they are extending culture in a different direction and are, thereby, in the midst of making culture anew. The claimants or subjects are in some respect making new experiences available and cultivating feelings that value sexuality differently as witnessed by the evocative and exhortatory rhetoric of their discourse.

This analysis, focused on the formative power of discourse, differs from the first by insisting on the cultural inscription and social character of feeling in a way that does not deny the role of sensation; on the contrary, sensation remains absolutely indispensable. This view further assumes historical relativity and accounts for the communicability characteristic of emotion necessary to the generation of a social movement. It also finds support in Lazarus's work on emotion and cognition in response to Zajonc's claims. Nevertheless, additional issues of historicization and moral relativization remain. Does an experience of sexual liberation simply compete with reigning sexual taboos for the hearts and minds of women and men until one wins out over the other by sheer dint of political power? Does there remain any sense in which experience, now understood in terms of its social structure, is authoritative? This brings us to the second reason why the body plays so significant a role in feminist thought, namely, the construal of pain and pleasure.

As Morton herself points out, women's experiences of liberation often begin "at the end of a diffused pain." As will shortly become clear, giving voice to pain makes the body itself both an authority and a resource for theoretical work. Analyzing experience in terms of giving voice to pain constitutes a third approach to assessing the issue of authority.

Construing Pain and Pleasure

In *The Body in Pain: The Making and Unmaking of the World,* Elaine Scarry structurally analyzes the role played by pain in relation to imagination in the human processes of creativity and destruction.[35] The study is remarkable, her argument multi-faceted and worth analyzing at great length for all its implications; its relevance to this discussion, however, lies in the authority Scarry grants the sensation of extreme physical pain and the moral urgency with which she invests imagination.

The first part of the book consists of her chilling examination of Amnesty International documents detailing the events of torture and war, notable in both cases for the defining role played by an intention to injure another. She explores how this intention must remain largely masked with respect to the agents of violence and their supporters in order for acts of violence to be initiated and sustained. The ultimate self-deception in the case of torture, for example, occurs when the victim breaks down and "confesses" to "crimes" real and imagined. At this moment the moral burden appears to shift such that the victim comes to be viewed by the torturer, by all those who hear later of the confession (regardless of their political loyalties), and by the victim herself or himself as culpable—a traitor, a quisling, a betrayer, a coward. An alleged end, namely intelligence gathering, masks the real end, namely, the creation or fiction of power of a regime by the reduction, indeed destruction, of the imaginative capacities of the tortured.

The administering of extreme pain upon another reflects the disembodiment of the torturer's identity and the destruction of the imagination, and thereby the identity and the world of the tortured. The torturer becomes imagination unable to imagine its own physicality, while the tortured becomes exclusively sensation, the sensation of pain. The "confession" reflects the ultimate destruction of the victim's imagination, the destruction of her or his voice in the moral sense. The non-participating witness (whether at long range or close range) becomes an accomplice in self-deception in her or his revulsion at the victim for having "confessed."[36]

Crucial to the success of this grotesque drama, the victim's body as the locus of pain becomes the chief enemy of the victim. For the victim, the sensation of pain furthermore provides paradoxically the one absolute certainty that remains to existence. For torturer and witness alike, the extent to which imagination distances itself from the body ironically determines the extent to which the pain of another is subject to doubt. The greater the distance, the more doubt, until imagination disengages altogether from the body of the victim such that a human being can inflict pain upon another over and over and over. This process of disengagement ("process" in that it requires elaborate and detailed symbol systems and ritual acts) reverses the process of creativity (which Scarry explores with the same appreciation for detail in the second half of the book).

Scarry's analysis of pain holds several implications worth pursuing in regard to the authority of experience. For the victims of torture, provided they survive and regardless of whether they ultimately "confess," voicing their pain is crucial to healing it. For the witness, a steadfast, conscious refusal to engage in the deception that torture is a means of gathering intelligence crucial to national security (hence the

"legitimization" of seeking a confession) becomes morally imperative. Such refusal necessarily requires that imagination remain related
to sensation so that the witness does not cease to imagine the pain of
another in spite of the fact that the witness may never have experienced such pain. This refusal depends as well upon being able to hear,
to listen actively, to the testimony of survivors and their loved ones,
irrespective of the witness's ideological loyalties. Imagining pain and
an active hearing of testimony are crucial for the bonding of those
who have not been tortured, or lost loved ones to torture, with those
who are its victims. Thus the experience of being tortured must be
granted authority.

This *voicing* of pain, experienced and witnessed, serves for Scarry in
contrast to torture-induced "confession" as the origin, the first moment so to speak, of creativity. Whereas destruction presupposes a
lack of relation between pain and imagination, creation assumes their
relationship to be intimate. Furthermore, physical pain and imagination set the framework for understanding the human psyche as a
whole. Of their interaction she writes:

> Physical pain, then, is an intentional state without an intentional object;
> imagining is an intentional object without an experienceable intentional
> state. Thus, it may be that in some peculiar way it is appropriate to think
> of pain as the imagination's intentional state, and to identify the imag-
> ination as pain's intentional object. . . . To be more precise, one can
> say that pain only becomes an intentional state once it is brought into
> relation with the objectifying power of the imagination: through that
> relation, pain will be transformed from a wholly passive and helpless
> occurrence into a self-modifying and, when most successful, self-
> eliminating one. . . . What may . . . be the case is that "pain" and
> "imagining" constitute extreme conditions of, on the one hand, inten-
> tionality as a state and, on the other, intentionality as self-objec-
> tification; and that between these two boundary conditions all the other
> more familiar, binary acts-and-objects are located. That is, pain and
> imagining are the "framing events" within whose boundaries all other
> perceptual, somatic, and emotional events occur; thus, between the two
> extremes can be mapped the whole terrain of the human psyche. (164–
> 165)

It is of fundamental importance to note that it is physical pain, not
sensation in general nor psychological pain in its various forms, that
provides (in conjunction with imagination) the framework for understanding creativity and destruction for Scarry. (The priority of pain
also receives support in Frijda's work.) This is not to devalue other
sensations or concomitant feelings, especially positive ones; rather it

is to place them in a context with respect to the processes of creation and destruction.

If one accepts this framework, some clarification to the authoritative status of experience follows. The voicing of pain, directly experienced or witnessed, lies at the very heart of making, most especially making value. As Scarry herself goes on to point out, human beings in their relations to the deities they themselves make, not only make artifacts, but continually make and unmake making as this is associated with value. Thus language or discourse itself is always in the process of changing. To return to Morton as an example, her entire journey as a feminist was born initially out of the pain produced by her awareness of her oppression and viscerally experienced by her. Her experiences, particularly her experiences of the Goddess, occur in contexts that maximize the possibility of such experiences. Her feelings are responses to cognitions, verbal and visual, and these feelings serve to make these cognitions vivid and forceful (what Zajonc would term "hot") in Morton's sense of her own identity. The feelings do not generate the concepts; rather as responses to visual and verbal imagery they serve to select or make real. From Morton's perspective, these experiences give voice to her pain and provide alternatives to oppressive conditions.

To extrapolate even further, unmaking or destruction occurs legitimately insofar as the sensation of physical pain remains in relation to imagination. Thus viewing the vulva under certain conditions "unmakes" patriarchal taboos. What originates as "diffused pain" ultimately renders patriarchal symbol systems and associated discourse anomalous for Morton, "unmakes" their power over her, yet she never forgets the pain and must live with what she considers to be its consequences.[37] The pleasure she takes in woman-centered imagery and concepts, in contrast to the pain, depends upon ongoing ritual reinforcement to be sustained.

Unmaking becomes morally unacceptable, however, where the relation between the sensation of physical pain and the imagining subject is broken. Human brutality and cruelty depend upon denying, avoiding, ignoring, doubting, displacing, and, worse still, enjoying the pain of another in order to create a fiction of power. Our earlier example of Alicia Partnoy provides a case in point.

In the context of religious or moral authority the sole absolute lies in preserving an overall framework within which sensation and imagination may interact in its various historically conditioned and relative ways. Annihilating this framework either locally with respect to individual persons, as in the case of Partnoy, or globally as in the cases of planetary destruction threatened by nuclear accident or by ecological devastation, destroys the possibility for both historical conditions and variable moral and religious values, indeed destroys even the possibilities for skepticism, cynicism, and nihilism. Faced with annihilation whether local or global, imagining the pain of another and experiencing pain, as necessary conditions for giving voice to it, take on added urgency.

The experience of oppression, whether suffered or borne witness to, thus becomes authoritative to the extent that the theologies, thealogies, philosophies, and other worldviews to which experience gives voice preserve the relation between pain and imagination. The proponents of experience as authoritative, whether this experience is specified with respect to class, race, or gender, lay valid claim to its authority to the extent that the social character of experience is preserved and the further end, namely the preservation of a framework for articulating pain, is held steadily in view. In other words, the particularity of one's experience must embody an impetus or momentum toward solidarity and inclusivity in order to carry moral and spiritual authority for others whose experiences are different. Returning to the example of Partnoy, recall that the prisoners in la Escuelita share their meager fragments of bread in part so that they may remember that true values are still alive.[38]

The critics of the authority of experience likewise lay valid claim to challenge any tendencies toward reducing this impetus or momentum toward inclusivity by neglecting the social and relative character of experience, in short, attempts to circumvent culture by appeals to individual inner states. They are correct in pointing to the determinative role of language or discourse, as it interacts with the will to power in the construction of reality. The will to power, divorced form a consideration of shared values and value making, is, however, precisely where human society runs amok and why pain, once voiced, provides a genuinely creative alternative authority.

The Ambiguity of the Body

The methodological implications of the authority of sensation for theory of religion and philosophical theology provide the focus for the concluding chapter of this book. Let us return for the moment to the ambiguity of the body as site for the imagination as well as object of the imagination. The significance of sensation, especially the sensation of pain, for the exercise of human imagination grants insight into

the relation between the body lived and the body imagined by indi-
cating limits that force themselves upon imagination and its construals. On the one hand, too much sensation, particularly pain, destroys the capacity to imagine self, world, and the possibility of
transcendent realities; in short, extreme sensation annihilates even
the possibility of subjectivity for the sufferer, as evidenced in the
examples of torture, severe physical injury, and certain diseases. On
the other hand, extreme distantiation of the imagination from the
body that locates it threatens or actually destroys the capacity of an
imagining subject to recognize the subjectivity of another; the body of
another ceases to signify potential and actual status of the other as
subject as well as object of cognition. Under these latter circumstances
the other, reduced solely to object, serves as icon to support a fiction
of power, an assertion of hegemony.

In short, extreme distantiation between the body lived and the
imagining subject produces an identification of the body imagined
with whatever or whoever is other at the expense of the other's
subjectivity. The figure of woman has suffered precisely this fate in
both textual and visual representation, certainly in Western civilization, and from all appearances, with few exceptions in Eastern civilization. Likewise, the figures of the "primitive," the peasant, and the
slave, whether denigrated or glorified, have served as a vocabulary or
iconography of hegemony in much of the world's literature and art.
Although the objectification of the other is not news, a moral imperative to hold sensation and imagination in right relation to one another, along with the distinction between acceptable and unacceptable "unmaking," provides insight, as we have just seen, into how the
body lived can become for a resource for insisting upon the subjectivity of the other. This claim carries with it a correlative view of the
body imagined, a view that presupposes a very specific relation between sentience and subjectivity, as represented through textual and
visual image, a view to which we now turn.

FOUR

The Body as Sign for Religious Imagination

What is the relation between sentience and subjectivity? This chapter focuses on the significance of the body for subjectivity. Verbal and visual images teach us to "see," to imagine; they do so in part by providing concrete, particular bodies that cue us to attribute subjectivity to the self or another, or to withhold it. In short, the body locates a human being as object of interpretation by the self and others; the body is a sign—a very ambiguous one. This chapter explores the role played by verbal imagery in the attribution or denial of subjectivity to self and other; the next chapter discusses the significance of visual imagery.

Voicing one's pain and bearing witness to the pain of another presuppose an agent who knows herself in some sense to be an agent. This self-knowledge constitutes the agent as subject. The body plays several roles in this self-knowledge. As we have seen in the case of Nelle Morton, it serves as a resource for the imagination through sensation; in this instance, in the long run, it serves as an ally. Where physical pain is inflicted on another without consent, as in the case of Alicia Partnoy, the body becomes a weapon against the subject by destroying, or threatening to destroy, the victim's capacity to imagine. Nevertheless, as both ally and weapon, the body provides a field of sensation, albeit culturally construed sensation, for imagination.

In addition, the body plays a role as object of imagination, including one's own body in relation to her or his own imagination. Even as her captors seek to use her body as weapon against her, Alicia Partnoy turns to her body and the bodies of other prisoners for metaphors to assert their shared status as subjects. Partnoy's capped tooth provides one of the clearest examples. While incarcerated, she is shoved against an iron gate by one of her guards, and the force knocks loose her capped front tooth. She stores her tooth in a matchbox, preserving it as an object of reminiscence and meditation. At one point she ponders:

> My mother locked herself in the bathroom to cry when my real tooth broke. It happened at an amusement park when I was twelve. I did not have it repaired until I turned fifteen. Then, along with that acrylic wonder that closed the embarrassing window of my mouth, came my first boyfriend, Roberto. It was in that age of perfect teeth that I started to feel it was okay to flirt, to want to be pretty. Now the acrylic wonder sleeps inside this Ranchera brand match box and I'm convinced that, with my eyes blindfolded, I deserve at least a mouthful of teeth.
>
> Do I want to look pretty for the guard, the torturers? I hope that what really matters to me is to be whole . . . meanwhile, I'm being destroyed. To be whole is to keep my tooth, either in my mouth or inside the match box, my sole belonging. My mattress could be removed, should they find me talking, as they did to Maria Angelica some nights ago. They could take my bread away. But the tooth . . . it's a part of me. If the guards realized how important the tooth is for me, they would seize it.[1]

This passage raises the issue of how sentience, sensuality, and subjectivity relate. The "acrylic wonder" provides Partnoy, as adolescent, with confidence in her budding sensuality—the appeal of her physicality to herself and to others—a sensuality denied her in captivity. Asleep in its Ranchera matchbox, the tooth ironically comes to symbolize wholeness, its existence as her "sole belonging," a conferral that she still numbers among or belongs to the world of subjects, its preservation an act of self-preservation. Literally part of her body, the tooth stands as synecdoche for her wholeness. "If the guards realized how important this tooth is" integrates the aesthetic, the political, and the moral realms as an assertion that there is no subjectivity apart from sentience (albeit an "acrylic wonder") and sensuality (albeit a remembered one). To seize the tooth would be finally to accomplish the destruction of Alicia Partnoy, the subject.

The assertion that there is no subjectivity apart from sentience (the body) and sensuality (the body as pleasurable) flies in the face of the dominant religious traditions, both Western and Eastern. The major traditions, although not monolithic, have tended through much of their recorded histories to ignore or to devalue the body's relevance, to view its relevance as almost exclusively negative, or to relegate any positive value to the purely instrumental role of altering consciousness. Though each tradition has its exceptions, exceptions have tended not to represent either elite or conventional views and practices.[2] Furthermore, sentience and sensuality have been set in opposition to subjectivity and, for the most part, identified with the female in both textual and visual materials representative of culture; subjectivity, by contrast, has been reserved for the males of the ruling classes. This restriction, among other things, has led some feminist theorists to reject subjectivity as itself essentially phallogocentric, therefore, inappropriate and undesirable for women. The issue of subjectivity poses dilemmas related to and parallel with the controversies surrounding the significance of sexual and gender difference and the status of experience. The body and its significance, once again, lie at the heart of the matter. The development of the naked female body, as symbol for sin in the history of Christian literature and art, serves as a case in point.

Margaret Miles concludes *Carnal Knowing: Female Nakedness and Religious Meaning in the Christian West* by raising the question of whether textual and visual representation of female nakedness can ever communicate female subjectivity in Western culture.[3] Her book is a sustained examination of the textual and visual depiction of female nakedness by both men and women from the time of the early Christian churches to the seventeenth century. Miles includes evidence of female interpretation that provides a view of the relationship between female subjectivity and female nakedness that differs in telling ways from its male counterparts; nevertheless, she notes that this evidence is scant and not historically dominant. She proceeds carefully to demonstrate how, in spite of some of its own earliest teachings to the contrary, the church moved from relative ambiguity in its representation of naked women in its baptismal practices and its confrontation with martyrdom, to a dominating identification of female nakedness with sin and evil through the figure of Eve. In short, the first seventeen centuries of Christendom reflect the gradual cultural construction of the concept "woman" as synecdoche for all that is material and therefore finite, as this is associated with evil and death. This process occurred by denying both textually and visually a symbolic attribution of subjectivity to female representation; it took place, according to Miles, as an exercise of social control, albeit often carried out unconsciously, based on male fear of male sexuality projected upon women. The process of representation thus served as self-reinforcing for both men and women, as women internalized the values and roles projected upon them.[4] Miles's conclusion stresses the need for building traditions of women artists and writers who depict women's subjectivity by focusing on female particularity; she suggests resisting the idealization of the female body by putting textual and visual faces on female figuration that force the reader and the viewer to look women in the eye, so to speak. Nevertheless, the question remains whether men and women can view female nakedness without titillation. Can female nakedness communicate female subjectivity, or is it doomed by past history to eliciting sexual voyeurism?

The question of the relation between representation of female nakedness and the attribution of subjectivity to women entails at least two further problems. One involves the meaning of "representation"; the destabilization of subjectivity wrought by the deconstructionists constitutes the second problem.[5]

"Representation," especially with reference to female human beings, is fraught with difficulties. What is implied in "presenting *again*"? Who is representing whom? For an artist to represent another as object of vision, does this mean he (usually male) stands in her (when naked, very often female) place? Does the painted image stand in the place of the model? Does the viewer stand in the place of the painter? Can one distinguish between representation and presentation? Representation implies falsely more referentiality than the occasion manifests, given the selective powers of artistic imagination, even in the most consciously mimetic of portrayals. Presentation implies not only that the artist selects, but perhaps the model as "object" minimally colludes, and therefore, retains some element of agency. Presentation leaves open the possibility that revelation can occur as an event presupposing the interaction of various subjects, namely artist, model, image, and viewer. But perhaps presentation gives too much autonomy to the image itself; certainly with respect to human nakedness "presentation" bespeaks a ribaldry and levity both appropriate and inappropriate to discussions of subjectivity. I suppose that "representation" will have to do, in that it preserves the awareness that we are dealing in images that bear witness to an other, rather than subjects speaking directly for themselves.

Provided that female nakedness can come to represent (bear witness to, or speak for) female subjectivity, and I shall shortly illustrate how I think it has already begun to happen, what kind of subjectivity are we talking about? If it is neither dependent upon some essence or substance, nor, from a deconstructionist perspective, so thoroughly an arbitrary human fiction, pernicious in its forced unity, as to make it meaningless, what is it? Does sentience, however culturally construed along lines of gender difference in the human realm, nevertheless force the act of construal itself such that human physicality *requires* interpretation by human beings? If so, representation of the human body, whether female or male, forces an interpreter to infer subjectivity or lack thereof.[6] I propose in this chapter to suggest partial and tentative answers to these questions by examining selected fictional characters from the works of Toni Morrison, a contemporary African-American writer. In order to accomplish this task, I need first to reframe the context for raising these issues.

There is little question that representation of female nakedness lies at the heart of the sociocultural construction of *woman*. Female nakedness, particularly as represented in a text, is informed by the wider context of representation of female sensuality in general, however. Thus it could be very useful to analyze how an author of a text uses representation of female sensuality in general to communicate subjectivity or the lack thereof. The female body in motion, clothed or unclothed, carries in addition reference to race or ethnic origin as well as signs of social role and class. If diversity is a value centrally cherished by women thinkers and artists, as Miles and others argue, the key to shifting from cultural voyeurism may lie in part in considering the overall context of sensuality. By "sensuality" I mean specifically a sexual quality attributed to sentience that signals pleasure to be sought, extended, or denied—pleasure that may be forbidden or accepted. In this chapter, rather than focus solely on nakedness, I shall consider female sensuality as represented by the body as a whole, a general category of analysis in relation both to sentience, understood as a sexually determined reference to the body, and to subjectivity. As for defining subjectivity, this is to some extent the task this discussion confronts.

There exist historically a number of different conceptions of subjectivity, each of which presupposes more or less explicitly some view of mind-body relations. Nevertheless, much current discussion takes place in the context of a polarity defined at one extreme by substantialist concepts of subjectivity and at the other extreme by the deconstruction of subjectivity. The former view in its simplest form asserts an autonomous self whose identity as subject is founded upon some substance or essence that perdures irrespective of historical or material conditions; this view is perhaps the most conventional notion of the self held in this country. The latter view challenges all conceptions of self as thoroughly fictive, heteronomous in origin, and deceived in any claims of the subject to self-determination; deconstructionist critique, particularly of substantialism, has focused much academic discussion on both sides of the Atlantic.

Substantialist views of the human self evolved historically out of a faculty psychology prevalent in some form at least since Augustine.[7]

The notion of a discrete individual autonomous human agent, whose agency includes the conscious determination of his or her thoughts, has emerged over time, primarily in the West, and it usually depends in theory, implicitly or explicitly, upon some perduring essence or substance that transcends and unifies any given manifestation of the self to itself or to others (for example, some concepts of "soul," and our more popular notions of finding our "true" selves or being our "real" selves). Evidence for the existence of subjectivity in these terms consists of an appeal to the inner life of the subject, as this is understood to be in some sense given, rather than acquired through culture. This inner life provides, through introspection, dependable self-knowledge that in theory promises to be in the future, if not the present, in some sense complete. Substantialist views of subjectivity subordinate, minimize, or in some cases deny altogether the relevance of the human body in terms of any influence it exerts upon the exercise of subjectivity.

The body is most likely to become relevant only when the issue of sexual difference arises, at which point female subjectivity, if it is even granted at all, is often subordinated to what is perceived to be female biology.[8] The substance or essence of female humanity lies "naturally" in other-directedness or heteronomy in contrast to male autonomy, because women are more "naturally" subsumed by care-giving activities, as witnessed by the very makeup of the female body. Thus, the exercise of female human agency is determined by and confined to the domestic realm. That women internalize these limitations as not only natural but also chosen reinforces for them a sense of control over their own destiny that only further supports, albeit ironically, the central tenet of substantialist conceptions of subjectivity as self-determined.

Such conceptions of subjectivity may or may not be amenable to theories of consciousness that include attention to unconsciousness or subconsciousness, depending on the extent to which one allows what is held to be unconscious to be accessible to consciousness. So, for example, the human potential movement in the United States assumes a substantialist view of the subject in its optimism that the subject not only need, but can and must, bring what is unconscious to consciousness in order to be healed or actualized.[9]

Even though it may at first seem similar, this view of consciousness stands in direct contrast to that of Freud, one of the master architects of the deconstruction of the human subject. Whatever the merits or demerits of his psychoanalytic theory, he was quite pessimistic in regard to what conscious retrieval from a subject's unconsciousness could accomplish.[10] Retrieval to some degree notwithstanding, the human subject according to Freud continues to be at the mercy of drives and forces over which he or she has, at best, a relative and minimal control, heavily dependent for survival not only upon conscious sublimation, but also upon unconscious repression. From Freud to B. F. Skinner, indeed from Hobbes and Hume to present-day deconstructionists, theorists have challenged the hegemony of the subject, viewed as a self-determining agent. Irrespective of their differences, these thinkers rejected the central premise of substantialist theory that humans as subjects are even relative masters of their fate.

Here, as with substantialist views, the significance of the human body varies from theorist to theorist, and so, for example, when it comes to the issue of sexual difference, someone like Freud is no less vulnerable to biologism than his substantialist counterparts. Indeed, much European feminist theory, greatly influenced by Freud, especially through Lacan, tends, as we saw in Chapter Two, in this direction. From this perspective subjectivity is irredeemably a patriarchal construct to be eschewed by women as cultural outsiders who signify alterity. This alterity rightly stands in critical relation to all construals of the self, construal by definition being a phallogocentric exercise. In short, it is woman's destiny in some sense to be *the* Other, now transvalued as perpetual anarchist or iconoclast in relation to culture, the man's world, peopled by mythological autonomous males.[11] Needless to say, a deconstructionist view, feminist or otherwise, challenges conventional notions of knowledge, moral responsibility, and individual immortality, as well as the value of individual human freedom to determine one's own destiny, central to democratic republicanism and to capitalism. This view further challenges concepts of a transcendent reality, symbolized primarily as a super subject who stands over against the world as its author.

I find deconstruction of substantialist views of human subjectivity to be compelling. Even so, I likewise find the extreme destabilization of the subject and the focus upon the arbitrariness of meaning, especially as exemplified in the writings of Derrida, unacceptable on several grounds.[12] For example, epistemological dependence on paradigms or models notwithstanding, some of these are simply more adequate than others—adequate in their usefulness, adequate in terms of what they can account for, and adequate to the material and spiritual enrichment of human life. Thus, in the realm of science, a theory of evolution accounts more adequately for the origin and extinction of species than does a theory of spontaneous generation. Likewise in the political realm, insofar as no alternative account of human agency or human responsibility to effect change, however limited, is provided by some currently writing deconstructionists, such theories ultimately undermine the efforts of people to seek alternatives to present socioeconomic injustice. In this context, deconstructionist theories, like their substantialist counterparts, can serve further to disempower. Whether intended or not, such theories logically conclude in nihilism; when they don't, they have the potential to default in support of the status quo, even as they presume to derail it.[13] Critique as an end in itself provides no safe haven from ideological abuse. Thus, the question remains whether there are alternative views of subjectivity emerging about us that overcome both the problems associated with substantialism and the problems of extreme destabilization of human agency.

A different way to approach the issue, from a semiotic perspective, is to ask whether "self" serves as an adequate sign for the whole of subjectivity.[14] It may be preferable to speak of the subject or of subjectivity as a relation, specifically an imaginative, interpretive interaction of "self" and "thought" (here used in its widest possible sense to include all cognitions, visual or verbal, including "self," "other," and "body").[15] In concurrence with deconstructionist critique, the human subject is the artifact of its thoughts rather than the author of them; nevertheless, the subject's agency remains, albeit in modified form.

"Thought" here also refers to the activity of cognition, as well as all cognitions present to individual consciousness. Furthermore even perception itself is mediated by cognition, such that all we are and all we have is physiologically or culturally generated, and in all respects culturally mediated, interpretation. "All" most especially includes the inner life, a life that develops over time rather than being given at birth, for inner life would not be possible without the acquisition of language.

Though its duration and power change, the self and its inner life of reflection, contemplation, and meditation, as these are often cultivated through bodily discipline, are no less profound for having been generated by thought. Nevertheless understanding the subject requires that the focus shift from a subject reified and isolated as unitary "self" to include a consideration of the thoughts or cognitions that constitute it through imaginative, interpretive activity and to this activity itself as a process. This view of subjectivity is, of course, congenial to the sociology of knowledge, as well as to semiotics, and therefore not novel. It is the view Miles assumes to some extent, and its historical roots lie in the work of George Herbert Meade, William James, John Dewey, and Charles S. Peirce, among others.

Its chief problem, from my perspective, lies in clarifying the relation between what I am here calling "thought," or cognition, and what we normally refer to as the "material order" in ways that prevent degeneration into biologism, on the one hand, and a lapse into ahistorical idealism, on the other hand. This problem is diminished, however, to the extent that one holds "body" as a genuine sign for sensuality and sensuality itself as crucial to any meaning of human subjectivity. What it means for an interpreter to hold "body" as a sign that forces an interpreter's construal of another as subject is what I intend to illustrate here.[16] An analysis of selected fictional characters created by Toni Morrison will illustrate more concretely what I mean.

Although Morrison no doubt did not create her characters in light of academic discussions of subjectivity,[17] some of these characters are particularly fitting precisely because they are outcasts and outlaws in relation to a culture that, because of white racism, is itself on the margins of political power.[18] Thus conventional subjectivity (what we ideally associate with the concept "man"), as this is construed in substantialist terms, is not always available to them. Poverty stricken African-American women, sometimes crazy and always ostracized by their own communities, such characters as Sula Peace from the novel *Sula* and Pilate Dead from *Song of Solomon*, represent strikingly contrasting views of women's subjectivity as reflected through female sensuality.[19] On the one hand, Sula Peace typifies the deconstructed subject, as played off against her substantialist counterpart, Nel Wright; on the other hand, Pilate Dead presents a third alternative, to my mind preferable to both Sula and Nel.

Substantial and Deconstructed Selves as Derived and Deviant Women

Sula narrates a fictional account of friendship between two black women.[20] The characters Nel Wright and Sula Peace grow up together as best friends, only later to part company over Sula's adultery with Nel's husband, Jude. Not until twenty-five years after Sula's death does Nel realize and grieve her true loss. The narrative contains no spare parts, no insignificant details, no structurally loose string; the text cries out to be read aloud and heard; the fierceness of imagery blisters the eyes. In ways reminiscent of Dostoevsky, Zora Neal

Hurston, and Flannery O'Connor, Morrison portrays the relation between Nel, the virtuous, and Sula, the outrageous. The relation is one of a woman whose value derives solely from her relations with others, who nevertheless regards herself as in control (namely, Nel), and a woman whose deviance from virtuous womanhood places her in the role of bearer of absolute evil in relation to a whole community, a *totaliter aliter* (namely, Sula).

The narrative depends heavily upon the irony of reversal. For example, an all-black community named "Bottom" provides the setting. Bottom, located in the hills *above* the all-white town of Medallion, draws its name from a scam pulled by a white slave holder who frees a slave and gives him ostensibly choice bottom land *up* in the rocky, leeched hills in return for a favor. Rather than give up prime, fertile land in the valley, the slave holder convinces his former slave to take hill country because "when God looks down, it's the bottom" (5). This location not only serves to keep the subsequent black population impoverished, it ironically provides a superior vantage point in relation to the white population in the valley. Theologically justified as "the bottom of heaven" (6), Bottom's location allows its black citizens to look down upon the white population living below.

Movement inside and outside Bottom plays a major role in both the development of Nel's virtue and the identification of Sula with vice. For example, Nel's childhood journey to the South with her mother at the death of her great-grandmother marks her only distinction from the rest of the women in her family. Upon her return home, before she goes to bed, she examines her face in the mirror: "'I'm me,' she whispered. 'Me. . . . I'm me. I'm not their daughter. I'm not Nel. I'm me. Me.' Each time she said the word *me* there was a gathering in her like power, like joy, like fear. . . .'Me'. . . .'I want . . . I want to be . . . wonderful. Oh, Jesus, make me wonderful'" (28–29). This self-encounter before the mirror reflects Nel's only serious instance of a subjectivity that commands face-to-face contact of the beholder (both Nel and the reader). As time passes Nel's identity becomes thoroughly derived from the expectations of others.

By conventional standards Nel does become wonderful in her virtue. It is Nel who marries, Nel who has children, Nel who becomes a good citizen and active participant in her church, Nel who does her duty, no matter how unpleasant, without flinching. Her service to others produces her strong sense of identity. It also produces the illusion that she is the author of her destiny, one who is in control, the Nel whose "back [is] so straight" (147). Her disclaimer to being "their daughter" notwithstanding, she grows up to become like her mother, a pillar of society, a matriarch, the supreme irony of most substantialist views of subjectivity for women. Her body, itself a pillar, lacks sensuality in its rigidity.

By contrast, Sula acknowledges no such "me." An outsider by physical appearance as well as role, she bears a birthmark above one eye that gains symbolic significance according to the beholder.[21] As an epigraph to the narrative, Morrison quotes from *The Rose Tattoo,* "Nobody knew my rose of the world but me. . . . I had too much glory. They don't want glory like that in nobody's heart." Sula's birthmark is alternatively viewed as a rose, a tadpole, and a serpent; it is, however, impossible to avoid, unless the beholder looks away entirely. What Nel views as a mark of Sula's distinctiveness, her glory, the populace of Bottom regards as a mark of Satan or Cain. This connection between birthmark and evil resembles the Western church's eventual identification of women, through Eve's nude body, with sin and death, just as Nel's derived identity parallels the successful socialization of women exercised by church authority.[22]

With Nel's marriage to Jude, Sula leaves Bottom, not to return until ten years later, during which time she goes to college and subsequently travels. Physical appearance and actual experience designate her as permanently outside the community. Bottom's experience of her uncontrollability warrants its citizens' identification of her with evil:

> Sula was distinctly different. . . . As willing to feel pain as to give pain, to feel pleasure as to give pleasure, hers was an experimental life. . . . [E]xperience taught her there was no other that you could count on . . . no self to count on either. She had no center, no speck around which to grow . . . free of ambition, with no affection for money, property or things, no greed, no desire to command attention or compliments—no ego. (118–119)
> [H]ad she anything to engage her tremendous curiosity and her gift for metaphor, she might have exchanged the restlessness and preoccupation with whim for an activity that provided her with all she yearned for. And like any artist with no art form, she became dangerous. (121)

As an African-American woman in the all-black neighborhood of Bottom, she is identified by her community as an incarnation of evil, for she has, to all intents and purposes, escaped even the socialization of a subculture, not to mention that of the dominating culture. Sula, the aesthete, is, in effect, out of control—the perfect deviant—totally other.

This quality of her otherness allows the community to create itself in terms of its identity, its characteristic virtues, and its actions. Order and decency as typified in Nel's virtue prevail in the community correlative to the degree of Sula's perceived deviance and criminality. The community's dependent morality furthermore takes on religious dimensions:

> Their conviction of Sula's evil changed [the members of the community] in accountable yet mysterious ways. Once the source of their personal misfortune was identified, they had leave to protect and love one another. They began to cherish their husbands and wives, protect their children, repair their homes and in general band together against the devil in their midst. (117–118)

In the eyes of the community Sula's most serious violation is to reject other-directedness as her primary lot in life. She, however, does not become a subject, a "self," as that is usually understood as the other extreme of a polarity. On the contrary, "[s]he had clung to Nel as the closest thing to both an other and a self, only to discover that she and Nel were not one and the same thing" (119). Indeed Sula's rejection of her allotted role stands as a total challenge to the very framework that seeks to control her. The only recourse left for the neighborhood is communally to acknowledge loss of control and identify her as an aberration, indeed as evil itself. This construction allows the community to realign itself in apparent self-control.

The community's responses to Nel and Sula have several implications. Because Sula defies cultural expectations and at the same time assumes no culturally recognizable role, not even a definable though inappropriate one, she becomes subject to the community's projection of its deepest fears and unmet needs. The moral quality of the community's self-control, individual and corporate, thus depends on its self-deception. Her otherness must be absolutized as evil in order for the members of the community to be good. In other words, she symbolizes the alienation of an entire community that its members dare not acknowledge as their own, lest acknowledgment rend the community's moral fabric. This alienation locates itself in exemplary fashion in the person of Nel, whose virtue lies in overwhelming other-directedness, whose identity, albeit strong and agential, is utterly derivative. Dependent upon absolutizing Sula's otherness as evil incarnate, the community requires Sula's existence as Other in order to sustain its own moral identity, and sure enough, with Sula's death, the community morally deteriorates.

The irony of the situation is not lost on Sula. Confronted by Nel, years after Sula's adultery with her husband, Sula, on her deathbed, raises the question that has come to plague Anglo-European thought obsessively throughout this century: "'How you know?' Sula asked. 'Know what?' Nel still wouldn't look at her. 'About who was good. How you know it was you? . . . I mean maybe it wasn't you. Maybe it was me'" (146).

The interaction of sameness and difference as each is projected, respectively, as good and evil, recurs throughout the narrative; the issue is one of control—its exercise and its loss. For example, Sula's adultery with Jude forces Sula and Nel to acknowledge unexpected differences between them, Nel representing self-control at all levels in contrast to Sula's "experimental life" exemplified especially in her casual sexuality. Just as Nel's posture radiates sentience without sensuality, Sula's exudes a sensuality that obliterates all other qualities. Nel visits Sula for the first time since the episode of infidelity, and in their final exchange as Sula is dying of cancer, Nel appeals to their previous friendship, "We were friends," to which Sula responds, "If we were such good friends, how come you couldn't get over it?" (145). At this point Sula raises the issue of the knowledge of good and evil. The issue remains hanging as an ironic twist as Nel departs and Sula imagines her walking home, "So she will walk on down that road, her back so straight in that old green coat, the strap of her handbag pushed back all the way to the elbow, thinking how much I have cost her and never remember the days when we were two throats and one eye and we had no price" (147).

Just as Sula's death forces an encounter with difference, Nel's visit with Sula's grandmother, Eva, in the final chapter forces Nel to acknowledge their sameness in their past complicity in an unspeakable childhood act. Earlier in the text an episode occurs in which Sula accidentally causes the drowning of a male playmate named Chicken Little. Nel, Sula, and Chicken Little are on a riverbank. Sula in the midst of swinging Chicken Little round and round through the air loses her grip on him and flings him into the river, where he is carried away by a rushing torrent. It becomes clear in the exchange between Nel and Eva that Eva saw what happened, perhaps from her second-story bedroom window. Nel as a fulfillment of duty visits Eva, who is declining in her mental capacities and living in a nursing home. In the midst of a superficial exchange, Eva simply states:

> "Tell me how you killed that little boy. . . . The one you threw in the water. . . . How did you get him to go in the water?"
>
> "I didn't throw no little boy in the river. That was Sula."
>
> "You. Sula. What's the difference? You was there. You watched, didn't you? Me, I never would've watched. . . ."

"You think I'm guilty?" Nel was whispering.

Eva whispered back, "Who would know that better than you? . . .
"Just alike. Both of you. Never was no difference between you. . . ."

Nel hurriedly leaves as Eva calls out to her "Sula?" (168–169)

The issue is again one of control. Nel the virtuous is, like Sula the vice-ridden, guilty of murder, albeit accidental and in spite of their both being children at the time. For it was Nel who stood by and watched, who then seized and maintained control, who took charge after the episode by orchestrating their silence and supporting Sula in her anguish at her deed. An act arising through loss of control becomes a commitment to remain silent—an act of taking control. The burden of knowledge of the difference between good and evil becomes burden of the knowledge of common guilt. Whether virtuous or vice-ridden, whether insider with respect to the townspeople or outsider, whether other-directed or totally isolated by a splendid deviance, both women of Bottom share a common guilt that renders them outlaws relative to their own culture.

Their very significant differences require one another, and the relation is one of irony; in dialectical fashion they form a coherent whole. This coherence, its extreme irony, and a mournful hope become clear in the final scene of the narrative. Having left Sula's grave, Nel suddenly stops: "'Sula?' she whispered, gazing at the tops of trees. 'Sula? . . . All that time, all that time, I thought I was missing Jude.' And the loss pressed down on her chest and came up into her throat. 'We was girls together,' she said as though explaining something. 'O Lord, Sula,' she cried, 'girl, girl, girlgirlgirl'. . . . It was a fine cry— loud and long—but it had no bottom and it had no top, just circles and circles of sorrow" (174).

In Nel's cry, albeit a wail of grief, lies hope. A revolutionary cry if ever there were one, bound by neither top nor bottom, it remembers the real losses, reconciles the differences, and surrenders all attempts to take possession at the expense of others. The loss? The loss of a friend, greater than that of a lover. The reconciliation of difference? Nel's recognition of their intimacy, precipitated by the dawning of her shared guilt with Sula. The surrender? The cry of sorrow finally cut loose after twenty-four years of misdirected anger, acted out in Nel's fulfillment of her "moral duty."

For the reader the text cries out to continue,[23] for our losses need to be remembered, our differences reconciled, our attempts to take possession at the expense of others surrendered. Imagine what it could have meant for Sula in her "experimental life," revealed in her amorphous birthmark, to have found an "art form." Imagine what it could have meant had Nel, with her valiant self-discipline, reflected in her very posture, been nevertheless free to create, to experiment, once she reached adulthood. As it stands, the text suggests that excessive exertion of self-control, represented in the figure of Nel, conjoins with a glorious anarchy, portrayed in Sula, to render as outsiders women, people of color in general, the poor, indeed all whose identities emerge through derivation and through projected deviance. Even what looks like a revolutionary act, the assumption of deviance in defiance of convention, remains futile because it occurs in isolation and without form. In short, Nel and Sula illustrate the limits of both substantialist conceptions and deconstructionist denials of human subjectivity, in their shared inability to address inclusively enough the particular needs and realities of all who constitute humanity. Their bodies, through posture and birthmark, destine them as women to be objects of vision, not subjects, and certainly not visionary—objects watched, whether by Eva or the reader, in their complicity in crime.

Hope lies in part in sustaining friendship and community among "others." It further lies in living the experimental life as a discipline, a practice. Although these do not prevent tragedy, nor guarantee victory, they imply an alternative subjectivity both to substantialist conceptions and to deconstructionist denials. In making a disciplined but experimental life, friendship, and community among "others" primary themes of *Song of Solomon*, Morrison picks up, in a sense, where she left off at the conclusion of *Sula*. Once again unconventional female sensuality figures centrally in conveying meaning.

A Shift in Vantage Point

In *Sula*, Nel Wright and Sula Peace share a friendship that unites them as "two throats and one eye and [they] had no price" (147). Once the friendship ends, each lives in isolated existence—Nel isolated by her loneliness in spite of her status as an insider in relation to the citizens of Bottom, Sula isolated by the deviance of her experimental life that warrants her the status of outsider in relation to the same community. Differences, albeit significant ones, do not militate against their shared role as Other, their shared function as screen upon which to project the alienation of black as well as white men, rich as well as poor ones. Sula suffers the additional ignominy of meriting the projections of women, including those of her own best friend. If Nel's mourning promises hope, it is a hope gained at the expense of friendship, intimacy, community, and personal identity, a hope for some future generation. Sula's glory was indeed too much for the people of Bottom, however promising it may be for the reader. By striking contrast Pilate Dead of *Song of Solomon,* outrageous in the distinctiveness of her character, also an outlaw in respect to much of her own family, not to mention the black establishment, creates community.[24]

Song of Solomon as the title suggests is Morrison's tribute to the power of love to create, to destroy, and to heal. The text narrates a mystery. The mystery is the mystery of identity in relation to one's unknown past, confused present, and unlikely future. The central figure is one Milkman Dead, whose self-discovery in relation to his people costs him the lives of those who love him most and whom he loves most. Pilate Dead, his aunt, plays the major role in facilitating his quest. In the true spirit of the biblical Song of Solomon the narrative is more a texture than a text—a sustained throbbing sensuality. As with any good parable the story depends on the enigmatic quality of the ordinary, the surprise that lurks behind and within the ostensibly mundane. As Milkman Dead himself put it, "[A]nything could appear to be something else, and probably was. Nothing could be taken for granted. . . . Smack in the middle of an orchid there might be a blob of jello and inside a Mickey Mouse doll, a fixed and radiant star" (335).

Like *Sula, Song of Solomon* raises the issue of freedom. Like *Sula, Song of Solomon* expresses what might loosely be called a theological stance, though the *Song of Solomon* extends Morrison's stance more explicitly in terms of its ethical consequences. The issue of life integrates the theme of freedom with its theological and ethical presuppositions as these are all in turn conditioned by love. As Milkman Dead muses toward the end of the narrative, "Perhaps that's what all human relationships boiled down to: Would you save my life? or would you take it?" (334).

Although the novel certainly merits full treatment in its own right,[25] what concerns us here is the character Pilate Dead, a renegade who embodies love, a love that frees both self and other. Her status as renegade and the qualities of the love she embodies, especially its fierceness and its mercy, illustrate a subjectivity that gives life in the midst of bondage, pain, and death.

Pilate Dead, like Sula Peace, bears the symbol of her subjectivity visibly, in her flesh. In Pilate's case she lacks a navel: "[H]er stomach was as smooth and sturdy as her back, at no place interrupted by a navel. It was the absence of a navel that convinced people that she had not come into this world through normal channels; had never lain, floated, or grown in some warm and liquid place connected by a tissue-thin tube to a reliable source of human nourishment" (28). Born from an already dead mother without the aid of contracting muscles, Pilate wears her name, chosen at random from the Bible by her father, written on brown paper, and jammed into her dead mother's snuffbox, converted into an earring dangling from one ear. A wine maker whose lips are permanently stained, dark with juice, she possesses the various powers of making things grow, of healing, of changing her own size if the occasion requires it, and of signing. Simultaneously witch and prophet, she serves as matriarch for her own immediate family, which includes her daughter, Reba, and granddaughter, Hagar. Together they live by their wits on the fringes of black culture without electricity, central heat, or running water.[26]

Pilate, wine maker and crone without a navel, merits her special status as wise woman, prophet, and priest precisely through her love. A woman born from a dead mother virtually by her own efforts, a woman who lives off the land, she is also a woman who can love her family, including her brother and his family from whom she is estranged. A creator of community—with winos and derelicts—she saves life, heals it, and mourns death without seeking to possess those whom she loves. Neither all-powerful, nor ever all-good (such categories would surely render her inaccessible and without humanity), she lives her own life simply, without need either to denigrate herself or others, or to take particular pride in her own worth. She lives her life experimentally as does Sula, but without the need to make it a project in its own right; rather the discipline of her wisdom, her folk ways, and her willingness to struggle intimately with others place her own status as outsider in striking contrast to the splendid, awesome, yet terrible isolation of Sula.

Nowhere does this become clearer than at the moment of Pilate's death at the conclusion of the text. In the arms of her nephew, Milkman, on Solomon's leap—the point of their mutual origin and the resolution to the mystery of their ancestry—she dies from a bullet wound to the back of her head as twilight turns to darkness. Dying, "[s]he sighed. 'Watch Reba for me.' And then, 'I wish I'd a knowed more people. I would of loved 'em all. If I'd a knowed more, I would a loved more'" (340). At her request, Milkman, who can hardly carry a tune, sings to her a song from their African past, itself a clue to the mystery of their ancestry as well as the first song sung in the opening of the narrative. When he finally realizes that she is dead, insight into her existence and his feelings for her befalls Milkman. As Morrison puts it, "Now [Milkman] knew why he loved her so. Without ever leaving the ground, she could fly" (340).

As with *Sula*, likewise with *Song of Solomon*, the characters live on regardless of their fictional death and in flagrant defiance of the conventions of a last page. Pilate, like Sula and Nel, haunts the reader because she leaves so many questions, because she forces a reader to imagine a different order of being, generous out of abundance, without suffocating. What does it mean for one's love to be limited only by one's knowledge of particular people? What is it about love that destroys as well as creates? What is it about life-giving, saving, healing love that conjoins anger, mercy, and delight? What does it mean to fly without one's feet ever leaving the ground?

Morrison's Theological Anthropology

From *The Bluest Eye* to *Jazz*, Morrison's novels reflect a theological stance, if by "theology" we mean a view of human-divine relations set in the context of a world that assumes some concept of deity, itself elaborated more or less explicitly. Black Christianity, faithful to its African roots as well as its biblical ones, forms the background and also provides some of the central images and themes governing her narrative. Morrison's stance is one that is both relentlessly tough and celebratory.

The religious tradition she portrays is characteristically "sick souled" in that evil simply cannot be gotten around. Although she directly challenges conventional dualisms of good and evil, *Sula* a case in point, she also challenges easy resolution, or for that matter any resolution, to the problem of evil, most especially the problem of innocent suffering. So, for example, Pecola's prayers for blue eyes in *The Bluest Eye* are answered cruelly and absurdly by her going mad, convinced that her eyes are indeed blue, and it becomes clear that such innocent suffering could not possibly be redemptive either for Pecola or for those who bear witness to her.[27] Her abuse, her pain, even the relative release granted by her psychological dissolution, loom in the air, posing unanswerable questions that refuse the reader the luxury of looking away.

Like Calvin and Edwards before her, Morrison locates the ultimate responsibility for human sin and evil not only within intra-human relations, but with the deity who created them. Unlike Calvin and Edwards, she makes no effort to clothe this aspect of the deity's creativity with the language of the unknowable greater good that, had we as humans access to the deity's perspective, we would see both its sensibility and its glory. Rather, for example in *Sula*, evil is present, to be avoided insofar as one can, survived where necessary, and triumphed over where possible (118). In further contrast, God is a god of four faces rather than three, the fourth being that of Satan himself (118). Furthermore, evil triumphs in spite of individual efforts, as the dedication to Morrison's novel *Beloved* bears testimony, a dedication that simply reads: "Sixty Million and more."[28] What this view means for the citizens who live out their lives in Bottom is that "the only way to avoid the Hand of God is to get in it" (66).

Against this backdrop characters of biblically epic proportions appear suddenly in stark relief.[29] They live and die with an orneryness that is simultaneously and inexplicably graceful. Often wise in the folk ways of their ancestors and equally often unaware of them, characters like Sula Peace and Pilate Dead, in their apparent anarchy, may bring death; yet they also bear witness to life in ways that leave questions everywhere. In short, even as these characters profoundly disturb, they also enchant, and in their very outrageous particularity, as well as their shared status of other par excellence, they lay claim to universality. The universality to which they lay claim, however, appears only in and through their particularity, not in spite of it; it is a universality of appeal rather than a universality of uniformity. In other words, they invite us one and all into their lives, even as they invite themselves into our lives, our differences to be acknowledged, in some cases repented, and in other instances celebrated. They finally refuse to die, at least in the reader's imagination, by insisting instead on the priority of life even in its absurdity.

Sula Peace and Pilate Dead present an amazing contrast regarding the vantage point of an outsider. Sula in her splendid deviance will not be loved until perversion takes place at a cosmic level: "when Lindbergh sleeps with Bessie Smith and Norma Shearer makes it with Stepin Fetchit; after all the dogs have fucked all the cats and every weathervane on every barn flies off the roof to mount the hogs . . ." (145–146). Even the little love left over for her will itself likely be a screw job. In contrast the "navel-less" Pilate lives in a community of outcasts while refusing to abandon her upwardly mobile, financially successful brother and his own strangely perverted middle-class family, in spite of their rejection of her and their embarrassment at her. In her refusal to wash her hands of either family or community, Pilate exhibits love that is both fierce and tender.

Anyone designated "other" by culture lives caught between these two possibilities, on the one hand, and adoption of the culture's conventions of virtue as exemplified by Nel Wright, on the other. Nel's virtue, based as it is on self-deception, provides no safer ground on which to stand. Protected for years by her sense of her own righteousness, she gives up all chance at a real struggle and therefore a real peace until she cuts loose with her revolutionary cry at the end. In her case, even the insiders are finally outside. Her derived identity indicates the failure of substantialist conceptions of subjectivity for those who live on the margins of public power. Their "substance" is doomed to remain forever defined and determined by others, even as the marginalized claim authorship for their own destinies. Their virtue is the virtue of recognizing their place and remaining in it. Such virtue is, wittingly or unwittingly, a move to control others, regardless of how much it results from socialization and regardless of how covert the control. The benefits of such virtue are short term and illusory at best.

Furthermore, Sula's consciously assumed deviance provides a logical correlate that is finally no real alternative either. So long as her deviance requires her being out of control, it is merely a reaction to control, not the transcendence of a power struggle. Sula thus remains an "artist without an art form," ultimately the negative support for a conventional dualism of good and evil. Meanwhile a racist sociocultural system that fosters both of the stereotypes of women (as derived and as deviant) groans on. In short, all attempts to reify difference as *the* Other, whether as black, as woman, or as God; whether by men or by women; whether on either substantialist grounds or on deconstructionist grounds, serve ultimately to reinforce oppressive sociopolitical systems and reflect the privileges of an elite.

Likewise an outsider, though on altogether different terms, Pilate Dead promises a creative alternative to prevailing views of subjectivity and their denial. As one who is born from her mother's corpse without a navel, she figures a subjectivity that is neither totally derived (her origin reflects that she is not fused to her mother's existence), nor isolated and deviant (had her mother died earlier than she did, Pilate could not have survived to struggle through the birth canal). Although her identity has no central, unchanging core, her agency nevertheless has a distinctive shape. Cherishing no illusions of her status in relation to her family or the culture that provides its context, her agency lies in her creative responses to the circumstances that befall her. She can adapt to an alien and alienating culture without assimilating its goals and values. She can do better than survive, for she can celebrate without trivializing her losses and the sorrow they bring her. She can effect change, and she can accept change. Her folk ways, her dedication to those she loves, and the community which she helps to foster grant her "experimental life" a discipline not available to Sula. Her refusal to give up the search for the details of her African heritage provides her a critical perspective on both white culture and the assimilation to it by members of her own family, that prevents her, in contrast to Nel, from being seduced into misplaced virtue. In short, though she is clearly shaped by her circumstances, she is not their victim; quite the contrary, she further lends her own peculiar shape to the lives of those people with whom she interacts.[30]

The Subject as Artifact of Thought

Pilate Dead presents us with a type of human subjectivity in which the human subject is an artifact of thought and for which the body serves as a sign that points to the ultimate limits of language as a system of signs.

By "artifact of thought" I mean that the human subject is its relations. These relations include, among others, past relations often inaccessible and, even when accessed, highly selected. They further include future relations at best anticipated, but for the most part altogether unknown. This kind of relationality makes the subject unavoidably agnostic, incomplete, and preferably humble, in terms of pretenses to full self-knowledge—ironically in certain respects better known by others than by herself. This subject's agency lies less in attempting to seize an illusory control than in maintaining an alert responsiveness to the particular circumstances of the surrounding environment and an openness to future possibilities. On the one hand, responsiveness (not to be confused with automatic reaction) implies responsibility and therefore the discipline lacking in Sula. On the other hand, openness grants much more room for creativity precisely because it frees the subject from exhaustive efforts, exemplified by Nel, to get and keep control over self and others. Hence, the freedom of the subject lies oddly in responsibly letting one thought lead to another, a profoundly ethical stance, governed neither solely by duty, nor solely by utility.[31] This type of subjectivity further entails a rich spirituality, if by "spirit" one means minimally that which energizes or enlivens a subject's existence beyond individual self-interest. As we see in the case of Pilate Dead, and in Morrison's theological viewpoint as a whole, what energizes is a love limited only by a confessed, partial knowledge.[32]

Such a subject, whether male or female, is necessarily sentient, seriously sensual. As we have seen, the body as sign has a very peculiar status in that it forces the beholder to attribute or deny subjectivity to another. Nel virtually effaces herself such that her very posture represents her struggle to control, in its slavery to others. By contrast, Sula and Pilate, as "marked women," communicate sensuality—Sula by her birthmark and Pilate by her belly, her earring, her wine-darkened lips, and her ability to change size as needed. These marks insist on interpretation; they refuse to be ignored. Though verbally communicated in this context, they force visual imagination and attribution of the reader. The ambiguous shape of Sula's birthmark that elicits conflicting interpretations from others, like her life as an undisciplined aesthete, reinforces her amorphous, deconstructed identity— her attribution as *totaliter aliter*. Pilate, no less outrageous than Sula, nevertheless does not deconstruct, as witnessed by her willfully changing her own body size in relation to circumstances (as opposed to becoming a projection screen for the interpretations of others); her sensuality by contrast is integrated with other qualities, especially her wisdom and her capacity to love. Just as Sula's body marks her for dissolution, Pilate Dead's allows her to fly without her feet ever leaving the ground.

The status of the body as sign for subjectivity is ironic in that it forces thought (in Peirce's broad sense of the term) that exceeds language, though it is constrained by language. Like music and the visual arts, sentience, particularly in the form of sensuality, comprises a non-verbal system of communication, for which language as a system of communication is simultaneously the best and worst analogy (hence we speak of body language). "Subjectivity" is a linguistic abstraction, to which the only access in regard to meaning comes through inference. This inference is heavily dependent upon the distinctiveness verbally or visually granted to the body of the subject. Hence an even greater irony, one must be a certain kind of perceived object (real or imagined) in relation to another likewise construed subject in order to warrant an attribution of subjectivity. This holds true irrespective of the gender of the subject.

The history of idealizing the female body in ways that efface women's subjectivity as women, and the voyeurism correlative with this effacement, require drastic measures, as attested by Morrison's use of the grotesque in the construction of her characters. Flannery O'Connor, another artist of the grotesque, when asked why her characters were so exaggerated, replied at the time, "When you can assume that your audience holds the same beliefs you do, you can relax and use more normal means of talking to it; when you have to assume that it does not, then you have to make your vision apparent by shock—to the hard of hearing you shout, and for the almost-blind you draw large and startling figures."[33] We might counter today by asking, Grotesque in relation to what and according to whom?

FIVE

Site, Sign, and Imagination

Morrison's characters illustrate in regard to text how the body cues an interpreter to respond to another's agency in relation to various cultural forces. Posture, skin color, body markings, and movement, portrayed through the medium of the written word, operate as evocative coding, the meaning of which emerges as a transaction from the interaction of sentience with an immediate context and an interpreter's past. An encounter among characters serves as the generative force for meaning that becomes only further complicated and enriched by what a reader of the text brings to bear upon it, as well as what other critics may have written about it. What the written word cannot do, however, no matter how vividly imagistic and evocative it may be, is elicit in a single frame what one scholar calls "content presented instantly with relations in place before action or sound begin to cue responses."[1] In short, a text cannot represent a contextualized figure, here the human figure, captured in its immediacy.

Partnoy implicitly acknowledges this difference when she writes in the introduction of *The Little School*, "I asked my mother, who is an artist, to illustrate this book. Her suffering during the years of repression has given her the tools to show this terrible reality in her powerful drawings" (18). The book contains three full-page illustrations, crafted by her mother, Raquel Partnoy.[2] Two of the illustrations portray blindfolded prisoners, while the third and final illustration presents a montage of images, one that seeks to capture the entire history of "disappearance" in Argentina in a single "moment." The two illustrations depicting blindfolded prisoners minimize perspective, whereas the montage denies it altogether.

The two illustrations of prisoners (Figures 1 and 3) capture the irony of a macabre struggle over identity. The prisoners are, with one exception, blindfolded in order to preserve the anonymity of the guards who appear in the background as a series of suspended masks, spying on the captives ("we are beaten whenever our blindfolds are loose" [106]). The prisoners whose very identities the guards seek to destroy appear in the foreground, elongated and grotesque in their particularity, eyes superimposed upon the surface of their blindfolds. It is they who remain connected, through touch, to one another— they who see clearly the "meaning" of the violence to which they are subjected. Indeed, it is they who through Partnoy's memory and her mother's art make meaning out of their very bodies.

Although these representations communicate the violence of the prisoners' situation, they also convey the prisoners' resistance to victimization and to a fetishizing of their pain. In the first illustration (Figure 1) one prisoner holds another as both begin to remove their blindfolds, while a third appears slightly behind them, face free. The third illustration (Figure 3) shows two figures facing each other blindfolded, hands extended toward each other. The one in the immediate foreground wears a slipper with a flower on it, a reference to the text titled "The One-Flower Slippers" (25–28). The flower, a plastic daisy, becomes an icon, sometimes an occasion for humor, that measures over one hundred days of Partnoy's trips from bed to latrine, from bed to shower. Left behind when Partnoy is transferred from the "Little School" to a public prison, the slippers, like those who do not survive captivity, disappear. The visual image even as it requires the text for a fuller understanding nevertheless augments it by depicting simultaneously the menace of the voyeurism of the guards with the absurdity of the flower in their midst. (The guards, for example, allow the prisoners to have sexual intercourse in order to masturbate as they watch [70–71].)

The second illustration (Figure 2) appears just before the last vignette simply titled "Nativity" (117–121). The montage is accompanied by a poem, written presumably by Alicia Partnoy, which commemorates the birth of a child, borne by Graciela Alicia Romero de Metz while she was incarcerated with Partnoy. Both mother and child permanently disappeared. Partnoy estimates that some four hundred children were kidnapped with their parents or born to the disappeared, most of whom have never been traced.[3] Raquel Partnoy juxtaposes what appears to be a tribunal that comprises four male heads with a baby, two military boots, and a series of females with kerchiefs around their heads, the mothers of the Plaza de Mayo.[4] The image of the baby, by virtue of its size and its positioning slightly to the left of center, visually dominates the montage; its right arm extends outward to its rightmost border; its left elbow rests on one of the boots, its

1. Untitled by Raquel Partnoy, 1985.

Black and white drawing, 8 ½″ x 11″.
Private collection of Alicia Partnoy, Washington, D.C.
Photographed by Patricia Ullmann.

2. Untitled by Raquel Partnoy, 1985.
   Black and white drawing, 8 ½" x 11".
   Private collection of Alicia Partnoy, Washington, D.C.
   Photographed by Patricia Ullmann.

3. *(above, right)* Untitled by Raquel Partnoy, 1985.
   Black and white drawing, 8 ½" x 11".
   Private collection of Alicia Partnoy, Washington, D.C.
   Photographed by Patricia Ullmann.

4. *(below, right) A Few Small Nips* by Frida Kahlo, 1935.
   Oil on sheet metal, 15" x 19".
   Courtesy of the Mexican Government,
   ARCHIVO-INBA, Mexico City.
   Photographed by Caesar Palomino.
   Reproduced by Cindy Weidemann.

5. *Tree of Hope* by Frida Kahlo, 1946.
   Oil on masonite, 22″ x 16″.
   Isidore Ducasse Fine Arts, New York.

6. *(above, right) The Little Deer* by Frida Kahlo, 1946.
   Oil on masonite, 9″ x 12″.
   Collection of Carolyn Farb, Houston.

7. *(below, right) Still Life with Melons* by Frida Kahlo, 1953.
   Oil on masonite, 15½″ x 10½″.
   Courtesy of the Mexican government,
   ARCHIVO-INBA, Mexico City.
   Photographed by Caesar Palomino.
   Reproduced by Cindy Weidemann.

8. *My Birth* by Frida Kahlo, 1932.
   Oil on sheet metal, 12 ⅜" x 14".
   Private collection, USA.

bottom on one of the mothers' heads. To the other side of the boot an arm reaches outward in the direction opposite that of the child's extended arm, this arm dissociated from any particular body, positioned as if beseeching, in a manner that geometrically complements the child's arm. Male tribunal and female protesters locate the child, contextualizing it, even as the opposing extended arms sustain and promote an almost unbearable tension. We know from the text that Graciela's child was male, in contrast to what appears to be deliberate obscuring of sexual identification through the abstract body of the visual image. The text of "Nativity," the last of the prose-poems, ends: "A new cry makes its way through the shadows fighting above the trailer. Graciela has just given birth. A prisoner child has been born. While the killers' hands welcome him into the world, the shadow of life leaves the scene, half a winner, half a loser: on her shoulders she wears a poncho of injustice. Who knows how many children are born every day at the Little School?" (121). The obvious textual use of Christian imagery of the Nativity is given a new dimension by its visual as well as verbal connection to a distinctive and much more recent history. The visual abstraction of the child, rendered without distinction between foreground and background, nevertheless centered by a specific history, communicates simultaneously that the child could be any child, including the Christ Child, yet is clearly an Argentine disappeared one. In short, the image holds in tension particularity with universality.

Human bodies appear textually and visually throughout most of human history as "gendered." Gender difference, as I have argued, is itself socially construed, in most known cultures, in ways that on the whole privilege the male of the species.[5] Cultural iconography often identifies the masculine gender with agency, mind, and spirit, in contrast to identification of the feminine gender with passivity, body, and nature, an iconography of power that we see reflected in Raquel Partnoy's montage in the positioning of males in relation to females, the obscuring of the child's sex notwithstanding. In a struggle to understand the near-universal subordination of women to men, feminists have alternatively affirmed and denied an epistemologically privileged connection between women and the female body or between women and nature. I have argued that neither position (affirmation nor denial) is satisfactory as presently developed, and have sought to provide a third alternative through close examination of how sentience and culture interact in the context of religious symbols.

I have further argued, in line with Elaine Scarry and others, that the body understood as sentience drives imagination through physical pain and pleasure to make selves, worlds, and their deities, while noting that even pain and pleasure are socially construed.[6] The body thus plays a major epistemological role as medium. It plays this role ambiguously; moreover, its ambiguity lies in its double role as site and as sign. Viewed as site, "body" focuses conceptually upon sentience as a field of pain and pleasure, experienced by imagining subjects. Viewed as sign, "body" forces the attribution or denial of agency to another, and therefore serves as a building block in the social construction of subjectivity, an attribution often denied particularly on grounds of racial, ethnic, class, and gender differences.[7] In either case, that of site or that of sign, we are working with body as cultural artifact, though the body analyzed as site exposes the limits of culture in human cries of pain and pleasure.[8]

Religious symbol systems play several roles in the social construction of reality, many of which are already well known to scholars of religion and society, and some of which are relatively unexplored, underestimated, or ignored. I shall return to a discussion of the latter in the conclusion. Before addressing the issue of religious symbol systems, however, three questions require further investigation: More precisely, what is the relationship between the body understood as site and the body understood as sign? Likewise, what is the relation between body and the imagining "bodied" subject? Finally, how does gender figure epistemologically in these relations? In response to these questions I intend to develop a twofold argument: First, the relation between site and sign can best be characterized as one of mapping; the sign "body," understood as pluri-vocal, on the one hand, maps sentience and, on the other hand, plays a role in mapping subjectivity, itself a pluri-vocal sign. Second, resistance in the relation between site and sign is of special importance, such that mapping, especially where resistance is intense, contributes in essential ways to the making of making itself and, therefore, the making of gender. Thus, the gendered body, understood everywhere and always as cultural artifact, when *it* becomes the explicit object of imagination, reciprocates by reshaping the social and personal processes of creativity and production which we call imagination.[9]

Mapping

"Mapping" as I use it metaphorically here refers to the interaction of site and sign in the conceptualization of "body."[10] The body as site provides the locus, ranging from battleground to theater, for signification. Recall, however, the previous discussion of the significance of pain and pleasure for imagination in which sentience is not at all passive; quite the contrary, pain or pleasure may serve as resistance to signification.[11]

I have deliberately chosen this metaphor for several reasons. Mapping is visual and spatial, as well as temporal and verbal. It further preserves a tension between materiality and discourse that I find lacking in such concepts as "interpreting" and "expressing," though "mapping" includes connotations of both. Furthermore, the activity of mapping captures simultaneously a visual detachment necessary to an aerial view and a sense of being in the middle of things seeking to convey direction.

Mapping is an act of symbolic construction, an act of imagination; nevertheless, real cartographers, however agential, are subject to material conditions that they cannot control. These constraints notwithstanding, the process of mapping focuses human agency on space in both analytical and synthetic ways not as explicitly conveyed by words like "picturing," which in present society connotes more passivity than I seek to convey. Furthermore, resulting maps serve to orient others in time and space, albeit they provide only provisional orientation. As provisional guides that may be more or less mimetic, maps are subject to critical judgment regarding their adequacy, depending on context; hence they should not be taken literally as the actual terrain represented.[12] Indeed, given the state of the art in computer technology, there need be no terrain beyond the map itself. Thus, both the process of mapping and any resulting maps are subject to modification, to differing interpretations at any given point in their history, and to dispute, revision, and rejection. Although some theorists object to the use of "map" and its cognates on the grounds that maps distort and are reifications, people who actually use maps, as well as those who make them, tend to recognize their limitations, even as they depend on maps to get to their destinations.[13] In short, most importantly, the process of mapping is social and material, therefore, historically conditioned. Compare, for example, a seventeenth-century map of the southwestern region of what is now the United States with a road map from a Texas filling station.

The metaphor is further applicable to a variety of different contexts, ranging from the interactive relationship between physicality and imagination to the processes that socially construct what we call "reality." For example, with specific reference to the body, mapping refers to historically conditioned processes of socialization that not only shape various attitudes toward the body, but to the extent that these attitudes are internalized, shape the way one experiences his own body with respect to ease, pride, shame, and guilt, as well as the way she experiences shared space, exemplified especially by touch, ranging from intimacy to menace.[14] At the most fundamental level of experience mapping designates what counts as pain as opposed to pleasure, what counts as tolerable bodily sensation as opposed to intolerable, and in some cases even what a society or culture is willing to acknowledge as sensation at all. Mapping further defines the borders that distinguish public from private, by plotting what counts as appropriate activity for public disclosure (for example, eating with your mouth closed) and what is restricted to the private domain (usually acts of sexual intercourse and biological elimination). Mapping most especially codes difference signified as gender, class, race, ethnicity, religious creed, level of education, and politics. Thus, the body is mapped from the outside in, as well as the inside out, and mapping, even at this most micro-logical level, reflects power struggles that are characteristically ideological.[15]

Because ideological struggle is characteristic, mapping as the interaction of site with sign can be analyzed in terms of resistance, that is, the extent to which socialization, for whatever reasons, does or does not "take." With respect to sentience resistance refers simply to the limits imposed by and on sentience itself; with respect to imagination (individual and social) resistance occurs at the level of interpretation. Like socialization, resistance is not necessarily conscious in those involved; however, resistance, whether intentional or unintentional, produces a range of possible responses marked with respect to an experiencing subject, at one extreme, by the transformation of the body into a weapon turned against the subject and, at the other extreme, by the transfiguration of pain and pleasure into a resource for changing the material conditions in which the subject finds herself. In the former case, a subject may lose his life; in the latter case she may seek to play a deliberate, imaginative role in the mapping process.

Partnoy's accounts of disappearance in Argentina, illustrated by her mother, provide ample evidence of the body turned into weapon against itself. Scarry's work, *The Body in Pain: The Making and Unmaking of the World,* not only discusses in detail how the body becomes a weapon, but the wider context of destruction as a mimicry of creativity in its dependence upon symbol, ritual, and myth in the activity involved in physical mutilation and killing that characterizes torture and warfare.[16] Mapping, precisely because it is symbolic activity that seeks to articulate space in time, likewise can destroy as well as create. Because mapping is symbolic activity that seeks to articulate, it presupposes language in addition to visual imagery, or, since language never exists simply in the abstract, discourses representing various perspectives. Thus how and why the body becomes a weapon disclose themselves in the various verbal and visual accounts rendered by victims, victimizers, and witnesses to events of physical cruelty.

These accounts further extend the relevance of mapping as a metaphor. As accounts they stand in dialogical relation.[17] Though verbal exchange in the context of violence will hardly be civil, competing voices compete to persuade, and failing this, perhaps to coerce an audience beyond those immediately involved. In destructive contexts the victim's body thus becomes the site for competing interpretations in the making of worldviews or ideologies, and the material provided by the "winners" serves as the dominant meaning in the cultural life of the body as sign. Nevertheless, as I shall shortly illustrate, even the "losers'" discourses remain latent in the resulting map, ready to serve in future struggles to create and to destroy meaning and value.

The structural resemblances between creativity and productivity, on the one hand, and institutionalized suffering and violence, on the other hand, raise the issue of how to communicate ethically or with justice.[18] For example, Partnoy's account of disappearance combines various modes of discourse, ranging from iconographic and poetic to a prose that varies in tone according to authorial aim. The prose-poems are framed by direct discourse in the first person, initially in the form of an introduction that seems to address a reader personally, and then in the conclusion as a witness giving testimony in the more public context of the courtroom. The prose-poems shift in perspective, including both male and female perspectives, as well as the positions of both prisoner and guard (very briefly in this latter case). The account compels to the extent that Partnoy avoids melodrama, rationalism, fetishism, and romanticism,[19] and to the extent that a reader is neither convinced by the ruling junta at the time,[20] nor predisposed to discredit pain.[21]

Multiple perspectives producing multiple interpretations suggest by their potential and actual disagreement a broadening of resistance, and likewise mapping, beyond the sentient that can also be generalized beyond contexts dominated by violence. Multiple interpretations presuppose a struggle over signification itself. Centered by a struggle that is ultimately substantiated by the body as site, whether various perspectives be external and conflictual or internally imagined by a single person, multiple interpretations suggest that mapping contains the potential for change. Socialization may not "take" in part because socialization itself is pluri-vocal in nature and always in the process of being made up and made real in part through substantiation by the body. In other words, resistance, whether between site and sign or within signification, indicates that the body, understood as artifact, reciprocates in the process of making itself. Mapping, then, as a comprehensive, historical process of constructing or making socionatural reality is neither arbitrary fabrication (due to resistance at any given point) nor unintentional.

This claim lies implicit in Scarry's work. She argues that violence is the occasion by which ideas are substantiated through human bodies. She further argues that made objects are extensions of the human body, made by the imagination driven by sensation. She points out that made objects reciprocate excessively in proportion to human need for them.[22] Though she does not fully consider the body itself as conceptual artifact and furthermore ignores the issue of gender difference altogether, I see no reason not to extend the process to include the body itself, particularly the gendered body, given the body's status as sign as well as site. In which case, the body gendered plays a role in the making of making additional to that of the body sensing and sensed—the role of reciprocating artifact. To understand what it means for the body as artifact to reciprocate in relation to imagination, and, in addition, to understand the relevance of gender, we need to turn to an instance in which a maker consciously makes and remakes her own body through visual representation. Frida Kahlo's preoccupation with portraying herself reflects the dialogical quality of mapping a body, marked by resistance, a body that as artifact reciprocates excessively not only in relation to Kahlo's own imagination, but also in relation to the social milieu her work subsequently shapes. Indeed her work involves nothing less than what one scholar calls the re-mapping of the female body.[23]

Frida Kahlo

Born on July 6, 1907, in Coyoacán, Mexico, to Guillermo Kahlo, a Hungarian Jew, and Matilde Calderon y Gonzalez, of Spanish and Mestizo descent, Frida Kahlo is one of Mexico's premier artists of this century.[24] Though she enjoyed brief international acclaim in the thirties and forties, especially among the surrealists, her work was overshadowed most of her life by the work of her husband, Diego Rivera, perhaps the greatest of Mexico's fabulous muralists. She spent much of her life in great physical pain caused by polio in early childhood and, later, a near-fatal accident while travelling on a bus when she was a young adult. In the bus wreck, Kahlo's pelvis and one leg were crushed, several ribs were broken, and she was impaled through her vagina by a metal rod. Though she underwent several operations, none was sufficient to correct her injuries. Toward the end of her life she suffered gangrene, requiring amputation of one of her legs at the knee. The last years of her life were especially marked by a hideous, unrelenting pain that required heavy use of narcotics.

Partially in response to physical disfigurement, she in many respects created herself in mythic proportions, devoting a great deal of time daily to her toilette, dressing in colorful Mexican peasant clothing. From her diaries it is clear that she identified herself, her body, its appearance, her pain, and her pleasure metaphorically with Mexico; the terms for this connection were not only patriotic, but also spiritual in relation to the natural order. From Kahlo's perspective, her mixed heritage and the events of her life reflected the history of struggle and suffering, as well as the hoped-for destiny of Mexico itself.[25] A Marxist nationalist (Mexicanidad) and atheist, she was part of a larger movement of intellectuals, artists, and politicians who supported Mexico's revolution of 1910 by embracing the indigenous culture in preference to imitating European culture. A political activist, she died shortly after participating by wheelchair in a march protesting U.S. intervention in Guatemala. She died in the house in which she was born, the *casa azul*, on July 13, 1954, leaving only about two hundred paintings, roughly seventy of which are self-portraits.[26]

Her paintings, remarkable as they are in their own right, when related to her life, have generated controversy among critics and scholars that represents an interesting ideological struggle over Kahlo herself as icon. She and her work provide therefore an outstanding illustration of mapping, the role played by resistance within mapping, the role played by the body in the making of gender, and the role played by the gendered body in the making of making.

Kahlo's Work

Mexican popular culture illustrates well how the discourses of "losers" remain latent in resulting maps, poised ready for future assertion, for it reflects already existing syntheses of various pre-Columbian cultures with European culture. One of the most striking examples consists of the assimilation of an Aztec belief that life emerges from death into Christian observance of All Souls Day (November 2). This observance, celebrated in Mexico and in southwestern Mexican-American cultures as the Day of the Dead, is marked by a carnivalesque ubiquity of dancing, leering skeletons and by the baking of bread in the shapes of the deceased in order to commemorate them, both of which reflect Aztec motifs. Although Kahlo had such examples as this at hand on which to draw, she also consciously synthesized Aztec, Zapotec, and popular Catholic images to construct an iconography that reinforced visual identification of her own person with her country. For example, Aztec imagery, especially the goddess Coatlicue, appears in several of her self-portraits.[27] It further serves as reinforcement to visually depicted conflict between Mexican cultural nationalism and modernization as represented by U.S. technological development.[28] The skeletons that appear throughout her work likewise derive from Aztec iconography in support of her own emphasis upon the emergence of life from death, though her diaries, as well as her paintings, register more ambivalence toward death than the Aztecs may have felt.[29]

In addition, Kahlo's husband, Diego Rivera, possessed one of the world's finest collections of pre-Columbian artifacts from western Mexico. Scholars assume that Kahlo drew directly upon this collection for the Zapotec images that, like the Aztec imagery, characterize her paintings.[30] One scholar notes that Kahlo's use of Zapotec imagery specifically symbolizes liberty in Mexicanidad iconography.[31] The Tehuana dress stands as Kahlo's most famous recurring Zapotec image.[32] Her own preference for Tehuana clothing marks her as performance artist as well as painter.[33]

Kahlo's atheism notwithstanding, she combined Aztec and Zapotec imagery with popular Catholic motifs, most notably the *retablo*, perhaps the most disturbing of her appropriations from the religious realm. *Retablo* refers to a genre of popular Christian artifacts that includes icons of various saints and members of the Holy Family and *exvoto* paintings, that is, small paintings that are hung on church walls to commemorate miracles. These paintings are usually done on tin and are slightly larger than postcards. The *exvoto* in particular records an event (usually life-threatening) that occasioned a miracle, an intervening agent (usually a saint or a member of the Holy Family), and a brief, written documentation, appearing as a banner, sometimes including historical dates.[34] Kahlo collected *retablos*, many of which can still be seen hanging in the stairwell of the *casa azul*. Her fascination with the *retablo* goes beyond a detached consideration of iconography in the production of images for a post-revolutionary Mexico, by being immediately associated with her own pain, for which there would be no miraculous cure.[35] In some cases, though not always, she painted directly on tin comparatively small paintings. These commemorated specific, often violent events that happened not only to her, but to others.[36] Her later self-portraits take on an added dimension of religious significance in her further appropriation of eighteenth- and nineteenth-century funeral portraiture of nuns.[37] One scholar notes that Kahlo's preoccupation with *retablos* and related religious art forms represents a *detournement* of religious images, a detouring from the supernatural order to the natural order, in order to transvalue the secular, a move I find similar to Partnoy's verbal use of religious imagery,[38] which I have characterized as parabolic.[39] However, Kahlo's *retablos,* like Partnoy's parables, disturb in part because they commemorate actual events for which there is no outside intervention depicted, no miracle to stop the wounding,[40] and like Morrison, Kahlo depends heavily upon the grotesque. One example will suffice.

In 1935, Kahlo painted *A Few Small Nips* (Figure 4), an oil on tin, framed. The painting depicts the event, recorded in the newspaper, of a drunken man throwing his girlfriend on a cot and stabbing her twenty times. The newspaper account quotes him as protesting before the court, "But I only gave her a few small nips." The painting depicts the immediate aftermath of the murder: The murderer, wielding a bloody knife, hovers over his victim's lifeless body, gashed and bloody, naked except for one nylon stocking and a high-heeled shoe; the victim's body lies posed, as scholars are quick to point out, in a manner reminiscent of the dead Christ descended from the Cross;[41] blood is splashed everywhere, spilling over onto the frame itself, as if to pull the viewer immediately into the scene as witness, if not accomplice. The "moment" appears so realistically that as one scholar puts it, "Comme dans la plus pure tradition des images miraculeuses ou s'écoule du sang des plaies du saint, l'image n'est plus simulacre, elle se fait chair."[42]

However realistically portrayed, the painting also depends heavily upon gender stereotypes, deliberately used by Kahlo to connect her own dissatisfaction with her life with Diego Rivera, who was having an affair with her sister at the time, with the event of the murder. Heydan Herrera, Kahlo's best known biographer in English, writes:

> Hand in pocket, fedora set at a jaunty tilt, the murderer looks as brutal as the woman looks brutalized. Indeed, the painting presents stereotypes,

the *macho* and the *chingada*, his victim. *Chingada*, literally the "screwed one," is Mexico's most familiar curse and a word used frequently by Frida. . . . Frida told a friend that she painted the murderer as he appears here "because in Mexico killing is quite satisfactory and natural." She added that she had needed to paint this scene because she felt a sympathy with the murdered woman, since she herself had come close to being "murdered by life." (180–181)

Herrera goes on to point out that the painting parodies the graphics of Jose Guadalupe Posada (1851–1913), a favorite of Kahlo's who satirized sensational horror scenes. Herrera interprets *A Few Small Nips* as Kahlo's *carcajada*, or burst of laughter, in the face of pain (not unlike what Partnoy referred to as "black humor" among the prisoners in the Little School).[43]

Biting laughter in the face of unrelieved pain deeply disturbs, in part because of its ambiguity; this ambiguity has implications for subsequent scholarship on Kahlo's work as well. One scholar notes that "[a] total willingness to reveal herself is perhaps her most definitive quality."[44] What Kahlo reveals through her paintings and her diaries is nevertheless highly ambiguous, producing multiple, often conflicting interpretations, particularly with respect to the significance of her sexuality, her politics, and her employment of religious iconography. What Kahlo reveals through her work and her diaries is a highly complex person of volatile temperament, constituted by loyalties so deep that she could be quite obsessive and possessive in her relations with others. Plagued by pain, she was ambivalent toward her body; known for her kindness toward children, she was ambivalent toward childbearing. Wife of Rivera and lover to several men, she is rumored to have had lesbian relations as well. Committed to the Bolsheviks, she and Rivera nevertheless sheltered Trotsky, with whom she is reputed to have had an affair; yet, she died before completing a portrait of Joseph Stalin, who was one of her heroes.[45] I have already alluded to her atheism, even as she deliberately drew upon religious sources for her iconography. Were one to seek to reconstruct a coherent worldview or ideology from what Kahlo reveals, one would be hard pressed to find the logical coherence, for what Kahlo reveals about herself for the most part is a person of strong political convictions, engaged in social struggle and defined by inner division, resolved only by a death that some have claimed was a suicide.[46]

Kahlo's studied ambiguity has played a role in generating subsequent controversy among scholars as well. Her complexity, her conscious engagement in self-creation, her deceptive transparence, and the lack of resolution of the conflicts that marked both her work and her life have won her a place as icon in her own right. As one scholar notes, "She was the main character in her own mythology, as a woman, as a Mexican, and as a suffering person. . . . [S]he knew how to convert each suffering into a symbol or sign capable of expressing the enormous spiritual [and I would add political] resistance of humanity and its splendid sexuality."[47] Stated differently, Kahlo's capacity to identify self with country and self with other is a two-way street that has allowed her to become a site for ideological struggle among those who identify reciprocally with her. Kahlo's conscious synthesis of Aztec, Zapotec, Catholic, and Marxist iconography, with specific reference to biographical and historical events of personal significance to her, elicits critical and scholarly responses ranging from allegorical to reductive. Her conscious appropriation and modification of religious and political iconography indicate that she intended allegory; critics and scholars who interpret her paintings in light of her diaries sometimes tend toward psychological reduction that denies or diminishes her politics. In other words, the scholarship her work and life have generated further manifests mapping, now modeled on dialogue characterized by conflicting interpretation. Because scholarship itself illustrates an extension of mapping, I shall relate the rest of my analysis of Kahlo to the issues of mapping, gender, and the nature of making with a critical analysis of relevant scholarship on the struggle to claim Kahlo as icon.

The Mapping of Frida Kahlo

Kahlo's paintings, like the art work of her Mexican peers involved in the Mexicanidad movement, as well as that of other contemporary international movements that turn to some kind of alleged primitivism (whether stylistic or substantive), reflect the rejection of one culture by drawing from and reconstructing one or more earlier cultures. Such movements tend to romanticize or fetishize the alternative cultures, a tendency that can lend itself to appropriation in the service of totalitarian interests, though this does not necessarily follow.[48] What I think distinguishes Kahlo's work from that of some of her national and international contemporaries lies in her general resistance to romanticization and fetishization. Though her work is dramatic and her concerns very programmatic, with few exceptions, Kahlo's images sustain sufficient ambiguity and tension to resist oversimplification and thereby avoid ready use for totalitarian interests.

Kahlo characteristically focuses intensely on struggle itself and, further, places struggle in a context that typically connects particular bodies in all their wonderful and horrible concreteness with a wider, public religiopolitical commitment. Many of her paintings reflect a recurring concern with polarities, sometimes expressed as dualities,[49] sometimes visualized in terms of division and demarcation,[50] and in any case, represented as unresolved tension.[51] In most of these paintings Kahlo's own body plays a central role in representing sustained tension among conflicting forces. Her preoccupation with her own body as icon for expressing unresolved tension in painting after painting illustrates what I mean by mapping with special reference to resistance. Over and over she projects her body as site, whether portrayed in multiple images in the same painting (as in the case of *The Two Fridas* [1939]), or straddling various borders (as in the case of *Self-Portrait on the Borderline between Mexico and the United States* [1932]), or split and supported by a Greek column in the process of crumbling (as in *The Broken Column* [1944]). Even as her sentience becomes record, the record becomes "n'est plus simulacre, elle se fait chair."[52] The polarities represented seem to be multiple responses to a previously posed question, for which there is either no definitive answer or at best an ambiguous one. The nature of the struggle may vary, sometimes overtly sexual, sometimes obviously political, usually on some dimension a struggle to express and perhaps to relieve pain.

Tree of Hope (Figure 5) serves as an excellent illustration for which resistance to pain is the central issue. Two Fridas appear, one superimposed upon the other in the foreground of a landscape divided down the center. One half is painted in daylight, the other at night. The sky is cloudy, the horizon marked by mountains, the earth fractured by crevices that possess a dendritic quality. Sun, moon, and the wheels of a gurney delineate a quadrilateral space within which two figures appear. The two figures, both images of Kahlo, are positioned just beyond a major crevice that borders the bottom of the painting. One Frida dominates the day; the other the night. The Frida of the day lies horizontally upon the gurney, her back to the viewer, long dark hair flowing over the side of the gurney. Her body is covered by a sheet except at the waist and upper pelvic region, which are naked, gashed, and bleeding. To the front of the gurney the second Frida with darker complexion appears seated upright in a wooden chair. This Frida of the night faces directly forward, her expression impassive. She wears a bright red dress of indigenous origin. Her hair is groomed and bound atop her head by a matching red bow, and she wears jewelry that also looks to be of pre-Columbian origin.[53] She appears to be supported by a back brace, a duplicate of which she holds in her lap with her left hand. In her right hand she holds a banner marked ARBOL DE LA ESPERANZA MANTENTE FIRME ("tree of hope hold firm"). Just as the gurney is not confined to the daylight, but extends as well into the night behind the upright figure, so the upright figure exceeds the boundary established by the line between night and day into the daylight.

Kahlo's bare back is quite literally mapped like the earth that supports both figures. The crevice that appears at the base of the painting suggests that the supporting earth could at any moment rend again and swallow both figures. The contrasts of horizontal figure with vertical figure, back view with front, and day with night suggest not simple and equally viable alternatives between illness and health, but serious and complex struggle against despair. Given that the figures exceed their respective boundaries of day and night, given that the upright figure is supported by a brace, and given the content of the banner, the struggle at this point (1946) is not so much to be restored fully to health as to be able to hope for any kind of future not entirely dominated by pain. The upright figure, supported by a brace, becomes all the more poignant in light of the knowledge that Kahlo painted at times from a wheelchair and, more difficult still, sometimes from a horizontal position in her bed, with the aid of a mirror.[54]

The indigencity of the red dress and jewelry and the content of the banner suggest that hope lies in turning to one's native and spiritual roots, which in the case of Mexican culture are more directly tied to nature. Herrera notes that paintings that show Kahlo twice are paintings of self-nurture.[55] Nevertheless, the brace supporting Frida of the night and the horizontal figure on the gurney leave no doubt that Kahlo is dependent on modern medical technology as well. Once again there are no simple choices; rather there is only resistance to despair in the midst of ambiguous and competing forces. This resistance in the face of ambiguity finds its clearest expression in the dendritic quality of the crevices that mark the earth, for they suggest simultaneously the earth quaking, scars, the human nervous system, and the roots of trees.

If the artistic subtleties along the borders of demarcation and duality go unobserved, the polarities characteristic of Kahlo's work lend it all too easily to Manichean interpretation. Scholars on occasion interpret these images in terms of an internal psychological conflict within Kahlo between good and evil.[56] Kahlo herself reinforces tendencies in this direction by speaking of herself in terms of dual personalities.[57] The psychological struggles of Kahlo notwithstanding, I find this kind of interpretation a distraction from the full richness of her work, as well as an obscuring of its value for understanding its place in the process of constructing culture itself. The strength of her use of polarities lies in the tension she generates and sustains in the interaction of opposing and broken images, a tension that brings together sentience and nature with history, psychology and spirituality with politics, artifact with performance. To psychologize this particular painting, for example, is to miss the political symbolism of the dress. In the long run psychologism privatizes and domesticates Kahlo, thereby making her more acceptable to an ideology of individualism.

The psychologizing of her work by scholars fixates especially upon Kahlo's sexuality and the related gender issues of childbirth and motherhood, again at the expense of the politics of her paintings, not to mention its aesthetic richness. One scholar claims on the basis of his analysis of her self-portraits that her political radicalism was "purely psychosomatic."[58] Another interprets the religious symbolism of one of her paintings in terms of her relationship with Rivera as it connects to an alleged Electra complex related to her father.[59] Often enough scholars who readily interpret her work in terms of her life, something to which she would probably not have objected per se, nevertheless ignore her politics and the indigenous religious elements of her painting altogether. This kind of psychologizing of her work by selecting sexual and maternal issues to the exclusion of other valid elements and issues succeeds in overemphasizing gender difference in highly stereotypic ways that run counter both to her work and to her life.

Kahlo would probably have espoused in a later time that the personal is indeed political, but "personal," as reflected in her paintings, encompassed issues of class and ethnicity. To identify gender with personal and all other distinctions with public and political constitutes a major conceptual mistake in the case of Kahlo's work. Second, her self-representation asserts adamantly that she is not simply female: She is a Mexican who is Euro-mestiza, and she makes this abundantly clear even in her most personal paintings. In this respect, she remakes gender difference by insisting that gender does not simply reduce to biology and that the concept "body" cannot be culturally identified solely with femaleness in some stereotypic sense. She accomplishes this reconstruction by means of two strategies. On the one hand, she represents her own body in ways that can be and have been appropriated by both sexes; on the other hand, she develops a distinctively female subjectivity or agency in tension with her attribution of traditional gender characteristics and concerns. *The Little Deer* (Figure 6) illustrates the first strategy; recurring motifs across a number of her paintings exemplify the second.

The Little Deer (1946) consists of a forest scene dominated by a figure of a wounded deer whose head is that of Kahlo, bearing antlers. The trees of the forest are cropped, showing only the trunks, ragged, gnarled, extending toward an unseen sky. The horizon at the very back of the line of vision is marked by what appears to be a body of water; the foreground is delineated by a broken young branch which symbolizes Aztec funeral practices revolving around belief in the resurrection of the dead.[60] The body of the deer is pierced by nine arrows and is bleeding. Combining the human figure with that of another creature reflects an identification of the human with all life forms characteristic of indigenous Mexican religious traditions, particularly Aztec traditions.[61] That the deer is wounded by arrows suggests further the *retablos* of San Sebastian. In addition, the wounded deer is a recurring theme of Mexican folklore and literature.[62]

Kahlo's assumption of the body of a deer extends her identification beyond the human to include nature, an identification of female with nature that would be entirely traditional, had she not chosen specifically the body of a stag. That she chose the body of a male creature, wounded in a somewhat phallic manner that further suggests an icon of a male saint, in short, that she crosses the lines of gender or sexual difference, extends the identification of sentience with female humanity to include males as well. Furthermore, a later generation of male Mexican artists would appropriate this image with conscious reference to this specific work in ways that clearly challenge conventional views of sexuality and gender difference.[63]

Even as she transgressed conventional gender boundaries, she also created a distinctively female subjectivity.[64] By "distinctively female" I mean two things: She undermined the objectification of the female body by objectifying female sexuality in unconventional ways; in addition, she took areas of reproductive life exclusive to females like childbirth and recast them in ways that resist, even defy, interpretations or ideologies that glorify motherhood and giving birth. Her still lifes show her undermining conventional sexual objectification. The painting titled *My Birth* by Herrera and *Childbirth* by Nancy Breslow[65] exemplifies dramatically Kahlo's transformation of the exclusively female domain.

Kahlo connected particular with wider concerns to express not only her pain, but also her joy, what Herrera calls her *alegría*. Among her most joyful paintings are still lifes, some of which are downright bawdy.[66] Very sensual in texture, color, and light, these works suggest through Kahlo's arrangement of fruit, vegetables, or flowers a raw and exuberant female sexuality, a sexuality in which the lines that distinguish pleasure from pain, like the lines that define sexual preference, blur.[67] One still life in particular, *Still Life with Melons* (1953),[68] represents an arrangement of cut red watermelons and assorted other yellow and white fruit, centered by half a mamey, a brown-pitted, yellow fruit related to the peach (Figure 7). The melon slices to either side of the mamey suggest labia on either side of a clitoris.[69] The dark, deeply ingrained wood upon which the fruit rests only further reinforces an overall tactile quality that elicits a desire to reach out and touch the fruit.

The painting strikes me as a joke, particularly a joke on the unsuspecting observer, not unlike the work of Kahlo's contemporaries, notably Edward Weston's peppers and Georgia O'Keefe's flowers. At first sight, the painting simply depicts an arrangement of vividly colored fruit. It can take more than one viewing before the light dawns that this is no ordinary still life, but once the light dawns, one can only wonder how she could have been so dull as to miss the obvious. The arrangement of fruit as female genitalia serves simultaneously as a joke and as a celebration of the connection of all life. Western representation of the female body has a long history of fragmenting the body and exposing it as object; Kahlo in this painting takes this tradition and stands it on its head. She depicts a fragment, indeed, some would argue *the* distinguishing, exclusively female body part visible to an observer and associated with female *jouissance*, by disguising it through its connections to other life. The joke is on the observer, schooled to view female bodies as isolated and obvious.

In her biography of Kahlo, Herrera comments that Kahlo's still lifes are chaotic and out of control, that her brush work is loose, that she has lost precision, and that the images she paints change from animate to agitated. Herrera attributes what appears to her to be a deterioration in painting to Kahlo's increasing dependence on narcotics in order to survive growing physical pain.[70] Kahlo's reliance upon painkillers notwithstanding, I find nothing chaotic about her 1953 still life (nor for that matter other paintings of this period). Although drugs no doubt altered Kahlo's perception, their presence in her body does not necessarily diminish the quality of her work any more than earlier constant pain necessarily enhanced it. Though it would be anachronistic to attribute consciously held feminism to Kahlo, *Still Life with Melons* celebrates female sexuality with a humor that liberates, that anticipates Judy Chicago's *Dinner Party* and Emily Culpepper's *Period Piece.*[71]

Even as Kahlo undermined conventional objectification of female sexuality, she reconstructed motherhood and childbirth in ways that fostered female agency. Painted oil on tin in 1932, *My Birth*, or *Childbirth* (Figure 8), symbolized several different events and meanings to Kahlo. The image is that of a woman giving birth, painted in the style of a *retablo*. The woman lies upon a bed, her face covered by a sheet, her body extended toward the viewer with legs raised at the knees. The head of a child with a face resembling Kahlo's emerges from the woman's vagina; there is blood beneath the infant's face and the mother's pelvis. Above the head of the bed hangs a *retablo* of the Virgin's head. The room is otherwise starkly empty of furniture or decoration. In true *exvoto* fashion the foreground of the painting is bound by a banner on which a documentation of the event would normally have been written; this banner, however, is blank. Kahlo completed this painting shortly after her first miscarriage and the death of her mother. She alternately viewed the image as her mother giving birth to her, the sheet covering her mother's face a symbol of her recent death; Kahlo's own miscarriage; and Kahlo's giving birth to herself.[72]

Of all her paintings I find this by far the most disturbing, by virtue of the absence of words to commemorate the event. Not only does this painting reflect the same *detournement* of religious icons characteristic of her *retablos;* interpreted as Kahlo's miscarriage or as her actual birth, it does so without recourse even to the ironic and satiric elements of humor that characterize *A Few Small Nips*. The bleakness of the room, the suppression of the mother's face, the stretching of the vaginal opening by the infant's head, and the image of the Virgin's head (with us at birth and at death) work together with verbal silence to communicate a fragmentation and wounding of female bodies not normally associated with the "naturalness" attributed to childbirth and the nobility consigned to motherhood in much of Western culture, especially in the context of the miscarriage of a chosen pregnancy. The painting is gruesome, depicting life-and-death struggle not verbalized by the participants and, therefore, unrelieved.[73]

Interpreted as Kahlo giving birth to herself, however, the painting not only takes on irony, but also communicates agency. The covered face of Kahlo as "mother," taken in conjunction with the protruding head of the infant, suggests that Kahlo has miraculously inverted her own head internally through the rest of her body so that it exits from her vagina. The "miraculous" nature of this act of contortion is reinforced by the image of the Virgin hanging on the wall at the head of the bed. The act is torturously painful but on the way to becoming triumphant. The banner is blank because the act is still in process. Female agency in this most exclusively female context resists patriarchal definition as passive, as derived from male power (no male is represented at this event), and as present as image primarily for male consumption. On the contrary, the act of giving birth becomes an act of female self-definition that conjoins pain, struggle, and hope. These latter qualities defy romanticizing for the act presupposes physical pain and the possibility of death at any "moment" throughout the process of birth.

While Kahlo avoids romanticizing, she nevertheless generates and cultivates a "new" sensibility in the viewer. By employing the *retablo* as her art form, a familiar form to her Mexican viewers at the time, she elicits, yet detours, feelings historically reserved for sacred objects and events; thus, she transforms in this instance an ostensibly natural event, that of giving birth. The painting further re-educates a viewer not only by its producing acute discomfort at the grotesqueness of the figures, perhaps experienced in conflict with feelings of piety, but, regardless of which interpretation one plays with, by the kind of visual exposure suffered by the figure giving birth. It forces the viewer to question his role in the production of meaning as observer (voyeur?), as critic and connoisseur (consumer?), and as co-sufferer (fetishizer of pain?). It forces the viewer to wonder what it means for her to witness and to bear witness (give testimony). For the painting as artifact further engages the beholder in some sense to collude in the act of giving birth through painting itself.

Frida Kahlo, unlike Sula, is an artist with an art form who furthermore, like Pilate Dead, gives birth to herself. Her relentless concern with her own body as metaphor reflects what I have been calling a mapping process whereby the body becomes site for struggle among multiple social and physical forces over its significance. This struggle continues to be conducted dialogically in the ideological struggles represented in the scholarship on her work. For example, her own refusal to de-politicize her work and her employment of religious symbolism conspire to re-contextualize gender difference by resisting cultural stereotypes; later scholars in some cases resist in turn this very transformation of images of female as object to female as subject by psychologizing her work in traditional, dualist fashion and by ignoring her politics and her use of religious imagery to transvalue the ordinary.[74]

The Making of Making

Kahlo's sentience as she lived it asserted itself upon her work through the hideousness of her pain and the euphoria chemically induced to relieve it, though whether pain and euphoria enhanced or diminished the quality of her work is a different issue. In any case her body resisted all efforts she made to heal it, ironic in that she originally wanted to be a doctor until the injury. Indeed she learned to paint while bedridden in order to alleviate boredom, and one can imagine that, had she not been injured so permanently, she might never have painted at all. Her sentience furthermore defied idealization, even as it drove her to paint, particularly to paint her body.

Her body painted, over and over, is an artifact, a made thing. As made thing it maps a relation between her lived body as site and a cultural process of signification in which she participated consciously, with great awareness of many, though probably not all, of the implications. This mapping, this interaction of site and sign, is marked by resistance—resistance to pain, resistance to conventional views of gender difference and female sexuality, and resistance to de-politicizing art, emotional life, and gender. A surprisingly enduring sense of joy, a wicked sense of humor, a flare for the melodramatic, and a deeply held political faith numbered among her more positive strategies for resisting; however, her most immediate artistic weapon for resistance lay in her deliberate use of a consciously created religious iconography to transvalue the ordinary and to commemorate the pain. As made things, Kahlo's body and the bodies of others whom she painted, especially in *exvoto* style, draw the beholder into the process of mapping, whether as one who colludes or as one who bears witness, depending on "viewer receptivity." Thus, as made things her bodies become sites for future mapping, marked by further resistance, in the ongoing ideological struggles that characterize scholarship on her work.

As made thing Kahlo's body reveals something about the process of making itself, different from the making of deities and from the making of other objects. Though all made objects reciprocate by making us, making histories, and making futures in return, only made bodies can reciprocate by asserting simultaneously our commonness as a species and our differences from one another. This potential only makes certain kinds of idealizations and objectification of the body more an affront insofar as they deny particularity and therefore individuality.

Kahlo's preservation of universality in tension with particularity through her representation of bodies depends heavily upon the use of religious symbols that assert her political loyalties as post-revolutionary Mexican nationalist. Although she was in no way religious in any conventional sense (on the contrary, she was strongly atheistic), her constant return to various religious art forms as well as symbols suggests a sensibility that might be called religious insofar as it is a ritualistic transvaluing of the ordinary that reflects a deeply held faith. Furthermore, though she eschewed supernaturalism, her paintings pose a visual critique of social injustice every bit as biblical as anything verbally hurled at the priestly classes by Hebrew and Christian prophets. Thus her employment of religious art forms and iconography provides a viewer with new contexts that restructure sometimes traditional, sometimes conventional, piety and values.

In addition, by making it virtually impossible for a viewer *not* to assume a consciously held position in response to her painting, she directly draws the viewer in to collude, whether as an advocate of the victims of violence or as an accomplice to the violence. This latter technique has interesting implications for scholarship—not only in art history or in the study of religion, but in any academic study of human beings and their behavior—for it raises discomfiting questions concerning the relation between scholar and subject matter in regard to voyeurism, fetishism, and other forms of intellectual consumption.

Last but not least, the implications of her work for the role of the human body as artifact in the making of making suggest an avenue worth exploring as a way out of current theoretical disputes between modernists and post-modernists. If the body as artifact potentially plays a unique role as arbiter between universality and particularity in the making of making, then human bodies, the most material of all human conditions, provide a conceptual starting point for uniting micro-theoretical and macro-theoretical concerns.

SIX

Mapping Religion

I have analyzed the production of religious meaning and value in terms of how the creators and the practicers of several traditions, including artists, theorists, and activists, have employed religious symbols, myths, rituals, and disciplines as strategies to empower self and others in the name of higher values or causes. In short, I have sought to articulate the interrelations of knowledge, power, and value—both religious and moral. All the figures I have chosen share the status of relative outsider to a dominant culture; as outsiders they have employed a variety of strategies grounded in what they view to be the religious or moral authority of their experience, as represented by some kind of appeal to the body as source or resource for knowledge. Morton's feeling in her stomach, Partnoy's tooth, and Kahlo's crippling pain serve as cases in point. In some of the examples that I have explored, the status claimed for this knowledge is that it is grounded in feeling, sometimes designated explicitly as religious, that transcends or circumvents culture. Recall, for example, Morton's account of her encounter with the Goddess. This claim to circumvent culture in particular has forced the central question governing this book: What is the relation between an imagining subject and the body in the context of religious life and practices?

Why "religious"? Because religious symbol systems provide one primary way, though, of course, not the only way, the human race has learned historically to make its cultures and therefore itself. Like the concepts "body" and "subjectivity," "religion" as a concept is a reciprocating artifact that not only makes us in return, but plays a significant role in the making of the processes of creativity and destructiveness themselves. Unlike "body," however, "religion" has no specifically material referent; rather, its "material" comprises discursive and non-discursive practices related in turn to economic, political, and other social structures. In addition, unlike "subjectivity," "religion" signifies no individual referent at all; rather, it designates communal, inter-subjective, and intra-subjective actions and states. As concept, "religion" depends for its realization or substantiation upon structuring or mapping actual bodies, as well as mapping human identities as subjects represented by human bodies. Thus religious narrative and practice produce various kinds of subjects who experience their bodies in ways highly, though not exclusively, determined by the symbol systems of the traditions in which they participate.

Precisely because of religious as well as other kinds of cultural construal, actual human bodies are almost never represented as sexually neutral, whether in texts, in visual imagery, or simply in daily interaction. Instead they are defined by sex and socialized by gender.[1] Furthermore, not all humans are extended the status of subject as the defining characteristic of their individual identity; on the contrary the subjectivity accorded some human beings depends upon an aberrational logic of power that subordinates much, indeed most, of the human race to the status of other, often visually depicted and religiously structured as object, for exploitation and consumption by the subjects. This logic selects on the basis of gender, racial, ethnic, and class difference with a view to sustaining various interests, particularly economic ones, of the subjects. Thus, for example, the body as sign, when representing or figuring "woman" as symbol or concept, tends to work against the attribution of subjectivity to women as a class, as well as to particular individual women, by denying agency as characteristic of human females. Throughout this century scholars have challenged the political logic and the ontological status presupposed by the category "subjectivity," even as activists have struggled to extend the status of subjectivity in part by redefining its meaning. Such conflicts have necessarily forced returning to questions that have provoked wide ranging intellectual conflict among scholars.

For example, what is the epistemological significance of gender in the relations between imagination and the body in a religious context? How do disestablished people employ gender difference and religious experience as strategies to establish their agency? What role does the body actually play in this experience? What kind of authority—ontological, epistemological, or moral—does this experience have? What roles then does the body play as site and as sign in dissolving, redefining, or establishing identity? Furthermore, what is the relation between the body understood as site and the body understood as sign?

Appeals to the body have emerged from within or have further complicated already existing intellectual debates over the epistemological status of gender, of religious experience, of subjectivity, indeed of the body itself. Thus I have framed discussion of these questions in the context of several ongoing intellectual debates: First, in respect to gender, feminist theorists have been divided over the issue of whether identification of the female and the feminine with the body provides a privileged knowledge, or alternative way of knowing, grounded in feeling. Second, theorists of religion, feminist and otherwise, have likewise debated the epistemological status of religious experience, again by exploring the relation of emotion to cognition, on the one hand, and to sensation, on the other hand. Third, social theorists from various disciplines have debated the status of subjectivity, particularly in respect to the subject's moral agency.

Each debate shares with the others certain formal similarities that may be described in the extreme as a conflict between essentialist and cultural determinist positions. Furthermore, whereas the essentialists are beset by tendencies either to biologism or to supernaturalism, the cultural determinists fail to articulate sufficiently clearly the relation between human physicality and the body as culturally constructed lens for the experience of imagining human beings. In addition, the debates waged over the status of the body have a further ideological significance beyond their manifest conflict in regard to the production of knowledge. Thus, I have returned again and again to raise the issue of the epistemological significance of the various debates themselves.

The complexity of these epistemological debates arises in part as a result of what I have been calling the ambiguity of the body, by which I mean that the body itself is a cultural artifact that is nevertheless the sentience we live as subjects of our experience. Our sensations appearing immediate and compelling to us, we often lapse, in our thinking, into the assumption that the body circumvents culture, such that experience is somehow more real than culture—especially the feelings we experience. Thus in the face of oppressive cultural authorities, religious or otherwise, we turn to the body as a foundation for an alternative knowledge that circumvents the oppressiveness of the cultures we wish to resist. Appeals to the body thus provide a compelling strategy for the empowerment of self and others, compelling in part because of a deep awareness of the extent to which human sentience serves as battleground or theater for making real and continually reproducing cultural meanings and values. To reclaim the body is to wrest away control over the self by others. But such appeals present us with certain internal contradictions as well. In fact, the body is not only a site that focuses major individual and social struggle. On the contrary, our very sensations are vulnerable to cultural structuring, thereby rendering culturally unmediated access to sentience impossible, except possibly at moments of such extreme pain and pleasure that imagination, and with it any power to make, is dismantled. In these contexts of extreme sensation the body works to limit, not to free, the imagination. In short, we are at every point subject to socionatural forces we do not control. The omnipresence of cultural construal, taken with sentience as limit to the imagination, raises perhaps the most important question of all: By what agency then does change occur?

Tentative Conclusions

I have argued throughout this discussion that the body serves as a compelling moral and religious authority to claims for justice. The body compels not because it provides through emotion an alternative knowledge or way of knowing unmediated by culture, but because of the various roles it plays in the making of culture, and more specifically the making of religious traditions. These roles can now be systematically elaborated in response to the issues of the epistemic significance of gender difference, the epistemological status of religious experience, and the meaning of subjectivity, after which I shall propose what I understand to be a central feature of the relations between imagining "bodied" subjects and the body itself. I shall then conclude by making explicit some of the implications of my proposal for understanding the position of the scholar in regard to the concept "religion," to the study of religious traditions, and to the work of theology and philosophy carried on from within the traditions themselves.

Gender

Actual bodies bear gender. All general claims about the relation between human physicality and the cultural or social context are qualified by gender differentiation. Gender itself is a cultural construal, often heavily dependent on religious symbol systems for reinforcement. The cultural construal, or production, of gender does not mean, however, that the body is irrelevant, nor that gender difference is incidental and subject to arbitrary reconstruction. On the contrary, differentiating according to gender has played a major and enduring role as a reciprocating cultural artifact in the continuing reproduction of culture itself. Thus, differentiating according to gender also produces, through sometimes conflicting processes of socialization, different avenues for knowing, though, because of conflict, not necessarily strictly along predictable lines. (In other words, socialization notwithstanding, actual men and women are not reducible in terms of their character traits to parallel categories of masculinity and femininity.)

More recently, however, direct attention to the sociopolitical significance of gender difference has operated as a discursive strategy to prescribe and perhaps to generate attending to and valuing positively periodically neglected and historically devalued features of knowing, for example, the relations between knowledge and power, the significance of sexual and spiritual self-exploration, and the positive role potentially played by emotion in moral decision making. In other words, women have used gender difference as one strategy, among others, for reevaluating and redefining knowing as a process of producing meaning, and knowledge as its result.

We have done this even when making misleading statements about the epistemological status of our claims, for example, that there is knowledge, gained through the body, that circumvents culture. Claiming privileged knowledge based on gender specification is significant not so much because it is somehow "true" in some ontological sense, but because the claim has played a very important role in the production of meaning and value. In other words, I think the claim itself, albeit misleading, has played a positive role in changing what counts as knowledge and how we value it. Evocative discourse on the female body, understood metaphorically as a land of emotion and a territory to be reclaimed by women through sexual and spiritual self-gratification, has served as a practice that has forced a change in cultural direction. The epistemological significance of gender difference then lies more in its employment as a strategy for change, than in its substantive meaning. Having now figured this out, however, we need to take more care in how we speak in recognition of the dilemma within which we who are women live.

On the one hand, the dichotomy that differentiates gender into masculine and feminine is at the heart of injustice toward women *as* women. Though this binary appears simply to designate cultural interpretation of perceived biological or sexual differences, the process of interpretation itself not only construes or constructs difference, but also historically does so in the interest of maintaining male privilege in relation to females. The process is not homogeneous, monolithic, and always successful; it furthermore operates in relation to other interpretive and equally construing patterns of differentiating along lines of age, race, class, and ethnicity from which gender cannot be isolated. Gender differentiation nevertheless appears to form a foundational binary underpinning such other problematic dichotomies as history and nature, mind or spirit and matter, and active and passive; it furthermore exemplifies dualistic thinking at its most pernicious. Gender differentiation thus lies at the heart of oppression, and overcoming it lies at the heart of feminism. Overcoming it at the level of theory and critique, therefore, depends in part upon rejecting all forms of essentialism.

On the other hand, to deconstruct "woman" and "man," dependent as they are for their meaning upon distinguishing gender as "feminine" and "masculine," in a way that leads to de-politicizing the concept "woman" ironically undermines the very attempt to transcend sexual and gender dualisms. So, for example, in *The Second Sex* Simone de Beauvoir rightly asserts, "One is not born a woman; one becomes one," insofar as this statement points to the social construction of "woman."[2] The same statement is highly problematic for women if it is taken to imply that actual women can at this time in history somehow choose not to be women. Although we may be human individuals confronting choices, however limited, we are not simply reducible to human individuals. As Toril Moi points out, if patriarchy oppresses us as women, defining us as "feminine" regardless of individual differences, we as feminists must struggle both to try to undo the patriarchal strategy that makes 'femininity' intrinsic to biological femaleness, and at the same time to defend women precisely *as* women.[3] We who are feminists thus seek to be women-centered women seeking to overthrow the oppressiveness built into the very concept "woman" in all its forms.

Religious Experience

The status of discursive strategy holds true likewise for similar claims made about religious experience. Just as claims that privilege female or feminine knowledge often serve in anti-authoritarian fashion to aid in redefining knowledge more richly by extending power more inclusively, so claims to the ontological status of truth gained from religious experience that circumvents culture likewise can destabilize and redefine familial, social, religious, political, economic, and aca-

demic institutions by democratizing religious authority. So, for example, Maxine Hong Kingston's bi-cultural experience authorizes her to
challenge both Chinese traditions and the cultural norms of the contemporary United States in a manner that does not so much collapse
the tension between the two as it reconciles them and strengthens her
to continue to struggle creatively in their midst. Though Anne Klein
as Buddhist convert differs from Kingston in that she consciously
embraces a tradition different from the one into which she was born
(therefore, her conflicts are not specifically bi-cultural), her experiences of the practices of her chosen tradition provide her an alternative that challenges the sexist assumptions of her tradition and culture
of origin. Stated negatively, narratives of experiences of religious
transformation may thus signal the lacunae and fissures of various
specific ideologies, both religious and secular, that are potentially
liable to subversion.

Analysis of the specific role of the body in an explicitly religious
context provides additional information about its significance as well,
by clarifying the body's religious and moral authority. Not only does
the body, as site for pain and pleasure, drive imagination to project
self, world, and transcendent realities, but, given extreme pain, it sets
limits on imagination's projections. The body as site and limit for
imaginative projection thereby plays a reciprocal role in relation to
religious symbol systems by providing a moral criterion to assess the
difference between creativity as this may include needed destruction,
on the one hand, and wanton damage that destroys the very possibility for further creation, on the other hand. Contrast, for example,
the needed iconoclasm in response to images that demean the female
body as experienced by Nelle Morton, with the acts of physical torture
intended to elicit "intelligence" and to "reeducate" Alicia Partnoy
and her co-workers.

The body as site serves, in addition, to substantiate or make real the
symbol systems and their associated practices, discursive and otherwise. That Kingston's and Klein's experiences depend upon and presuppose narrative articulation or discursive practice re-defines the
terms of authority but does not de-authorize the significance of experience for either subject, nor any potential significance for those with
whom experiences are shared. On the contrary, it substantiates their
respective particularity while connecting them to larger or wider realities than their own individual egos. Furthermore substantiation depends in part upon sentience, in these cases, respectively, the cut
frenum and breathing. Experiences of pain and pleasure, themselves
culturally mediated, carry religious and moral authority insofar as

they teach and heal us, and they perform such pedagogical and recon-
ciling roles only insofar as they can be communicated. Communication presupposes discourse, at least one voice, and a listener who
seeks to imagine what she or he has quite possibly never experienced,
hence, particularly with reference to the peculiar nature of pain, the
necessity for voicing one's own pain, crediting others' accounts of
pain, and bearing witness to the pain of others. These activities both
presuppose and further sustain the symbol systems that frame them.
In addition, they may refine, alter the direction of, or create anew
such systems. So, for example, Morton's experience of Goddess both
logically presupposes and, through the practice of worship, actually
substantiates the symbolic reality of Goddess. Her experiences and
others like it push the culture in which it occurs and to which it
opposes itself in a new direction by challenging the already existing
traditions characteristic of that culture.

Thus the claim that religious experience verifies extra-cultural realities does not follow from the nature of the experiences themselves.[4]
Rather, religious and political movements, especially newly emerging
ones, cultivate experiences in response to the cultures they counter,
experiences that alter consciousness through various practices. Such
movements appeal for their authority to such complex and symbolically structured emotions as sorrow and grief for past loss, righteous
anger at present and past conditions, joy in self-discovery and in the
discovery of solidarity with others. This emphasis on experience by
appeal to the authority of specific, prescribed emotions nevertheless
ultimately reveals less about extra-cultural realities than it discloses
how we engage continually in creating and substantiating the cultures and counter-cultures, including their religious traditions, of
which we are part and which reciprocally create and destroy us. This
drama of reciprocity, or in many cases battle for hegemony, is played
out by means of ritual and discipline enacted upon and through the
body as its site. The epistemic authority of such experiences lies not in
their ontological foundation in some absolute truth, but in their possible moral status: Namely, to what extent do such experiences sustain,
advance, enhance, or extend a socionatural environment conducive
to perpetuating further human creativity itself? In short, the ultimate
epistemological issue is justice itself.

Subjectivity becomes an issue in part because of the role played by
religious symbol systems in the formation of identity, and in part
because of the issues of moral agency and human responsibility or
lack thereof for effecting change. Subjectivity is further problematic
because our conventional ways of thinking about the identity of a

subject rarely, and almost never sufficiently, take into account the possible significance of the body in the production of subjectivity in particular, or of individual and social identity in general.

Subjectivity

Subjectivity, functionally defined, is one among several possible ways of construing identity, one that focuses on psychological unity, individuation, and agency with reference to human beings. Not all religious traditions cultivate subjectivity; indeed because of its potential, if not always actual, association with autonomy, some traditions, for example Buddhist, Hindu, and Confucian, represent certain types or kinds of subjectivity as problematic to spiritual growth and health, rather than as a desirable feature of human religious identity. Other traditions, chiefly Western monotheistic and some goddess-centered ones, exhibit more ambivalence toward subjectivity as a structure of identity. On the one hand, subjectivity refers to inner states of consciousness (especially feelings), self-reflection, and moral agency, all of which qualities and activities are seen within these traditions as essential to piety, faithfulness, or sanctity. On the other hand, subjectivity, insofar as it refers to self-reliance to the exclusion of human-divine relations and intra-human relations, once again becomes a problem as a source of egocentricity manifested positively in pride, gluttony, and avarice, and negatively in sloth and underachievement.[5] Furthermore, in either case, subjectivity in many religious contexts presupposes some concept of an immutability of the self, for example, a cosmic self or soul (Atman), an individual immortal soul (as in Islam), or some other form or state of eternal life.

The body, connected directly to an economic context and the constant reminder of mutability and lack of individual control, suffers, at best, lack of attention and, at worst, outright denigration within these various symbolic frameworks. Furthermore the kind of moral agency fostered by the view of the subject as an autonomous individual who is responsible for the consequences of his or her actions has, at least in the United States, been subverted into ideological support for a highly selective individualism and ironically a form of social control. This ideology, by mis-reasoning backward from social effects to individuals as causes, blames poverty on the poor, racism on racial minorities, and sexism on women. In this construal in particular subjectivity depends on a logic of self and other in which the status of the self as subject depends for its continuation upon maintaining illusory or actual control over the self and the other. The self exercises this control in part through the structuring of the other's body so that its otherness is recognizable as such and the denial of its subjectivity is sustainable. In this process, the body serves as sign by which to identify and to distinguish subjects from others whom they designate as objects. Of course, the body as sign ironically renders every person as in some sense an object, such that the attribution or denial of subjectivity is really an attribution or denial of value, power, and agency to another, made in part by inference from the body.

As we saw in the discussion of Partnoy's reflections on her sensuality and from Toni Morrison's construction of her characters Sula Peace, Nel Wright, and Pilate Dead, there are problems for women with the dissolution of subjectivity altogether, as well as problems with subjectivity as it is conventionally assumed. Furthermore there are alternative, possibly desirable kinds of subjectivity as well. On the basis of the example of Pilate Dead, I have suggested a qualifiedly communitarian type of subjectivity that emphasizes agency as an inter-relational quality manifested as moral and spiritual responsiveness. This responsiveness to others, to circumstances, and to one's own self rests on claims to provisional rather than to absolute knowledge. In seeking, as Pilate Dead did, to love all whom one knows, the orientation of such a subject is one of universality of intention marked by humility (exemplified by Pilate Dead's wish to have known more people that she might love more), as distinguished from a universality that projects as normative one's own particular experience. This type of subjectivity further depends upon a view of sensuality as the ability to take pleasure in physicality.[6] This type of subjectivity is also commensurate with voicing one's own pain, crediting others' accounts of pain, and bearing witness to the pain of another.

In addition, membership in multiple communities characterizes this type of subject, a multiplicity which performs several roles. For example, membership in multiple communities relativizes any given community for Pilate Dead, thus qualifying a strictly communitarian subjectivity. This relativity produces in turn multiple positions from which she speaks and acts in response to others, hence the fluidity of her shape.[7] Outsider to the world of privilege though she may be, she can move around as a subject within the world of privilege, as well as other worlds, with relative independence or detachment at any given point, because she is always related by her loyalty and by her commitment to trustworthiness to other groups and individuals beyond any given immediate context. The multiplicity of her communities and her positions further performs a self-critical role that reinforces her humility.[8]

From dissolution to preferred type, subjectivity is in any case linked to attribution or to denial in a relation between oneself and another, and attribution and denial are both indissolubly linked to the body as sign, albeit always ambiguous and transactional in the act of interpretation. Thus the body as site serves both as a means for substantiating reality and, through sensation, as a driving force for projecting or imagining it; the body as sign serves as vocabulary in establishing and evaluating agency and relations of power and powerlessness by eliciting or cuing responses of attribution and denial. The body thus as sign most clearly manifests the extent to which the body itself is in all contexts cultural artifact, subject to multiple interpretations.

The "Bodied" Imagining Subject and the Body

What then, in contexts defined by religious symbol systems, is the epistemological relationship between a "bodied," imagining subject and the body imagined? From the most micro-logical to the most macro-logical level, I suggest that the relationship is one of mapping, where mapping is understood as a metaphor for a highly pluri-vocal and reciprocal social process in which individual persons participate. This process is furthermore multi-directional and includes potential and actual resistance at all levels as one of its features. Resistance, as I suggested earlier,[9] rather than an element in its own right, which would render it a reification, emerges inherently as a consequence of multiple forces and directions at play, including both the intended and unintended participation of individual imagination itself.

At the micro-logical level of human existence, mapping refers to the interaction between body as site and body as sign in the making of the body's significance for human experience and identity. Resistance at this level may occur as sensation itself in response, for example, to touch, the context for which may be perceived as threatening or pleasurable. Mapping thus not only gives one a sense of her body, but also a sense of a self in a world, dependent in part upon some view of the body; thus, this sense of self may be submerged in physicality or highly distanced from it, depending on cultural, especially religious, forces of socialization at play in the formation of identity. This sense of self, or identity, may take any one of a number of forms of subjectivity, or may take an altogether different form of identity, perhaps more bound by tribal, familial, or other collective configurations; in addition, these configurations presuppose and reflect significant economic structures and forces at play. Whatever form the self takes, the form may be viewed by the particular person or by any of its communities as either desirable or undesirable, positively valued or negatively valued. Resistance at this level further entails resistance to socialization, in other words, in response to conflicting interpretations within a self, among others, or between self and others.

The forms of identity available, and their culturally established relations to physicality or sentience, reflect the cultures in which they occur. The religious traditions characteristic of a particular culture, interacting with other forces of socialization, play a central role in the formation and cultivation of identity. By structuring relations between sensation and imagination, especially by cognitively cultivating complex emotions, religious traditions in particular play explicit pedagogical roles in specifying acceptable and unacceptable relations between physicality or sentience and identity, between self as subject and self as object of reflection, between self and others, between self and a socionatural environment. Specifically in contexts informed by religious symbol systems, the symbolic projection of central or ultimate realities, that serve as what Peirce called "place setters," that limit or anchor narrative and practice, establishes a horizon that provides both an orientation within an available reality and some sense of a "beyond," thereby relating particularity or the micro-logical order to universal or macro-logical concerns, even if the relation be a negative one.

The macro-logical forces at play here in charting reality nevertheless require not only human agency, but human sentience as well, to create and substantiate their reality. Furthermore, socialization itself is not monolithic. On the contrary, the forces at play in establishing human reality, religious and otherwise, are hardly harmonious in relation to one another; rather, they collide with each other as well as with human sentience itself, in ways that produce resistance as inherent within any given symbol system of meaning and value, as well as across systems. Frida Kahlo and her art serve well as a case in point. She sought deliberately to integrate her own pain and pleasure with the multiple religious traditions, cultures, and forces that went into the making of Mexico by projecting her body, indeed, multiple, conflicting representations of herself, as metaphor for Mexico's past and hoped-for destiny. By seeking to represent herself as a religious and political icon, she sought not only to make meaning from her pain, but to resist what she considered to be the injustice of Mexico's northern neighbor. In her resistance to capitalism and colonialism, represented by the United States to the north, and in her resistance to her own despair, she succeeded, probably without intending, in helping to alter the making of making itself.

In short, resistance as a quality of mapping at the most fundamental level of sentience itself produces change, or novelty, however imperceptible it may be; thus, change is a salient feature of the making of culture, indeed of all creativity, rather than external to it. I hasten to add, however, that resistance carries with it no guarantees that resulting change will necessarily be for the better. Furthermore, even when resistance is conscious in agents committed to what they value as a primary good, there are no guarantees, indeed, in all likelihood not even provisionally unambiguous results. Witness Kahlo's infatuation with Stalin as part and parcel of her resistance to capitalism. Thus resistance, the agency by which change is effected, operates throughout the various processes, human and otherwise, that create, sustain, and destroy the socionatural environment, including cultures and their religious traditions. Within this matrix of forces, the human role as agent of change, albeit severely limited and often unintentional, is ironically one of major responsibility with limited authority to "keep true values alive."

The Concept "Religion" and the Study of Religion

Religious symbol systems serve as primary instances of cultural making in both a subjective and an objective sense. That is, humans make and change culture, including religious traditions, as a way of making and changing themselves as both individual persons and communities. To return to some of the questions raised earlier in Chapter One, irrespective of whether these traditions stand outside culture or point beyond it (and I have argued that they do not), religious symbol systems and the institutions that constitute them are inextricable from culture, though they may be distinguished, albeit in certain respects arbitrarily, from other kinds of symbol systems that go into the making of culture, economic, political, familial, artistic, scientific, and so forth. For the student of religion what distinguishes religious symbol systems from other symbol systems lies not in the ontological status of the claims to extra-cultural realities, but in the roles played by such claims and their historical effects in the making of culture. In *Map Is Not Territory* Jonathan Z. Smith focuses on religion as practiced as an exercise in mapping. He writes:

> Religion is the quest, within the bounds of the human, historical condition, for the power to manipulate and negotiate ones [sic] "situation" so as to have "space" in which to meaningfully dwell. It is the power to relate ones [sic] domain to the plurality of environmental and social spheres in such a way as to guarantee the conviction that ones [sic] existence "matters." Religion is a distinctive mode of human creativity, a creativity which both discovers limits and creates limits for humane existence. What we study when we study religion is the variety of attempts to map, construct and inhabit such positions of power through the use of myths, rituals and experiences of transformation.[10]

I would also point out that one might likewise define politics, and in either case, the processes involved are social and communal in ways not sufficiently explicit in this quotation. Therefore, I would further add that as a distinctive mode of human creativity, religious symbol systems seek to extend and to transcend the limits of human existence, and it is precisely in this area that religious institutions, life, and practice can manifest both their most revolutionary and their most totalitarian aspects.

Mapping, however, does not end with religious faith and practice; rather, the anti-establishment discursive practices surrounding gender difference and religious experience, Partnoy's poetic prose, Kahlo's consciously held political values and artistic intentions, and subsequent scholarship on Kahlo's life and work, taken together, illustrate how mapping occurs as more and less explicitly ideological struggle or, more ideally, through dialogue at the macro-logical level. In other words, mapping extends beyond the mapping of bodies, selves, deities, and worlds to include even the theoretical discourses that seek to articulate, to analyze, and to evaluate them. Several implications for the concept "religion" and for religious studies, as well as for theological and thealogical method, follow from this extension.

In the first place, the concept "religion" is itself a cultural artifact with a history reflecting several agendas.[11] As with all concepts, "religion" is best understood as a heuristic device. Whether defined in terms of function (for example, religion is a symbol system that serves pedagogical purposes in the making of culture), or in terms of substance (for example, religion originates in a feeling of absolute dependence upon the whence of all existence), this concept is ironic. Its etymology denotes boundedness, ligature, but its actual scope, depending on method of approach, is almost boundless in the possible data it comprehends. If religious traditions are made real in part through the bodies of those who practice them, "religion" itself is a highly fluid concept always in the process of being made up by many methods borrowed from several disciplines, in no small part by the scholars, especially the theoreticians, who seek to study religious traditions. Furthermore the concept reciprocates with the phenomena it classifies.

In other words, scholarship is in part a constitutive act, a discursive practice, though not exclusively so and not without limits. For example, at a national meeting of the American Academy of Religion I heard a paper by a scholar who argued cogently that Hinduism is a European homogenization of quite diverse religious systems, in some cases only loosely related at best—in short, a fabrication or distortion of those practices not otherwise classifiable or recognizable as Buddhist, Muslim, Christian, Sikh, or Jain. The designation, the initial context for which was the colonization of India, has in turn been appropriated by the indigenous population to whom it was first applied as a category by which they themselves now describe themselves to Westerners.[12] In contrast to this "sin of commission," scholars of religion have also constituted what counts as religious by way of omission as well. Witness, for example, the extent to which women's practices and roles were, and often still are, overlooked or subordinated in status to men's, even in egalitarian populations, thereby reflecting the androcentric assumptions of the male and female scholars rather than the values of the communities studied. Furthermore consider the scholarly bias toward textual and elite manifestations of traditions as opposed to their oral, visual, and popular counterparts. Last but not least, consider that any given scholar's work is itself a symbolic structuration, re-presenting, not presenting a tradition, and possibly modifying the phenomena by reflecting it from a definite particular perspective, whether that of outsider or insider. This is not to say that our scholarship is worthless; rather I mean to emphasize the extent to which it requires a very high level of *self-critique* in relation to very material referents, namely, the phenomena we study, with a special view toward the extent to which our discourse reciprocates with the phenomena themselves.

The act of study fortunately places the scholar in the role of one among many scholars, one among many witnesses, one among many voices, whose work reciprocates not only with the phenomena we seek to explain, but also with the work of one another. The plurivocal quality of religious studies produces the possibility for cooperation, dialogue, and mutual self-criticism under the best of circumstances, even as it renders explanation of religious phenomena necessarily ridden with intellectual conflict and laden with value.

Under less happy and more likely circumstances, the pluri-vocal condition in which we live as scholars makes us necessarily contenders when our attempts to persuade one another with civility break down—the latter case being more likely than the former precisely because our scholarship presupposes an economic structure defined by seeking, getting, retaining, and keeping sufficiently scarce our positions, first as graduate students and, later, as tenured faculty.[13] Explanation (as I have characterized theory) differs, then, from evocation (as I have characterized theological and thealogical discourse) not so much in kind as in degree and intention,[14] for the one explaining is always positioned as one among many who differ, often greatly, from one another. Furthermore by virtue of being accountable to a community or multiple communities of scholars, the one explaining often stands outside not only what he seeks to explain, but also outside the views of those in the academy with whom she differs.

In the second place and perhaps more importantly, regardless of one's specific area of scholarship, scholars of religion explain to students; we teach. We seek to extend students' imaginations to include worlds new to their experience, thereby extending the concept "religion" even further. That what we do as teacher-scholars helps constitute the meaning of the concept itself requires of us a moral alertness to the implications of our own individual positions and approaches within the overall field, coupled with a humble agnosticism that makes us open to those students with whom we may differ far more greatly than we may differ with one another, even as we stand outside the data we claim to explain. In short, the fluidity of the concept calls us to exemplify in our work, especially in our teaching, many of the same qualities possessed by Pilate Dead.

Within this context of ideological and dialogical struggle in which the sole common ground is pedagogical, much more needs to be done in the way of explicit, constructive feminist theory of religion. Gender analysis and feminist critiques of sexist religious practices within various religious traditions and of male-centered approaches to religious symbol systems have revolutionized religious studies in the last two decades. Furthermore, feminists have sought not only to construct alternatives within existing traditions, but also to create new religious symbol systems. Much of this work has focused explicitly on the body.[15] Nevertheless, our work needs to engage more with critical theory, cultural studies, feminist epistemology in philosophy (especially cognitive science), and sociology of religion as we articulate distinctively feminist stances. Likewise, theorists in these fields who are not focused on the religious studies could benefit from our work in return.

For example, assuming the social construction of reality as a starting point, it would be interesting to explore the ontological implications of being able to imagine different possible worlds in relation to what we call "*the* real world" in terms of the significance of gender, with special reference to the category of time.[16] We live in socially constructed realities which we assume as finite and given, from which we imagine alternative worlds "before," "after," and ongoing with, but different from, life in this world, worlds in which the status of sexuality is even more ambiguous than it is in "*the* real world." What role does sentience play in the assumption of a shared "real world"; how fragile is this assumption; and to what extent is this really a safe assumption to make?[17] What do we do with bodies in these other worlds, these heavens, hells, next lives, eternal life, utopias, dystopias, and "virtual realities," and what is the significance of imagined other worlds for human lives as they are actually lived? Are there significant differences in how these various worlds function along lines of race, class, and gender or, likewise, in how one imaginatively projects or appropriates these worlds? What does it tell us about religious identity and behavior, especially, though not exclusively, in the context of an ostensibly secular and certifiably pluralistic society? How does how we think about time and space interact with our responses to ethical and social issues posed by conflicts surrounding reproductive choice, aging, disease, poverty, dying, family, and sexual preference, not to mention many other "domestic" issues? Indeed why do we in a Western secular society distinguish public from domestic in the social order and public from private in individual life? Once again, what difference do race and class identification make in how we draw these fundamental gender distinctions?[18]

We have only just begun to map theory or, for that matter, antitheory of religion from a feminist perspective. Meanwhile we, who as feminists are engaged in other areas in religious studies, often hold contradictory and unexamined theoretical assumptions about the origin, status, and nature of religious phenomena, reflected in and through our work.[19]

Theology and Thealogy

Whether theology, thealogy, and other forms of theological discourse belong within religious studies is currently subject to debate.[20] This debate itself exemplifies the mapping of the concept "religion." Much, of course, depends on how one defines both "theology" and its cognates, as well as "religion," and I do not intend to enter into this debate at this time. Nevertheless, let us assume that these discourses properly belong to religious studies. Theological and thealogical work in particular depends heavily upon theoretical assumptions surrounding the concept "religion," whether these assumptions are positive or negative, conscious or unconscious. In some cases these assumptions are sometimes self-contradictory and often left implicit in the work itself. For example, post-modern critics have of late been quick to challenge all efforts at constructive thought, whether theoretical, theological, or thealogical.[21] A systematic analysis in response to post-modern critiques of contemporary efforts at constructive thought is beyond the scope of this discussion; further, this concluding chapter is not the appropriate context for developing a fully blown apologetics. Suffice it to say that the post-modern critics' own problems with nihilism and counter-charges of elitism notwithstanding, their challenges especially with respect to epistemological naivete, theoretical totalism, and ontological presumption are often right on the mark, whether in regard to male-centered thought or to feminist thought, as I have tried to demonstrate. Nevertheless, concerns for material justice, human liberty, and universal peace drove the grand theories and theologies of the modern era, even when they drove the theorists and theologians to project as universal their own conditions and characteristics. Although the worthiness of theological goals does not justify their intellectual imperialism, itself commensurate with the historical colonialism that served as its economic underpinning, their very claims have fueled revolutions, intellectual and otherwise, that sought and still seek to overthrow material and spiritual injustice.

Whether we now live in the middle of a serious paradigmatic break with modernity or its extension in a new direction, we in any case confront the question, What does the universality of our intentions (should we still share them) have to do with the particularity of our circumstances? The theoretical equivalent of responding to this question takes the form of addressing the relation between micro-logical and macro-logical concerns; the theological and thealogical equivalent of responding to this question addresses at least two issues: (1) the relation between particularity and universality in the context of the central symbols of the traditions, religious and academic, to which theologians and thealogians adhere, and (2) the relations of the many communities, religious or academic, which each thinker represents, to one another. In both cases, if we accept the partial if not total validity of post-modern challenges, the questions must be raised from the bottom up and the inside out. If we have learned nothing else from one another we have surely learned not to presume to speak for everyone else.

I have claimed that theology and thealogy differ from theory of religion by seeking to evoke, rather than to explain, the realities of which their authors speak.[22] Evocation presupposes that theological and thealogical critique serves the further end of constructive work from within any given symbol system. In contrast to explanation, evocation requires much more self-conscious involvement in making itself. In other words, theologians and thealogians work specifically with the central symbols of their traditions, the deities characteristic of each. We are concerned with the content of these symbols in terms of the role they play in the lives of those who seek relation to the realities they evoke. Concern with this issue may lead to the question of the significance of the body for experiences of self-transcendence. For believers throughout history the body may be manipulated under the right circumstances to help produce experiences of self-transcendence, self-expansion, or self-knowledge. Given what we now at least think we know about human sexuality, several questions worth pursuing follow: What role does eroticism play in mystical experience? Given contemporary claims that sexual exploration liberates and empowers, are there material and historical relations between mystical self-transcendence and disciplined transgression of sexual taboos, and, if so, what are they? What kinds of meaning and value do such experiences produce? How does acknowledging the involvement of sexuality in mystical experiences, whether sexuality is suppressed or exercised, materially affect the central symbols or concepts themselves? Does acknowledging the involvement of the body in mystical experiences tell us anything new about the role of central symbols as place-setters, or the prescription of limits on language itself? Given that transgression may include violence perpetrated by a self upon the self or others, how does disciplined transgression of sexual taboos (for example, sadomasochistic practices) relate to other contexts of violence (for example, torture, war, domestic violence, and rape)? Does the occurrence of sexual transgression in the context of a religious symbol system substantively differ from any other context? What does it mean that believers attribute wrath, carnage, sexual transgression, erotic behavior, and sexual acts to their deities? Does the absence of such attributions simply mask and deny the reality of the violence of human existence?

If theologians and thealogians are more directly and self-consciously involved in the process of making the traditions, the ontological status of the realities evoked is drastically relativized in part by their human origin and in part by the plurality of communities and positions interacting with one another. Although it provides no single all-purpose solution, the body, in all its particularity and in its ambiguity as artifact in relation to sentience, serves nevertheless as one common condition shared by us all, a condition that relates us to all other sentience, a condition that further stands as an ethical criterion by which to assess the significance of our work, one from which we should not detour.

Once again, Kahlo's life and work serve as a case in point. A Mexican Euro-mestiza, whose parents were Catholic and cultural Jew, a Marxist woman who saw her pain and pleasure, represented by multiple projections of her body, as metaphor for her country and its relation to an oppressive neighbor, she deliberately sought to bring into interrelation differing and, in some cases, conflicting religiopolitical images and religious genres of those she viewed as most dispossessed by Mexico's history, those she viewed as dispossessing, and those most celebratory of Mexico's possible future. Her body projected came to represent many cultural voices in tension within her, holding in common only a detouring of any religious and political tendencies to de-materialize human values. Her images became no longer simulation, but flesh itself, groaning with value. She thus resisted easy temptations both to empty universalism and to an anarchic nominalism.

Repeated *detournement* constitutes the single most important feature of her work for a discussion of theological and thealogical method, to my mind. That she drew on indigenous and popular religious symbols and practices, while detouring all traditional tendencies to mystify power and romanticize gender difference, serves as a stunning model for theological and thealogical critique and construction. One could make an interesting case, I think, that Kahlo was doing what her Italian contemporary Antonio Gramsci was calling for at the time (in all likelihood unbeknown to her, by the way). Namely, she was fashioning from popular culture a new, critical *common sense*.[23]

Theology from a feminist perspective and thealogy require nothing less today. We have ample evidence that the work we do as theologians and thealogians is imaginative construction, particularly, though not exclusively, the construction of deity; thus we map the faces of our own values.[24] Yet, we have only begun to map the theological and thealogical significance of bodies, either for imagination or for the imaginative construction of religious symbols. I have proposed that the body as artifact, especially in a religious context, plays what I think is an important role in the making of making itself, namely, the role of presenting simultaneously our individual particularity with our common human conditions of vulnerability and finitude.[25] As we seek continually to substantiate through history these briefly glimpsed, necessarily plural, and always provisional images, the images serve nevertheless to beckon us onward toward a more just future. The provisional image lies for me right now in the brown eyes, the toothy grin, and the large nose of Alicia Partnoy, speaking softly the unspeakable to roughly six hundred first-year college students and their associated faculty on a hot autumn day at Trinity University in San Antonio. Alicia Partnoy, once disappeared, reappeared and lived to tell about it.

Notes

Preface

1. Immanuel Kant, *Religion within the Limits of Reason Alone*, trans. with an intro. and notes by Theodore M. Greene and Hoyt H. Hudson, with an intro. by Greene and John R. Silber (New York: Harper & Row, 1960), 7–10.

2. When one has both philosophical and doctrinal concerns, relations with religious and secular communities and belief systems become much more complicated, however.

3. See Elaine Scarry, *The Body in Pain: The Making and Unmaking of the World* (New York: Oxford University Press, 1985). Scarry does not formally address issues of gender difference. For working definitions of the central concepts and a rationale for this approach, see Chapter 1. For another, excellent discussion of the epistemological problems raised by such conepts as "body" and "gender difference," see also Zillah R. Eisenstein, *The Female Body and the Law*, especially Chapter 1 "Politics and/or Deconstruction: Thoughts on Method" (Berkeley: University of California, 1988), 6–41.

4. See Mary Daly, *Gyn/ecology: The Metaethics Of Radical Feminism* (Boston: Beacon Press, 1978).

5. See not only Toni Morrison, *The Bluest Eye* (New York: Washington Square Press, 1970), but also Kathleen M. Sands, "Uses of the Thea(o)logian: Sex and Theodicy in Religious Feminism," *Journal of Feminist Studies in Religion* 8/1 (Spring 1992): 7–33.

Chapter One

1. All information on Partnoy, unless otherwise noted, comes from her book *The Little School: Tales of Disappearance and Survival in Argentina*, trans. Partnoy with Lois Athey and Sandra Braunstein (Pittsburgh: Cleis Press, 1986). Relevant pages hereafter cited in the text.

2. Elaine Scarry, *The Body in Pain: The Making and Unmaking of the World* (New York: Oxford University Press, 1985), 162–172.

3. I recognize that I am using "body" as an abstraction in a precarious manner throughout this text. "Body" is particularly problematic, for, as an abstraction, it can imply a normative or ideal form, when it is precisely this kind of thinking I seek to undermine. However, the alternatives seemed to me to be far more problematic. For example, "physicality" used over and over seems burdensome and jingoistic. "Embodiment" implies a Platonic dualism of mind or soul somehow "planted" in bodies. To avoid as best I could both jargon and dualism I have tried to qualify "body" as an abstraction in terms of its role: the body as artifact, "body" as sign, the body as site, and so forth.

4. For examples, see *Poetics Today* 6/1–2 (1985) and, more recently, *History of Religion* 30/1 (August 1990).

5. See Peter L. Berger and Thomas Luckmann, *The Social Construction of Reality: A Treatise in the Sociology of Knowledge* (New York: Doubleday, 1966).

6. See Scarry, *Body in Pain*, especially part 1, "Unmaking."

7. Michael Taussig wrestles with the complicity of our attempts to communicate the urgency of violence with the actual events of violence in *Shamanism, Colonialism, and the Wild Man: A Study in Terror and Healing*, where he writes of those who seek to communicate with justice, "And we are watching the watchers so that with our explanation we can pin them down and then pin down the real meaning of terror, putting it in the stocks of explanation. Yet in watching in this way we are made blind to the way that terror makes mockery of sense making, how it requires sense in order to mock it, and how in that mockery it heightens both sense and sensation" (Chicago: University of Chicago Press, 1987), 132.

8. Scarry, *Body in Pain*.

9. Taussig, *Shamanism, Colonialism and the Wild Man*.

10. I am speaking here of how we imagine "human body," for biology itself is far more various in terms of physiology and hormonal output than human imagination usually entertains, though Plato struggles with this issue at least implicitly in the *Timaeus* and the *Symposium*. Our efforts to imagine a human nature that is not biologically determined have perhaps met with limited success; so, for example, Augustine and C. G. Jung propose a psychological androgyny and Samuel Taylor Coleridge and Virginia Woolf suggest an androgyny of imagination.

11. See Lori Heise, "The Global War against Women," excerpted from *World Watch* 2/2 (March–April 1989): 12–21 in *Utne Reader* 36 (November–December 1989), 40–45.

12. My approach here is heavily influenced by the work of H. Richard Niebuhr and Ernst Troeltsch. See, for examples, Niebuhr, *Christ and Culture* (New York: Harper & Row, 1951), and Troeltsch, *The Social Teaching of the Christian Churches*, 2 vols., trans. Olive Wyon (Chicago: University of Chicago Press, 1981).

13. November 12, 1989.

14. Scholars have often attributed such a view to Schleiermacher, mistakenly, I think. Although he claims that the feeling of absolute dependence is not accessible directly to language (and therefore culture), he also argues that it is therefore only mediately experienced. In other words, for Schleiermacher, the feeling of absolute dependence plays a role similar to that of Kant's postulates in that it constitutes a necessary condition for piety to be what it appears to us to be. See *The Christian Faith*, 2 vols., eds. H. R. Mackintosh and J. S. Stewart, with an intro. by Richard R. Niebuhr (New York: Harper & Row, 1963). Furthermore, one could view his *Speeches* as a defense of religion's rightful place within culture. Certainly Schleiermacher's neo-orthodox successors perceived him to be far too cosy and at ease with culture, rather than staking a claim outside it. See *On Religion: Speeches to Its Cultured Despisers*, trans. John Oman, with an intro. by Rudolf Otto (New York: Harper & Row, 1958), especially "The Nature of Religion," 26–118.

15. See, respectively, Emile Durkheim, *The Elementary Forms of the Religious Life: A Study in Religious Sociology*, trans. Joseph Ward Swain (New York: Free Press, 1965), and Ludwig Feuerbach, *The Essence of Christianity*, trans. George Eliot, with an intro. by Karl Barth, and a foreword by H. Richard Niebuhr (New York: Harper & Row, 1957).

16. See Chapter Three, 57–62.

17. See Clifford Geertz, "Religion as a Cultural System," in *The Interpretation of Cultures: Selected Essays* (New York: Basic Books, 1973), 87–125.

Chapter Two

1. Male theorists for whom the body is significant rarely take on the significance of gender difference and sexual difference in relation to the body itself. So, for example, Foucault does not attend to gender as central to his discussion of *anatomo-politics* of the human body (*The History of Sexuality Volume One: An Introduction*, trans. Robert Hurley [New York: Vintage Books, 1980], 139) or of *biostruggle* to reinvent the body (157). Nor do Deleuze and Guattari address gender in their development of a politics of desire (*Anti-Oedipus: Capitalism and Schizophrenia*, trans. Robert Hurley, Mark Seam, and Helen R. Lane, with a preface by Michel Foucault [Minneapolis: University of Minnesota Press, 1983], 293) that is set in opposition to power (*A Thousand Plateaus: Capitalism and Schizophrenia*, trans. and with a foreword by Brian Massumi [Minneapolis: University of Minnesota, 1987], 151).

2. See Lori Heise, "The Global War against Women," excerpted from *World Watch* 2/2 (March–April 1989): 12–21 in *Utne Reader* 36 (November–December 1989).

3. The terms "sexual difference" and "gender difference" elude definition, precisely because their significance is subject to dispute. By and large, "sexual difference" refers to differences due to nature (usually reproductive) as opposed to "gender difference," which is the sociocultural interpretation of

sexual difference that is in turn reified as "natural" and imposed through socialization upon humans according to their perceived sexual identity, a socialization that itself produces differences in experience. But how do you distinguish one from the other? From a thoroughgoing cultural determinist perspective, we have no sexual differences available to us unmediated by cultural construal, no "raw data," so to speak. From the perspective of a dedicated essentialist, gender differences, by virtue of being interpretations of nature, are themselves natural, such that the concept of sexual difference tends to absorb the meaning of gender difference. To add further confusion (or enrichment as the case may be), supposedly self-evident biological distinctions break down, thanks to defective Y chromosomes which produce apparent females who are hormonally male and who cannot become pregnant. See the May 1992 issue of *Discover* magazine, devoted entirely to a discussion of sexual definition.

4. Distinguishing between "language" and "discourse," as in the case of sexual difference and gender difference, proves to be a difficult, if not impossible, task. "Discourse" tends to refer to the contextualization of language; hence the same language manifests itself in a variety of different ways according to different contexts. But if, as some theorists claim, language is itself inherently patriarchal, then context becomes secondary in significance at best and altogether irrelevant in the extreme.

5. For similar analyses of the concept "woman," albeit formulated in different terms and coming to different conclusions, see the following: Linda Alcoff, "Cultural Feminism versus Post-Structuralism: The Identity Crisis in Feminist Theory," *Signs* 13/3 (Spring 1988): 405–436; Teresa de Lauretis, *Alice Doesn't: Feminism, Semiotics, Cinema* (Bloomington: Indiana University Press, 1984); and Denise Riley, *War in the Nursery: Theories of the Child and Mother* (London: Virago, 1983).

6. Sherry B. Ortner, "Is Female to Male as Nature Is to Culture?" in *Woman, Culture, and Society,* eds. Michelle Zimbalist Rosaldo and Louise Lamphere (Stanford: Stanford University Press, 1974), 67–87. While Ortner herself makes no such argument in this essay, it is one of the most frequently cited essays in the ongoing discussion of the relation between sexual difference and identity.

7. See Penelope Washbourn, *Becoming Woman: The Quest for Wholeness in Female Experience* (New York: Harper & Row, 1977), for an American example.

8. Ann Rosalind Jones, "Writing the Body: Toward an Understanding of *l'Écriture féminine,* " in *The New Feminist Criticism: Essays on Women, Literature, and Theory,* ed. Elaine Showalter (New York: Pantheon, 1985), 361–377, provides an excellent overview. See also Elaine Marks, "Women and Literature in France," *Signs* 3/4 (Summer 1978): 832–842.

9. Jones, "Writing the Body," 362.

10. *New French Feminisms: An Anthology,* eds. Elaine Marks and Isabelle de Courtivron (Amherst: University of Massachusetts Press, 1980), 36, note 8.

See also Roland Barthes, *Image-Music-Text,* trans. Stephen Heath (New York: Farrar, Straus and Giroux, 1977).

11. Luce Irigaray, "Ce Sexe qui n'en est pas un," translated in *New French Feminisms: An Anthology,* eds. Elaine Marks and Isabelle de Courtivron (Amherst: University of Massachusetts Press, 1980), 103.

12. Alice A. Jardine's *Gynesis: Configurations of Woman and Modernity* (Ithaca: Cornell University Press, 1985) provides an excellent examination of feminine writing characteristic of male authors.

13. Julia Kristeva's *"Stabat Mater"* is an excellent example which concludes with a call to women to be heretics who create "her-ethics." See *Poetics Today* 6/1–2 (1985): 133–152. For American counterparts see Audre Lorde's "Uses of the Erotic: The Erotic as Power," in *Sister Outsider: Essays and Speeches* (Freedom, Calif.: Crossing Press, 1984), 53–59, and everything by Mary Daly written since *Beyond God the Father: Toward a Philosophy of Women's Liberation* (Boston: Beacon Press, 1972), but especially *Pure Lust: Elemental Feminist Philosophy* (Boston: Beacon Press, 1984).

14. Important conceptual differences notwithstanding, theories of *jouissance* strongly resemble Foucault's concern with technologies of the self-constituting self and Deleuze and Guattari's politics of desire in their shared insistence upon desire as productive and the body as central to rebellion against totalitarian and totalistic assertions of power.

15. For examples of this argument see Kaja Silverman, *"Histoire d'O:* The Construction of a Female Subject," in *Pleasure and Danger: Exploring Female Sexuality,* ed. Carole S. Vance (Boston: Routledge & Kegan Paul, 1984), 320–349, and Susan Rubin Suleiman, "(Re)Writing the Body: The Politics and Poetics of Female Eroticism," *Poetics Today* 6/1–2 (1985): 43–65.

16. Quoted in Jones, "Writing the Body," 370.

17. Ibid., 367–370.

18. For Heilbrun's position see *Toward a Recognition of Androgyny* (New York: Knopf, 1973), and "Androgyny and the Psychology of Sex Differences," in *The Future of Difference,* eds. Hester Eisenstein and Alice Jardine (Boston: G. K. Hall, 1980), 258–266. For Suleiman's position see "(Re)Writing the Body," 43–65.

19. Psychoanalytic theory (particularly Freudian and Lacanian, and feminist theory rooted in this tradition) attempts to take seriously both culture and physicality with varying degrees of success. See, for example, Nancy Chodorow, *The Reproduction of Mothering: Psycho-Analysis and the Sociology of Gender* (Berkeley: University of California Press, 1978). For an anthropological approach to the issue without specific reference to sexual difference see Mary Douglas, *Natural Symbols: Explorations in Cosmology* (New York: Random House, 1973).

20. For an excellent critique of the failure of socialist theory to take gender, the body, and nature sufficiently seriously, see Mary Mellor, "Eco-Feminism and Eco-Socialism: Dilemmas of Essentialism and Materialism," *Capitalism, Nature, Socialism: A Journal of Socialist Ecology* 3/2 (10 June 1992): 43–62.

21. This insight formed the bedrock of feminist consciousness raising in the late sixties on into the seventies. Feminist consciousness raising finds its historical roots in Latin American liberation movements. See Paulo Freire, *Pedagogy of the Oppressed*, trans. Myra Bergman Ramos (New York: Continuum, 1984), and Gustavo Gutierrez, *A Theology of Liberation: History, Politics and Salvation*, trans. Caridad Inda and John Eagleson (Maryknoll, N.Y.: Orbis, 1973). For the relation between consciousness raising and feminist theology see Judith Plaskow, *Sex, Sin and Grace: Women's Experience and the Theologies of Reinhold Niebuhr and Paul Tillich* (New York: University Press of America, 1980), especially Chapter 1, "Women's Experience," 9–50; and "The Coming of Lilith: Toward a Feminist Theology," in *Womanspirit Rising: A Feminist Reader in Religion*, eds. Carol P. Christ and Plaskow (San Francisco: Harper & Row, 1979), 198–209. More recently, focus on experience plays a major role in de Lauretis's work cited previously, whereas Alcoff stresses women's positionality (also see preceding discussion).

22. How emotion mediates between body and discourse, as well as nature and culture, is the subject of the next chapter.

23. For the beginning of such a theory see Paula Cooey, "The Power of Transformation and the Transformation of Power," *Journal of Feminist Studies in Religion* 1/1 (Spring 1985): 23–36. Work done in this area by Valerie Saiving, Mary Daly, Judith Plaskow, Rosemary Ruether, and Carol P. Christ is invaluable. Nevertheless much remains to be done, particularly with respect to the significance of differences among women—ethnic, racial, class, and creedal differences. Furthermore, there is insufficient communication between theorists involved in the study of religion and theological studies, on the one hand, and theorists engaged in the so-called secular disciplines, on the other.

24. See Clifford Geertz, "Religion as a Cultural System," in *The Interpretation of Cultures: Selected Essays* (New York: HarperCollins, 1973), 87–125; Suzanne K. Langer, *Philosophy in a New Key: A Study in the Symbolism of Reason, Rite, and Art* (Cambridge, Mass.: Harvard University Press, 1957); and Mary Douglas, *Natural Symbols*.

25. For an interpretation of faith as an act of and response to value, see H. Richard Niebuhr, *Radical Monotheism and Western Culture* (New York: Harper & Row, 1960), especially "Faith in Gods and in God," 114–126. For an analysis of the relation between religion and change, see Alfred North Whitehead, *Religion in the Making* (New York: New American Library, 1954).

26. I shall return to the issue of religious symbol systems as pedagogical in Chapter Three. Regarding technologies and the care of the self, see *The Care of the Self*, vol. 3, *The History of Sexuality*, trans. Robert Hurley (New York: Vintage, 1988), "Technologies of the Self," in *Technologies of the Self: A Seminar with Michel Foucault*, eds. Luther M. Martin, Huck Gutman, and Patrick H. Hutton (Amherst: University of Massachusetts Press, 1988); and *The Use of Pleasure*, vol. 2, *The History of Sexuality*, trans. Robert Hurley (New York: Vintage, 1986).

27. Nelle Morton, *The Journey Is Home* (Boston: Beacon Press, 1985).

28. Maxine Hong Kingston, *The Woman Warrior: Memoirs of a Girlhood among Ghosts* (New York: Random House, 1976).

29. Paule Marshall, *Praisesong for the Widow* (New York: E. P. Dutton, 1983), relevant pages hereafter cited in the text. For an extended analysis of the role played by ritual in both the structure and the content of the novel, see Barbara Christian, "Ritualistic Process and the Structure of Paule Marshall's *Praisesong for the Widow*," in *Black Feminist Criticism: Perspectives on Black Women Writers* (New York: Pergamon Press, 1985).

30. For those more comfortable with non-fiction see Carol P. Christ's "Why Women Need the Goddess: Phenomenological, Psychological, and Political Reflections," in *Womanspirit Rising: A Feminist Reader in Religion*, eds. Christ and Judith Plaskow (San Francisco: Harper & Row, 1979), 273–287.

31. Anne Carolyn Klein, "Finding a Self: Buddhist and Feminist Perspectives," in *Shaping New Vision: Gender and Values in American Culture*, eds. Clarissa W. Atkinson, Constance H. Buchanan, and Margaret R. Miles (Ann Arbor: UMI Research Press, 1987), 191–218.

32. For discussions of realization of emptiness the following texts are helpful: Frederick J. Streng, *Emptiness: A Study in Religious Meaning* (Nashville: Abingdon Press, 1967); Osel Tendzin, *Buddha in the Palm of Your Hand* (Boston: Shambala, 1982).

Chapter Three

1. Alicia Partnoy, *The Little School: Tales of Disappearance and Survival in Argentina*, trans. Partnoy with Lois Athey and Sandra Braunstein (Pittsburgh, Cleis, 1986), 18.

2. See, for example, Judith Plaskow, "The Coming of Lilith: Toward a Feminist Theology of Liberation," in *Womanspirit Rising: A Feminist Reader in Religion*, eds. Carol P. Christ and Plaskow (San Francisco: Harper & Row, 1979), 198–209.

3. Sheila Greeve Davaney, "Problems with Feminist Theory: Historicity and the Search for Sure Foundations," in *Embodied Love: Sensuality and Relationship as Feminist Values*, eds. Paula M. Cooey, Sharon A. Farmer, and Mary Ellen Ross (San Francisco: Harper & Row, 1987), 79–95; Linell E. Cady, "Theories of Religion in Feminist Theologies," paper presented to the Women in Religion section at the national meeting of the American Academy of Religion, Boston, December 1987.

4. See, for example, Wilfred Cantwell Smith, *Faith and Belief* (Princeton: Princeton University Press, 1979).

5. Immanuel Kant, *Critique of Pure Reason*, trans. Norman Kemp Smith (New York: Saint Martin's, 1965), 549–70.

6. Alfred North Whitehead, *Process and Reality: An Essay in Cosmology*, eds.

David Ray Griffin and Donald W. Sherburne, corrected edition (New York: The Free Press, 1978).

7. Wayne Proudfoot, *Religious Experience* (Berkeley: University of California Press, 1985), Chapter 6, "Explanation," 190–227.

8. William James, *The Varieties of Religious Experience: A Study in Human Nature*, with an intro. by Martin E. Marty (New York: Penguin, 1982), 449–501.

9. See, for example, Friedrich Schleiermacher, *On Religion: Speeches to Its Cultured Despisers*, trans. John Oman, with an intro. by Rudolf Otto (New York: Harper & Row, 1958), esp. "The Nature of Religion," 26–118, and *The Christian Faith*, 2 vols., eds. H. R. Mackintosh and J. S. Stewart, with an intro. by Richard R. Niebuhr (New York: Harper & Row, 1963), chap. 1, "The Definition of Dogmatics," 3–93. See also Smith, *Faith and Belief*.

10. See, for example, Alan Heimert, *Religion and the American Mind: From the Great Awakening to the Revolution* (Cambridge, Mass.: Harvard University Press, 1966).

11. See, respectively, Rosemary Radford Ruether, *Women-Church: Theology and Practice of Feminist Liturgical Communities* (San Francisco: Harper & Row, 1985); Starhawk, "Witchcraft and Women's Culture," in *Womanspirit Rising: A Feminist Reader in Religion*, eds. Carol P. Christ and Judith Plaskow (San Francisco: Harper & Row, 1979), 259–268; Mary Daly, *Gyn/ecology: The Metaethics of Radical Feminism* (Boston: Beacon Press, 1978).

12. See Schleiermacher, *On Religion*, 36, 43; also *Christian Faith*, 5–26.

13. Paula Cooey, "The Power of Transformation and the Transformation of Power," *Journal of Feminist Studies in Religion* 1/1 (Spring 1985): 23–36.

14. Wayne Proudfoot, *Religious Experience*.

15. Ibid., 124–148; William James, *Varieties of Religious Experience*, "Mysticism," Lectures XVI and XVII, 379–429.

16. See Daryl J. Bem, "Self-Perception Theory," in vol. 6, *Advances in Experimental Social Psychology*, ed. Leonard Berkowitz (New York: Academic Press, 1972), 1–62; Kelly G. Shaver, *An Introduction to Attribution Processes* (Cambridge, Mass.: Winthrop, 1975).

17. The chief participants included R. B. Zajonc, "Feeling and Thinking: Preferences Need No Inferences," *American Psychologist* 35/2 (February 1980): 151–75, relevant pages hereafter cited in the text, and Richard S. Lazarus, "A Cognitivist's Reply to Zajonc on Emotion and Cognition," *American Psychologist* 36/2 (1981): 222–223.

18. Thus, for example, as my colleague Dr. Paula Hertel, also a cognitivist, points out, a feeling of repugnance in response to the smell of feces or to the smell of rotting corpses appears to be initially a biological mechanism for survival, given the potential for feces and decaying flesh to carry disease. Such repugnance constitutes a "natural" feeling necessary to the survival of species before the development of chemical treatments for excretion. Although this does not mean that repugnance is not taught, it does indicate that its origin is natural, not cultural. Feelings such as trust and loyalty, by contrast, appear to

depend upon highly complex belief systems and processes of socialization. It is worth noting in either case, however, that minimal cognition of an object is required.

19. See James's discussion of the psychology of conversion, *Varieties of Religious Experience,* lecture X, 217–258.

20. See, for example, *Miscellany 782,* in *The Philosophy of Jonathan Edwards: From His Private Notebooks,* ed. Harvey G. Townsend (Eugene: The University Press [University of Oregon], 1955), 113–126.

21. Clifford Geertz, "Religion as a Cultural System," in *The Interpretation of Cultures: Selected Essays* (New York: Basic Books, 1973), 87–125.

22. K. Jill Kiecolt and Hart M. Nelsen, "The Structuring of Political Attitudes among Liberal and Conservative Protestants," *Journal for the Scientific Study of Religion* 27/1 (March 1988): 48–59.

23. Nico H. Frijda, "The Laws of Emotion," *American Psychologist* 43/5 (May 1988): 349–358.

24. Ibid., 353. Emphasis in the original.

25. Ibid., 353. Emphasis in the original.

26. Ibid., 354.

27. Sheila Greeve Davaney, "Problems with Feminist Theory," 79–95; Linell E. Cady, "Theories of Religion in Feminist Theologies," unpublished.

28. Linell Cady, "Theories of Religion in Feminist Theologies."

29. See the Select Bibliography for publication information on all authors and texts just cited.

30. See, for classic examples of French feminist thought, the essays in *New French Feminisms: An Anthology,* eds. and with an intro. by Elaine Marks and Isabelle de Courtivron (Amherst: University of Massachusetts Press, 1980).

31. Nelle Morton, *The Journey Is Home* (Boston: Beacon Press, 1985), 123.

32. Ibid., 125, 127; emphasis in the original text.

33. Ibid., 155–157.

34. Davaney, "Problems with Feminist Theory," 79–95; Cady, "Theories of Religion in Feminist Theologies," unpublished.

35. Elaine Scarry, *The Body in Pain: The Making and Unmaking of the World* (New York: Oxford University Press, 1985), relevant pages hereafter cited in the text.

36. For different, though not altogether incompatible views, see Michel de Certeau, "The Institution of Rot," in *Heterologies: Discourse on the Other,* trans. Brian Massumi, with a foreword by Wlad Godzich (Minneapolis: University of Minnesota Press, 1986), 35–46; and Michael Taussig, *Shamanism, Colonialism, and the Wild Man: A Study in Terror and Healing* (Chicago: University of Chicago Press, 1987), esp. "The Economy of Terror," 51–73.

37. Nelle Morton suffered throughout her life a blood disorder which she attributed in part to internalized patriarchal attitudes toward female bodies. See *Journey Is Home,* 162–164.

38. Partnoy, *The Little School,* 84–85.

Chapter Four

1. Alicia Partnoy, *The Little School: Tales of Disappearance and Survival in Argentina*, trans. Partnoy with Lois Athey and Sandra Braunstein (Pittsburgh: Cleis, 1986), 88.

2. The exceptions have, on occasion, been popular (not to be confused with conventional), as in the case of Bhakti.

3. Margaret R. Miles, *Carnal Knowing: Female Nakedness and Religious Meaning in the Christian West* (Boston: Beacon Press, 1989), "Nakedness, Gender, and Religious Meaning," 169–185.

4. *That* this process has occurred throughout the history of Western Christianity is not news; an historical overview of specifically *how* it occurred is fascinating.

5. In regard to the meaning of "representation" Miles distinguishes between nakedness and nudity as different modes of representation, preferring the latter to the former. She does not address other philosophical implications of representation, however. Rightly critical of all attempts to shore up conceptions of the human self as grounded in substance, the deconstructionist movement has challenged virtually all views of subjectivity by associating them with philosophical substantialism or essentialism. Miles is aware of this problem and identifies herself as a social theorist of the self. Her aim is to understand socialization "as a process in which subjectivity is created and informed by relationships and by the symbolic provisions of culture" (*Carnal Knowing*, 187). She argues for a "carnal knowing," a knowledge that celebrates particularity, within this context. She contrasts this process with essentialist theories that masculinity and femininity are innately related to a person's gender. Unlike the deconstructionists, however, she seeks an alternative subjectivity. Thus she stands in opposition both to essentialists and to deconstructionists, though she leaves the question of the epistemological status of her alternative open.

6. An alternative view of subjectivity implies alternative views of its environment, therefore, "world" and "God." A discussion of these lies beyond the scope of this chapter, however. Suffice it to say that the view of subjectivity that I suggest is not amenable to conventional conceptions of personal immortality in an eternal realm after death.

7. See, for an example of faculty psychology, Augustine, *The Trinity*, trans. Stephen McKenna (Washington, D.C.: Catholic University of America Press, 1963). For one of the most recent discussions of the historical and philosophical development of subjectivity in North America from the colonial period to the present, see James Hoopes, *Consciousness in New England: From Puritanism and Ideas to Psychoanalysis and Semiotic* (Baltimore: Johns Hopkins University Press, 1989). For a geographically more extensive discussion, see the work of Peter Abs.

8. Paula M. Cooey, "The Word Become Flesh: Woman's Body, Language, and Value," in *Embodied Love: Sensuality and Relationship as Feminist Values*,

eds. Cooey, Sharon A. Farmer, and Mary Ellen Ross (San Francisco: Harper & Row, 1987), 17–33.

9. Hoopes, *Consciousness in New England,* esp. 260–274.

10. See, for a classic example, *Civilization and Its Discontents,* in *The Standard Edition of the Complete Psychological Works of Sigmund Freud,* ed. and trans. James Strachey (London: Hogarth Press,1961). For a discussion of Freud's expectations of psychoanalysis as a therapeutic process, see Mary Ellen Ross, "The Ethical Limitations of Autonomy: A Critique of the Moral Vision of Psychological Man," in *Embodied Love: Sensuality and Relationship as Feminist Values,* eds. Paula M. Cooey, Sharon A. Farmer, and Ross (San Francisco: Harper & Row, 1987), 151–168.

11. See the discussion of French feminism in Chapter Two. Theorists who hold this view stand in the ironic position of simultaneously deconstructing the male subject and insisting that women are *in essence* others in relation to this fabrication.

12. See, for examples, Jacques Derrida, *Of Grammatology,* trans. Gayatri Chakravorty Spivak (Baltimore: Johns Hopkins University Press, 1974), and *Writing and Difference,* trans. with an intro. and notes by Alan Bass (Chicago: University of Chicago Press, 1984).

13. For a recent, very brief critique of Derrida's nihilism see Carl A. Raschke, "Fire and Roses: Toward Authentic Post-Modern Religious Thinking," *Journal of the American Academy of Religion* 58/4 (Winter 1990): 671–689.

14. This is the same approach Hoopes takes in *Consciousness in New England.* My analysis of self as sign, like Hoopes's, depends heavily, though not entirely, upon Charles Sanders Peirce's semiotics. See especially "The Law of Mind," in *Collected Papers of Charles Sanders Peirce,* vols. I–VI eds. Charles Hartshorne and Paul Weiss; vols. VII–VIII ed. Arthur W. Burks (Cambridge, Mass.: Harvard University Press, 1931–58), 86–113, vol. VI; and "Questions Concerning Certain Faculties Claimed for Man," 135–155, and "Some Consequences of Four Incapacities," 156–189, both in vol. V. See also Vincent Michael Colapietro, *Peirce's Approach to the Self: A Semiotic Perspective on Human Subjectivity* (Albany: State University of New York Press, 1989). For a recent application of Peirce's logic to construct a critical methodology for interpreting religious experience, see Wayne Proudfoot, *Religious Experience* (Berkeley: University of California Press, 1985).

15. Peirce's philosophical view of "thought" as inclusive of all cognitions functions similarly to Lazarus' psychological conception of "cognition" in that in both cases "cognition" tends to absorb all human mental processes except sensation. See Chapter Three, 46–51.

16. Chapter Three discusses at length a hypothesis for the relation between cognition (imagination) and the material order (sensation). See also Paula M. Cooey, "Experience, Body, and Authority," *Harvard Theological Review* 82/3 (July 1989): 325–342.

17. I don't wish to reduce Morrison's characters to serve solely as typologi-

cal approaches, nor to imply that this discussion exhausts all possible approaches to subjectivity. I am claiming only that the characters analyzed here wonderfully illumine different views of subjectivity and their limitations.

18. Toni Morrison's fiction celebrates African-American life and history without glossing the tragedy of white racism. More recently she has shifted her gaze to a critical analysis of the effects of racism against African-Americans upon white people. She writes in a collection of lectures, delivered originally at Harvard University: "The well established study [of the impact of racism upon its objects] should be joined with another equally important one: the impact of racism upon those who perpetuate it." In the collection of lectures she proceeds to analyze the cultural effects of white racism on the works of Hawthorne, Cather, and Hemingway, among others. She is not, by the way, attributing racism to the authors she analyzes. See *Playing in the Dark: Whiteness and the Literary Imagination* (Cambridge, Mass.: Harvard University Press, 1992). The same might be said of sexism; see John Stoltenberg, *Refusing to Be a Man: Essays on Sex and Justice* (New York: Penguin Books/Meridan, 1989).

19. Claudia Tate, "Toni Morrison," in *Black Women Writers at Work*, ed. Tate (New York: Continuum, 1983), 117–131.

20. Toni Morrison, *Sula* (New York: New American Library, 1973), relevant pages hereafter cited in the text. For the most current and exhaustive bibliography of commentary on Morrison see David L. Middleton, *Toni Morrison: An Annotated Bibliography*, Garland Reference Library of the Humanities vol. 767 (New York: Garland Publishing, 1987).

21. See C. Lynn Munro, "The Tattooed Heart and the Serpentine Eye: Morrison's Choice of an Epigraph for *Sula*," *Black American Literature Forum* 18/4 (Winter 1984): 150–154.

22. Miles, *Carnal Knowing*, esp. "Adam and Eve: Before and After," 85–116.

23. This lingering of the power of the characters over a reader beyond the end of the text is deliberately cultivated by Morrison. See Marsha Jean Darling, "A Conversation with Toni Morrison," *The Women's Review of Books* 5/6 (March 1988): 6, where Morrison states:

> The whole point is to have those characters . . . move off the page and inhabit the imagination of whoever has opened himself or herself to them. I don't want to write books that you can close . . . and walk on off and read another one right away. . . . It's that the writing be as understated and as quiet as possible, and as lean as possible in order to make a complex and rich response come from the reader. They always say my writing is rich. It's not—what's rich if there is any richness is what the reader gets and brings him or herself. . . . The folk tales are told in such a way that whoever is listening is in it and can shape it and figure it out. It's not over just because it stops. It lingers and it's passed on. It's passed on and somebody else can alter it later. You can even end it if you want.

24. Toni Morrison, *Song of Solomon* (New York: New American Library, 1977), relevant pages hereafter cited in the text.

25. For the particular significance of names in Morrison's work see Charles Fishman, "Naming Names: Three Recent Novels by Women Writers," *Names* 32 (1984): 33–44.

26. Susan Willis, "Eruptions of Funk: Historicizing Toni Morrison," *Black American Literature Forum* 16/1 (Spring 1982): 34–42.

27. Toni Morrison, *The Bluest Eye* (New York: Washington Square Press, 1970).

28. Toni Morrison, *Beloved* (New York: Alfred A. Knopf, 1987). For a discussion of Morrison's view of evil and her ability to provoke outrage in the reader in response to the defeat of another, see Sharon D. Welch's recently published *A Feminist Ethic of Risk* (Minneapolis: Fortress Press, 1990), esp. 67–70.

29. "Biblically epic" refers to the kind of biblical realism discussed by Erich Auerbach in *Mimesis: The Representation of Reality in Western Literature*, trans. Willard R. Trask (Princeton: Princeton University Press, 1953), a sense of realism lost to biblical hermeneutics during the modern period. See Hans W. Frei, *The Eclipse of Biblical Narrative: A Study in Eighteenth and Nineteenth Century Hermeneutics* (New Haven: Yale University Press, 1974).

30. This analysis of subjectivity is in certain respects amenable to Welch's analysis of an ethic of control in contrast to an ethic of risk; see *A Feminist Ethic of Risk*, especially the distinction, borrowed from Mildred Taylor, between "bending" and "bowing and scraping," 80.

31. See Peirce, "The Law of Mind," 280–283.

32. Though not identical in all respects, this kind of subjectivity closely resembles H. Richard Niebuhr's "responsible self." See *The Responsible Self: An Essay in Christian Moral Philosophy*, eds. James M. Gustafson and Richard R. Niebuhr, with an intro. by Gustafson (New York: Harper & Row, 1963). See also Welch, *Feminist Ethic of Risk*.

33. Quoted by Sally Fitzgerald in the introduction to *Three by Flannery O'Connor* (New York: National American Library, 1983), xxi.

Chapter Five

1. Horace M. Newcomb, "On the Dialogic Aspects of Mass Communication," *Critical Studies in Mass Communication* 1/1 (March 1984), 41. See also Jiri Veltrusky, "Some Aspects of the Pictorial Sign (1973)," *The Semiotics of Art*, eds. Ladislav Matejka and Irwin R. Titunik (Cambridge, Mass.: MIT Press, 1976), 245–264; and W. J. T. Mitchell, *Iconology: Image, Text, Ideology* (Chicago: University of Chicago Press, 1986).

2. In addition, a small image of her blindfolded daughter appears at the beginning of each vignette, and a map of the buildings in which the prisoners were held is included in the conclusion. For an interpretation of the possible

significance of the image of Alicia Partnoy blindfolded, see Alicia Partnoy, *The Little School: Tales of Disappearance and Survival in Argentina*, trans. Partnoy with Lois Athey and Sandra Braunstein (Pittsburgh: Cleis, 1986), intro., 16–17. The map (132) presumably reflects Partnoy's memory of her surroundings and appears in the final portion of text, which is devoted to her testimony given during national and international hearings.

3. Partnoy, *Little School*, 16.

4. The mothers and grandmothers of the disappeared formed a human rights group that marched daily in the Plaza de Mayo in protest against disappearance. Because they refused to be intimidated by the government, they too were threatened, and some of them disappeared (see Partnoy, *Little School*, 16).

5. See Chapter Two.

6. See Chapter Three, 57–61.

7. See Chapter Four, 67–71.

8. My colleague in art history, John Hutton, wisely points out that the body as site, like the body as sign, has an externalized reading because it is the intersection of external, material forces like wind, sun, heat, cold, and physical objects to bump into.

9. See Denise Riley, "Does Sex Have a History?" in *New Formations* (Spring 1987): 38–40.

10. This conceptualization of "mapping" is in part a response to Fredric Jameson's call for "cognitive mapping," and in part a response to the critique of Jameson's concept of "cognitive mapping" launched by Steven Best and Douglas Kellner. See especially Jameson, "Cognitive Mapping," in *Marxism and the Interpretation of Culture*, eds. Cary Nelson and Lawrence Grossberg (Urbana: University of Illinois Press, 1988), 347–360. For a critique see Steven Best and Douglas Kellner, *Postmodern Theory: Critical Interrogations* (New York: Guilford Press, 1991), 188–192.

11. See Chapter Three, 59.

12. See, for example, Jonathan Z. Smith, *Map Is Not Territory* (Leiden, Netherlands: Brill, 1978), 289–309.

13. See Pierre Bourdieu, *Outline of a Theory of Practice*, trans. Richard Nice (Cambridge, U.K.: Cambridge University Press, 1977), 2, 37–38, 105; and Terry Eagleton, *Ideology: An Introduction* (London: Verso, 1991), especially his treatment of Althusser and Geertz, 150–156. For a more sympathetic view, see Clifford Geertz, "Ideology as a Cultural System," in *The Interpretation of Cultures: Selected Essays* (New York: Basic Books, 1973), 193–233.

14. For an analysis of the significance of touch in the formation of identity, see Paula M. Cooey, "The Word Become Flesh: Woman's Body, Language, and Value," in *Embodied Love: Sensuality and Relationship as Feminist Values*, eds. Cooey, Sharon A. Farmer, and Mary Ellen Ross (San Francisco: Harper & Row, 1987), 17–33. See also Elaine Scarry, *The Body in Pain: The Making and Unmaking of the World* (New York: Oxford University Press, 1985), 165.

15. For an excellent discussion see Terry Eagleton, *Ideology*.

16. See "Introduction" and Scarry, *Body in Pain*, 27–157.

17. I use "dialogical" here as I understand M. M. Bakhtin to have used it. See *The Dialogic Imagination: Four Essays*, esp. "Epic and the Novel," ed. Michael Holquist, trans. Caryl Emerson and Holquist (Austin: University of Texas Press, 1981), 3–40.

18. For an extended discussion of this issue, see Michael Taussig, *Shamanism, Colonialism, and the Wild Man: A Study in Terror and Healing* (Chicago: University of Chicago Press, 1987), "Part One: Terror," esp. 127–135.

19. There are points, albeit very few, where she does not avoid these tendencies.

20. An Argentine who waits the table where I regularly sit at lunchtime in a Trinity dining hall once told me that the disappeared ones were communist thugs who deserved what they got.

21. Scarry notes that those who are not in pain have difficulty finding those who suffer it credible when they seek to communicate their pain, in part because pain in the extreme becomes an entirely objectless and therefore totally subjective state of consciousness. See *Body in Pain*, 4, 7, 56–57.

22. Scarry, *Body in Pain*, 315–326.

23. Michael Newman, "The Ribbon around the Bomb," *Art in America* 71/4 (April 1983): 168.

24. I am deeply indebted to the assistance of two of my colleagues in the Department of Art History, as well as to student assistance, for helping me develop a critical appreciation of Kahlo's work and the scholarship it has generated. Lisa Reitzes initially suggested that I might find Kahlo's art relevant to my own work in after-dinner conversation at our home in the spring of 1990. In the summer of 1991, John Hutton provided me with extensive bibliographical materials, which our own department work-study student, John Mendoza, compiled for me.

25. See, for example, her painting *My Grandparents, My Parents, and I*, 1936.

26. All biographical information, unless otherwise noted, comes from Hayden Herrera, *Frida: A Biography of Frida Kahlo* (New York: Harper & Row, 1983).

27. Janice Helland, "Aztec Imagery in Frida Kahlo's Paintings: Indigeneity and Political Commitment," *Woman's Art Journal* 11/2 (Fall 1990/Winter 1991): 8–13. See in particular the self-portraits dedicated to Sigmund Firestone (1940), with thorn necklace and hummingbird (1940), dedicated to Dr. Eloesser (1940), with braid (1941), and dedicated to Marte R. Gomez (1946). The jagged lines around the neck that suggest or in some cases actually denote severing provide the recurring Aztec motif here.

28. Helland, "Aztec Imagery in Frida Kahlo's Paintings." See, for example, *They Ask for Planes and Only Get Straw Wings* (1938) and *Self-Portrait on the Borderline between Mexico and the United States* (1932).

29. Ibid. See, for example, *Luther Burbank* (1931), *The Dream* (1940), and *Roots* (1943).

30. Ibid. See also, Nancy Deffebach Breslow, "Frida Kahlo's 'The Square Is Theirs': Spoofing Giorgio de Chirico," *Arts Magazine* 56/5 (January 1982): 120–123. Breslow notes, "This [western] area of Mexico is unusual in that the ancient sculpture is more frequently secular than religious. It was a nonelitist culture and the only area of pre-Conquest Mexico known for erotic art. (The Aztecs, who were quite a prissy group, considered both adultery and drunkenness capital crimes)" (120).

31. Helland, "Aztec Imagery in Frida Kahlo's Paintings."

32. See, for, examples, *Memory* (1937), *My Dress Hangs There* (1933), *Remembrance of an Open Wound* (1938), *The Two Fridas* (1939), and *The Love Embrace of the Universe, the Earth (Mexico), Diego, Me and Senor Xolotl* (1949).

33. Michael Newman connects her painting to her self-presentation in "The Ribbon around the Bomb" by noting, "There is no denying that for Kahlo . . . the adoption of a naive manner and the use of pre-Hispanic and Catholic iconography was a deliberate choice. . . . It was a form of role playing, like when she wore the Tehuana costume" (164).

34. For a study of *retablo* art, see Gloria Fraser Giffords, *Mexican Folk Retablos: Masterpieces on Tin* (Tuscon: University of Arizona Press, 1974).

35. See, for example, *Henry Ford Hospital* (1932), which commemorates one of several miscarriages. My colleague John Hutton notes that the contrast in scale between Kahlo's small *retablos* and Rivera's murals reflects implicitly an ideological breach of Kahlo. At the time she was painting, the political movement to which she was connected, as exemplified by Rivera, despised easel paintings as "private" and "Bourgeois" and called for massive public art (conversation, November 6, 1992).

36. See, for example, *A Few Small Nips* (1935) and *The Suicide of Dorothy Hale* (1939).

37. See Emmanuel Pernoud, "Une Autobiographie Mystique: La Peinture de Frida Kahlo," *Gazette des Beaux-arts*, 6th series, 101 (January 1983): 43–48.

38. Ibid., 48.

39. By "parabolic" I mean "operates as a parable." See Chapter One, 3–4 for a discussion of this technique in Partnoy.

40. Though there is no outside intervention in a supernatural sense, at least three of her paintings in the *retablo* genre do depict faith in the intervention by other human beings: *Self-Portrait with the Portrait of Doctor Farill* (1951), where the doctor assumes the role of intercessor, *Marxism Will Give Health to the Sick* (1954), in which Frida is saved by Karl Marx, and *Frida and Stalin* (1954), in which Stalin intervenes on Frida's behalf.

41. Herrera, *Frida*, 180–181.

42. Pernoud, "Une Autobiographie Mystique," 47.

43. Herrera, *Frida*, 188.

44. Nancy Breslow, "Frida Kahlo: A Cry of Joy and Pain," *Americas* 32/3 (March 1980): 33.

45. Of her communism in relation to Rivera's she declared to her friend the

journalist Rosa Castro: "I was a member of the Party before I met Diego and I think I am a better Communist than he is or ever will be" (quoted in Herrera, *Frida,* 396). Kahlo's and Rivera's relations with the party were stormy. Rivera was kicked out in 1929, and Kahlo followed him. She was later reinstated in 1948.

46. Herrera, *Frida,* 189.

47. Raquel Tibol, "Frida Kahlo," in *Art of the Fantastic: Latin America, 1920–1987* (Indianapolis: Indianapolis Museum of Art, 1987), 216.

48. One very obvious example I have in mind here is Leni Riefenstal's brilliant cinematography in the service of the Third Reich.

49. See, for examples, *What the Water Gave Me* (1938), *The Two Fridas* (1939), and *Tree of Hope* (1946).

50. See, for examples, *Self-Portrait on the Borderline between Mexico and the United States* (1932) and *My Dress Hangs There* (1933).

51. See, in addition, *Memory* (1937) and *The Broken Column* (1944).

52. Pernoud, "Une Autobiographie Mystique," 47.

53. In the paintings in which two images of Kahlo appear, one figure tends to be more European and the other more indigenous in dress and complexion.

54. Her home, which is now a museum, retains all of the furnishings from the time of her death. Her canopied bed seems so very small and fragile, the wall directly opposite the head of the bed covered with photographs of her favorite communist heroes.

55. Herrera, *Frida,* 279.

56. For example, Herrera does this on occasion.

57. Herrera, *Frida,* 279.

58. Francis V. O'Connor, "The Psychodynamics of the Frontal Self-Portrait," *Psychoanalytic Perspectives on Art* 7/1 (1985): 208.

59. Salomon Grimberg, "Frida Kahlo's *Memory:* The Piercing of the Heart by the Arrow of Divine Love," *Woman's Art Journal* 11/2 (Fall 1990/Winter 1991):4–5.

60. Herrera, *Frida,* 357.

61. See Anita Brenner, *Idols behind Altars* (New York: Harcourt, Brace and Company, 1929), 155; see also Herrera, *Frida,* 357–358.

62. Herrera, *Frida,* 358.

63. See also *Self-Portrait with Cropped Hair* (1940), as well as early family photographs, in which she "cross dresses." A number of artists exhibited their work under the title *Aspects of Contemporary Mexican Painting* at the Blue Star Gallery in San Antonio, Texas, May 24–June 30, 1991. Among them were several paintings that exhibited this motif with reference to male homosexuality. Unfortunately, I did not write down names of specific artists or titles. The artists exhibited included Rodolpho Morales, Alejandro Colunga, Arturo Marty, Ismael Vargas, Julio Galan, Nahum B. Zenil, Dulce Maria Nunez, Rocio Maldonado, and Georgina Quintana. Several of these artists also appropriated Kahlo's extension of the painting to include the frame.

64. This "transgression" challenged class as well as gender difference. Her emphasis on facial hair (upper lip and exaggerated eyebrows) in her self-portraits not only "masculinizes" her, but locates her solidarity with peasant and working class women as well.

65. Herrera, *Frida*, plate VI, 157–158, 221–223, 231; Breslow, "Frida Kahlo," 33–39.

66. See, for example, *Fruits of the Earth* (1938), *Still Life* (1942), *Flower of Life* (1944), and *Viva la Vida* (1954).

67. She was familiar with the works of Georgia O'Keefe; indeed, Rivera claims that she flirted with O'Keefe at Stieglitz's gallery (Herrera, *Frida*, 198).

68. *Naturaleza Muerta* translates literally to "dead nature," the point being lack of motion.

69. The mamey is held sacred in Cuban culture because it is believed to possess dark and evil power. (It apparently also has the power to cure colitis.) I don't know whether Kahlo knew this, since this belief is not indigenous to Mexico. See Lydia Cabrera, *El Monte: Igbo Finda Ewe Orisha, Vititinfinda* (Havana: Ediciones C. R., 1954), 483. I am indebted to my colleague Frank Garcia, professor of Hebrew Bible in the Department of Religion, Trinity University, for pointing this out to me.

70. Herrera, *Frida*, 398.

71. See Chapter Three, 53–56.

72. Herrera, *Frida*, 158–159.

73. Recall that Scarry stresses the importance of voicing pain in order to transform it. See Scarry, *Body in Pain*, esp. 27–38.

74. One controversy over the significance of Kahlo's work with which I have not dealt here focuses on her status as a surrealist, a status about which she at least felt ambivalent, and which she is reputed to have disclaimed. The best treatments of this issue I have found include Breslow, "Frida Kahlo's 'The Square Is Theirs'; and Newman, "The Ribbon around the Bomb." I have not dealt with this controversy because it bears only indirectly on the issues I am raising. It is, however, one more instance of ideological struggle through interpretation of a body of work.

Chapter Six

1. There are, of course, exceptions, for example, cross dressing, eonism, and unisex fashions.

2. Trans. H. M. Parshley (Harmondsworth: Penguin, 1972) and cited in Toril Moi's *Sexual/Textual Politics: Feminist Literary Theory* (London: Methuen, 1985), 92.

3. Moi, *Sexual/Textual Politics*, 82. Lest there be any misunderstanding, I am not suggesting that in some realist sense we are all androgynous. On the contrary, I think that the gender polarity as presently construed represents reduction and polarizing of a rich biological spectrum that might more ade-

quately be gendered along the line of at least five possible different distinctions. See, for a similar suggestion in regard to biological sex, the geneticist Anne Fausto-Sterling's article "Myths of Gender: Biological Theories about Women and Men" (*The Sciences,* March/April 1993), an abridged version of which appeared on the editorial page of *The New York Times,* March 12, 1993, p. A15.

4. It also does not necessarily follow that there are therefore no extra-cultural realities, by the way. Arguments for what these might be and how we as products of culture could know this, however, would have to be developed altogether differently from the way we have heretofore developed them.

5. "Positive" egocentricity presupposes an inflated sense of self-worth at the expense of other; "negative" egocentricity depends upon a lack of or deflated sense of self-worth. Both are nevertheless egocentric in their preoccupation with self-worth.

6. Taking pleasure in one's own physicality notwithstanding, this type of subjectivity is not characteristically narcissistic. One of the critics of feminism, Christopher Lasch, for example, criticizes the women's movement along with other groups for promoting narcissism, in part because he confuses women's refusal to define themselves centrally in terms of self-sacrifice with an egocentric obsession with self-fulfillment. See *The Culture of Narcissism: American Life in an Age of Diminishing Expectations* (New York: W. W. Norton, 1979).

7. One could interpret fluidity as characterological virtue as suspect. Can such a character be trustworthy and trusting? One would have to look at the context in order to respond. Furthermore, a unified autonomous self as an alternative, taken likewise in the abstract, does not inherently carry the ability to trust or the moral virtue of trustworthiness, unless in the case of trustworthiness, one simply means consistency. In regard to Pilate Dead, her trustworthiness lies in her commitment to love all whom she knows. Furthermore, she herself is capable of taking risks precisely because she is able to trust. For a discussion of the relation between identity and trust in the high modern era, see Anthony Giddens, *Modernity and Self-Identity: Self and Society in the Late Modern Age* (Stanford: Stanford University Press, 1991).

8. For a fuller treatment of the ethical implications of multiple communities, see Sharon D. Welch, *A Feminist Ethic of Risk* (Minneapolis: Fortress, 1990).

9. See Chapter Five, 92.

10. Jonathan Z. Smith, *Map Is Not Territory* (Leiden, Netherlands: E. J. Brill, 1978), 291.

11. For examples, see the work of Jonathan Z. Smith, Wilfred Cantwell Smith, and Wayne Proudfoot, as cited in the Select Bibliography.

12. Gerald J. Larson, "Discourse about 'Religion' in Colonial and Post-colonial India," paper presented to the Critical Theory Group at the national American Academy of Religion meeting, Kansas City, November 24, 1992.

13. For an interesting attempt to confront these issues in relation to scholarship see "'If I Perish, *We* Perish': A Collective Interpretation of Competi-

tion," by Charlene A. Galarneau, Jessica G. Gugino, Deborah J. Haynes, Elizabeth B. Lemons, Margaret R. Miles, Rachel C. Rasmussen, Kathleen P. Skerrett, and Karen-Marie Yust, *Union Seminary Quarterly Review* 45/1–2 (1991): 1–15.

14. See Chapter Three, 46–48. I intend this distinction between theory as explanation and theology and thealogy as evocation simply as a convenience and a matter of rhetorical tendency, rather than as some kind of hard and fast rule of genre. Schleiermacher, who was a theologian who theorized about the origin of religious faith, did so by consciously trying to evoke piety in his audience's imagination; furthermore, we all know how truly unevocative some theology can be. I think of explanation and evocation not as standing in oppositional relation to one another but as setting limits of a continuum, limits exemplified at their best by the theoretical writings of Ernst Troeltsch at the explanatory end and someone like Soren Kierkegaard or Mary Daly at the evocative end of the continuum.

15. Examples include Penelope Washbourn's *Becoming Woman: The Quest for Wholeness in Female Experience* (New York: Harper & Row, 1977), Mary Daly's *Gyn/ecology: The Metaethics of Radical Feminism* (Boston: Beacon Press, 1978), Mary Ellen Ross and Cheryl Lynn Ross's "Mother, Infants, and the Psychoanalytic Study of Ritual," *Signs* 9/11 (1983): 25–39, and Naomi R. Goldenberg's *The Changing of the Gods: Feminism and the End of Traditional Religions* (Boston: Beacon Press, 1979). For a recent example, see Victoria Lee Erikson, "Back to Basics: Feminist Social Theory, Durkheim and Religion," *Journal of Feminist Studies in Religion* 8/1 (Spring 1992): 35–46. This article is excerpted from Erikson's forthcoming book titled *Speaking in the Dark: Towards a Feminist Social Theory of Religion* (Minneapolis: Fortress Press, 1993). The article, which is excellent on the whole, concludes by distinguishing between *religion* as the domain of "masculine forces" and *spirituality* as the "life experience of women and other excluded people" (45), a distinction left undeveloped in the article, which I find puzzling for posing what appears to be either a Manichaean dualism of masculinity and femininity or a troubling relation between epistemology and ontology.

16. For a philosophical and somewhat indirect consideration of this issue see Jean-François Lyotard, *The Inhuman: Reflections on Time*, trans. Geoffrey Bennington and Rachel Bowlby (Stanford: Stanford University Press, 1991).

17. Thomas Pynchon's fiction raises these issues in a variety of different ways. Consider, for example, Oedipa Maas's question *"Shall I project a world?"* which drives *The Crying of Lot 49* (New York: Harper & Row, 1966), 82. See also Brian McHale, *Postmodernist Fiction* (New York: Methuen, 1987).

18. For the very practical problems that result in the courts and in public policy formation from isolating race and gender from one another, see Kimberle Crenshaw's "Demarginalizing the Intersection of Race and Sex: A Black Feminist Critique of Antidiscrimination Doctrine, Feminist Theory, and Antiracist Politics [1989]," in *Feminist Legal Theory: Readings in Law and Gender*,

eds. Katharine T. Bartlett and Rosanne Kennedy (Boulder: Westview Press, 1991), 57–80.

19. See Chapter Three.

20. In 1992, the program of the national American Academy of Religion included at least three full sections devoted exclusively to the status of theological discourse in relation to religious studies.

21. "Modern," "post-modern," and their respective cognates mean so many different things to so many different theorists. For clarification (whether by way of agreement or disagreement) see Steven Best and Douglas Kellner, *Postmodern Theory: Critical Interrogations* (New York: Guilford Press, 1991).

22. See Chapter Three, 47 and Chapter Five, 123–124 with n. 14.

23. See *Selections from the Prison Notebooks of Antonio Gramsci*, eds. and trans. Quintin Hoare and Geoffrey Nowell Smith (New York: International Publishers, 1971), esp. 348, 365, 370, 376. Gramsci had a very strong sense that constructive work required the voices of those most likely silenced throughout history, in order for change to be valid. Thus, on issues of sexual practice, he insisted that no discussion for cultural change could occur without a change in the status of women, making them fully equal, so that they might have direct input to proposing change. See 294–298.

24. See, of course, Gordon D. Kaufman, *An Essay on Theological Method* (Missoula, Mont.: Scholars Press, 1975), and *The Theological Imagination: Constructing the Concept of God* (Philadelphia: Westminister, 1981).

25. See Chapter Five, 107–108.

Select Bibliography

Adorno, Theodor W. "The Actuality of Philosophy." *Telos* 10/31 (Spring 1977): 120–133.

———. *Against Epistemology: A Metacritique: Studies in Husserl and the Phenomenological Antinomies*. London and Cambridge, Mass., 1983.

———."Husserl and the Problem of Idealism." *Journal of Philosophy* 37/1 (January 4, 1940): 5–18.

———. "The Idea of Natural History." *Telos* 17/60 (Summer 1984): 111–124.

———. *Kierkegaard: Construction of the Aesthetic*. Minneapolis, 1989.

———. *Negative Dialectics*. London, 1973.

Alcoff, Linda. "Cultural Feminism versus Post-Structuralism: The Identity Crisis in Feminist Theory." *Signs: Journal of Women in Culture and Society* 13/3 (Spring 1988): 405–436.

Aristotle. *Categories*. In *Aristotle's* Categories *and* De Interpretatione. Trans. with notes J. L. Ackrill. London, 1963. 3–42; notes 71–112.

———. *De Poetica*. In *The Basic Works of Aristotle*. Ed. and intro. Richard McKeon. Trans. Ingram Bywater. New York, 1941. 1453–1487.

Auerbach, Erich. *Mimesis: The Representation of Reality in Western Literature*. Trans. Willard R. Trask. Princeton, 1953.

Augustine. *The Trinity*. Trans. Stephen McKenna. Washington, D.C., 1963.

Badu, Fabienne. "Un poema de Frida Kahlo." *Literatura Mexicana* 1/1 (1990).

Bakhtin, M. M. *The Dialogic Imagination: Four Essays*. Ed. Michael Holquist. Trans. Caryl Emerson and Holquist. Austin, 1981.

———. *Rabelais and His World*. Cambridge, Mass., 1968.

Barrett, Michele. "Ideology and the Cultural Production of Gender." In *Feminist Criticism and Social Change: Sex, Class, and Race in Literature and Culture*. Ed. Judith Newton and Deborah Rosenfelt. New York, 1985.

Barthes, Roland. *Elements of Semiology*. New York, 1968.

———. *Image-Music-Text*. Trans. Stephen Heath. New York, 1977.

Belsey, Catherine. "Constructing the Subject: Deconstructing the Text." In *Feminist Criticism and Social Change: Sex, Class, and Race in Literature and Culture*. Eds. Judith Newton and Deborah Rosenfelt. New York, 1985.

Bem, Daryl J. "Self-Perception Theory." In *Advances in Experimental Social Psychology*, vol. 6. Ed. Leonard Berkowitz. New York, 1972. 1–62.

Benhabib, Seyla. "Epistemologies of Postmodernism: A Rejoinder to Jean-François Lyotard." *New German Critique* 33 (Fall 1984): 103–126.

———."The Generalized and the Concrete Other: The Kohlberg-Gilligan Controversy and Feminist Theory." In *Feminism as Critique: On the Politics of Gender*. Eds. Benhabib and Drucilla Cornell. Minneapolis, 1987. 77–95.

Benjamin, Walter. *Illuminations*. New York, 1968.

Berger, Peter L., and Thomas Luckmann. *The Social Construction of Reality: A Treatise in the Sociology of Knowledge*. New York, 1966.

Best, Steven, and Douglas Kellner. *Postmodern Theory: Critical Interrogations*. New York, 1991.

Bloch, Ernst, et al. *Aesthetics and Politics*. Trans. ed. Ronald Taylor. Afterword Fredric Jameson. London, 1977.

Bourdieu, Pierre. *Outline of a Theory of Practice*. Trans. Richard Nice. Cambridge, U.K., 1977.

Borgmann, Albert. *Crossing the Postmodern Divide*. Chicago, 1992.

Brenner, Anita. *Idols behind Altars*. New York, 1929.

Breslow, Nancy Deffebach. "Frida Kahlo: A Cry of Joy and Pain." *Americas* 32/3 (March 1980): 33–39.

———. "Frida Kahlo's 'The Square is Theirs': Spoofing Giorgio de Chirico." *Arts Magazine* 56/5 (January 1982): 120–123.

Breton, Andre. *Surrealism and Painting*. Trans. Simon Watson Taylor. New York, 1972.

———. *What Is Surrealism? Selected Writings*. Ed. and intro. Franklin Rosemont. New York, 1978.

Bynum, Caroline Walker, Stevan Harrell, and Paula Richman, eds. *Gender and Religion: On the Complexity of Symbols*. Boston, 1986.

Cabrera, Lydia. *El Monte: Igbo Finda Ewe Orisha, Vititinfinda*. Havana, 1954.

Cady, Linell E. "Theories of Religion in Feminist Theologies." Paper presented to the Women in Religion section at the national meeting of the American Academy of Religion, Boston, December 1987.

Carrion, Jorge. *Mito y Magia del Mexicano: Ensayos Sobre el Mexicano*. Editorial Nuestro Tiempo S.A., Mexico D.F., 1952.

Castro, Rosa. "Cartas de Amor: Un Libro de Frida Kahlo." *Siempre* June 12, 1954.

de Certeau, Michel. *Heterologies: Discourse on the Other*. Trans. Brian Massumi. Foreword Wlad Godzich. Vol. 17, *Theory and History of Literature*. Eds. Wlad Godzich and Jochen Schulte-Sasse. Minneapolis, 1986.

Chadwick, Whitney. "The Muse as Artist: Women in the Surrealist Movement." *Art in America* 73/7 (July 1985): 120–129.

———. *Women Artists and the Surrealist Movement*. London, 1985.

Chinas, Beverley. *The Isthmus Zapotecs: Women's Roles in Cultural Context*. New York, 1973.

Chodorow, Nancy. *The Reproduction of Mothering: Psychoanalysis and the Sociology of Gender.* Berkeley, 1978.

Christ, Carol P. "Why Women Need the Goddess: Phenomenological, Psychological, and Political Reflections." In *Womanspirit Rising: A Feminist Reader in Religion.* Eds. Christ and Judith Plaskow. San Francisco, 1979. 273–287.

Christian, Barbara. "Ritualistic Process and the Structure of Paule Marshall's *Praisesong for the Widow.*" In *Black Feminist Criticism: Perspectives on Black Women Writers.* New York, 1985.

———. "The Race for Theory." *Feminist Studies* 14/1 (1988): 67–80.

Cixous, Helene. "The Laugh of the Medusa." In *New French Feminisms: An Anthology.* Eds. Elaine Marks and Isabelle de Courtivon. Amherst, 1980.

———. "Sorties." In *New French Feminisms: An Anthology.* Eds. Elaine Marks and Isabelle de Courtivron. Amherst, 1980.

Coetzee, J. M. *Age of Iron.* New York, 1990.

Colapietro, Vincent Michael. *Peirce's Approach to the Self: A Semiotic Perspective on Human Subjectivity.* Albany, 1989.

Cooey, Paula M. "Experience, Body, and Authority." *Harvard Theological Review* 82/3 (July 1989): 325–342.

———. "The Power of Transformation and the Transformation of Power." *Journal of Femininist Studies in Religion* 1/1 (Spring 1985): 23–36.

———. "The Word Become Flesh: Woman's Body, Language, and Value." In *Embodied Love: Sensuality and Relationship as Feminist Values.* Eds. Cooey, Sharon A. Farmer, and Mary Ellen Ross. San Francisco, 1987. 17–33.

Cowart, David. "Pynchon's *The Crying of Lot 49* and the Paintings of Remedios Varo." *Critique: Studies in Modern Fiction* 18/3 (1977).

Cowie, Elizabeth. "'Woman as Sign'." *M/F* (1).

Crenshaw, Kimberle. "Demarginalizing the Intersection of Race and Sex: A Black Feminist Critique of Antidiscrimination Doctrine, Feminist Theory, and Antiracist Politics [1989]." In *Feminist Legal Theory: Readings in Law and Gender.* Eds. Katharine T. Bartlett and Rosanne Kennedy. Boulder, 1991. 57–80.

Culpepper, Emily Erwin. "Contemporary Goddess Thealogy: A Sympathetic Critique." In *Shaping New Vision: Gender and Values in American Culture.* Eds. Clarissa W. Atkinson, Constance H. Buchanan, and Margaret R. Miles. Ann Arbor, 1987. 51–71.

Daly, Mary. *Beyond God the Father: Toward a Philosophy of Women's Liberation.* Boston, 1973.

———. *The Church and the Second Sex.* New York, 1975.

———. *Gyn/ecology: The Metaethics of Radical Feminism.* Boston, 1978.

———. *Pure Lust: Elemental Feminist Philosophy.* Boston, 1984.

Darling, Marsha Jean. "A Conversation with Toni Morrison." *The Women's Review of Books* 5/6 (March 1988): 6–7.

Davaney, Sheila Greeve. "Problems with Feminist Theory: Historicity and the

Search for Sure Foundations." In *Embodied Love: Sensuality and Relationship as Feminist Values*. Eds. Paula M. Cooey, Sharon A. Farmer, and Mary Ellen Ross. San Francisco, 1987. 79–95.

Debroise, Oliver. *Figuras en el Tropico, Plastica Mexicana 1920–1940*. Barcelona, 1984.

De Lauretis, Teresa. *Technologies of Gender*. Bloomington, 1987.

———. *Alice Doesn't: Feminism, Semiotics, Cinema*. Bloomington, 1984.

Del Conde, Teresa. "Lo Popular en el Arte de Frida Kahlo." Universidad Nacional Autonoma de Mexico, Mexico, D.F., 1976.

Deleuze, Gilles. *Logic of Sense*. New York, 1989.

———, and Felix Guattari. *Anti-Oedipus: Capitalism and Schizophrenia*. Trans. Robert Hurley, Mark Seam, and Helen R. Lane. Preface by Michel Foucault. Minneapolis, 1983.

———. *Kafka*. Minneapolis, 1986.

———. *A Thousand Plateaus: Capitalism and Schizophrenia*. Trans. and foreword Brian Massumi. Minneapolis, 1987.

Derrida, Jacques. *Of Grammatology*. Trans. Gayatri Chakravorty Spivak. Baltimore, 1974.

———. *Writing and Difference*. Trans. with intro. and additional notes Alan Bass. Chicago, 1984.

Diamond, Irene, and Lee Quinby. *Feminism and Foucault: Reflections on Resistance*. Boston, 1988.

Douglas, Mary. *Natural Symbols: Explorations in Cosmology*. New York, 1973.

Dreyfus, Hubert L., and Paul Rabinow. *Michel Foucault: Beyond Structuralism and Hermeneutics*. Chicago, 1982.

Duran, Gloria. "The Antipodes of Surrealism: Salvador Dali and Remedios Varo." *Symposium: A Quarterly Journal in Modern Foreign Literatures* 42/4 (1989).

Duran, Jane. *Toward a Feminist Epistemology*. Savage, Md., 1991.

Durkheim, Emile. *The Elementary Forms of the Religious Life: A Study in Religious Sociology*. Trans. Joseph Ward Swain. New York, 1965.

Eagleton, Terry. "Capitalism, Modernism and Postmodernism." *New Left Review* 152 (July/August 1985): 60–73.

———. *Ideology: An Introduction*. London, 1991.

———. *Literary Theory: An Introduction*. Minneapolis, 1983.

Eco, Umberto. *The Open Work*. Trans. Anna Cancognia. Cambridge, Mass., 1989.

———. *Semiotics and the Philosophy of Language*. Bloomington, 1984.

Edwards, Jonathan. *Miscellany 782*. In *The Philosophy of Jonathan Edwards: From His Private Notebooks*. Ed. Harvey G. Townsend. Eugene, Ore., 1955. 113–126.

Eisenstein, Hester, and Alice Jardine, eds. *The Future of Difference*. Boston, 1980.

Eisenstein, Zillah R. *The Female Body and the Law*. Berkeley, 1988.

Eliade, Mircea. *The Sacred and the Profane: The Nature of Religion*. Trans. Williard R. Trask. New York, 1961.

Erikson, Victoria Lee. "Back to Basics: Feminist Social Theory, Durkheim and Religion." *Journal of Feminist Studies in Religion* 8/1 (Spring 1992): 35–46.

Fauchereau, Serge. "Surrealism in Mexico." *Artforum* 25/1 (September 1986): 86–91.

Felski, Rita. *Beyond Feminist Aesthetics: Feminist Literature and Social Change*. Cambridge, Mass., 1989.

Ferre, Frederick. *Shaping the Future: Resources for the Postmodern World*. New York, 1976.

Feuerbach, Ludwig. *The Essence of Christianity*. Trans. George Eliot. Intro. Karl Barth. Foreword H. Richard Niebuhr. New York, 1957.

Fiorenza, Elisabeth Schussler. *In Memory of Her: A Feminist Reconstruction of Christian Origins*. New York, 1984.

Firestone, Shulamith. *Dialectic of Sex*. New York, 1971.

Fishman, Charles. "Naming Names: Three Recent Novels by Women Writers." *Names* 32 (1984): 33–44.

Fitzgerald, Sally. "Introduction" to *Three by Flannery O'Connor*. New York, 1983. vii–xxxiv.

Flores, E. "Varo, Remedios." *Goya* 208 (1989).

Foucault, Michel. *The Care of the Self*. Vol. 3, *The History of Sexuality*. Trans. Robert Hurley. New York, 1988.

———. *Discipline and Punish: The Birth of the Prison*. New York, 1979.

———. "The Ethic of Care for the Self as a Practice of Freedom: An Interview with Michel Foucault on January 20, 1984." Trans. J. D. Gauthier. In *The Final Foucault*. Eds. James Bernauer and David Rasmussen. Cambridge, Mass., 1988. 1–20.

———. "Final Interview." *Raritan* 5/1 (Summer 1985): 1–13.

———. *The History of Sexuality Volume One: An Introduction*. Trans. Robert Hurley. New York, 1980.

———. *Power/Knowledge: Selected Interviews and Other Writings, 1972–1977*. New York, 1980.

———. "The Subject and Power." In *Michael Foucault: Beyond Structuralism and Hermeneutics*. Eds. Hubert L. Dreyfus and Paul Rabinow. Chicago, 1982.

———. "Technologies of the Self." In *Technologies of the Self: A Seminar with Michel Foucault*. Eds. Luther M. Martin, Huck Gutman, and Patrick H. Hutton. Amherst, 1988.

———. *The Use of Pleasure*. Vol. 2, *The History of Sexuality*. Trans. Robert Hurley. New York, 1986.

———. "What Is Enlightenment?" In *The Foucault Reader*. Ed. Paul Rabinow. New York, 1984.

Francis, Mark. *Frida Kahlo and Tina Modotti*. London: Whitechapel Art Gallery, 1982.

Franco, Jean. *Plotting Women: Gender and Representation in Mexico.* New York, 1989.

Fraser, Nancy, and Linda Nicholson. "Social Criticism without Philosophy: An Encounter between Feminism and Postmodernism." *Theory, Culture and Society* 5/2–3 (1988).

Frei, Hans W. *The Eclipse of Biblical Narrative: A Study in Eighteenth and Nineteenth Century Hermeneutics.* New Haven, 1974.

Freire, Paulo. *Pedagogy of the Oppressed.* Trans. Myra Bergman Ramos. New York, 1984.

Freud, Sigmund. *Civilization and Its Discontents.* In *The Standard Edition of the Complete Psychological Works of Sigmund Freud.* Ed. and trans. James Strachey. London. 1961.

———. *The Future of an Illusion.* Trans. James Strachey. New York, 1961.

Frijda, Nico H. "The Laws of Emotion." *American Psychologist: Journal of the American Psychological Association* 43/5 (May 1988): 349–358.

Fromm, Erich. *Escape from Freedom.* New York, 1941.

Fulkerson, Mary McClintock. "Sexism as Original Sin: Developing a Theacentric Discourse." *Journal of the American Academy of Religion* 59/4 (Winter 1991): 653–675.

Galarneau, Charlene A., Jessica G. Gugino, Deborah J. Haynes, Elizabeth B. Lemons, Margaret R. Miles, Rachel C. Rasmussen, Kathleen P. Skerrett, and Karen-Marie Yust. "'If I Perish, *We* Perish': A Collective Interpretation of Competition." *Union Seminary Quarterly Review* 45/1–2 (1991): 1–15.

Gallego, J., Manuel Alvarezbravo, Vincente Rojo, and Frida Kahlo. *Insula-Revista de Letras y Ciencias Humanas* 40/463 (1985).

Geertz, Clifford. "Religion as a Cultural System." In *The Interpretation of Cultures: Selected Essays.* New York, 1973. 87–125.

———. "Ideology as a Cultural System." In *The Interpretation of Cultures: Selected Essays.* New York, 1973. 193–233.

Giddens, Anthony. *Modernity and Self-Identity: Self and Society in the Late Modern Age.* Stanford, 1991.

Giffords, Gloria Fraser. *Mexican Folk Retablos: Masterpieces on Tin.* Tucson, 1974.

Goldenberg, Naomi R. *The Changing of the Gods: Feminism and the End of Traditional Religions.* Boston, 1979.

Gramsci, Antonio. *Selections from the Prison Notebooks of Antonio Gramsci.* Eds. and trans. Quintin Hoare and Geoffrey Nowell Smith. New York, 1971.

Griffin, David Ray. *The Re-enchantment of Science: Postmodern Proposals.* Albany, 1988.

———. *Spirituality and Science: Postmodern Visions.* Albany, 1988.

Grimberg, Salomon. "Frida Kahlo's *Memory:* The Piercing of the Heart by the Arrow of Divine Love." *Woman's Art Journal* 11/2 (Fall 1990/Winter1991): 3–7.

Guattari, Felix. "A Liberation of Desire: An Interview with George Stambolian." In *Homosexualities and French Literature: Cultural Contexts/Critical*

Texts. Ed. with an intro. George Stambolian and Elaine Marks. Preface Richard Howard. Ithaca, 1979. 56–69.

———. *Molecular Revolution.* New York, 1984.

Guattari, Felix, and Toni Negri. *Communists Like Us.* New York, 1990.

Gustafson, James. *Ethics from a Theocentric Perspective.* 2 vols. Chicago, 1981.

Gutierrez, Gustavo. *A Theology of Liberation: History, Politics and Salvation.* Trans. Caridad Inda and John Eagleson. Maryknoll, N.Y., 1973.

Habermas, Jurgen. *The Structural Transformation of the Public Sphere.* Cambridge, Mass., 1989.

———. *Theory of Communicative Action.* 2 vols. Boston, 1984 and 1987.

Harding, Sandra. *The Science Question in Feminism.* Ithaca, 1986.

Harlow, Barbara. *Resistance Literature.* New York, 1987.

Hartman, Joan E., and Ellen Messer-Davidow. *(En)Gendering Knowledge: Feminists in Academe.* Knoxville, 1991.

Heilbrun, Carolyn G. "Androgyny and the Psychology of Sex Differences." In *The Future of Difference.* Eds. Hester Eisenstein and Alice Jardine. Boston, 1980. 258–266.

———. *Toward a Recognition of Androgyny.* New York, 1973.

———. *Writing a Woman's Life.* New York, 1988.

Heimert, Alan. *Religion and the American Mind: From the Great Awakening to the Revolution.* Cambridge, Mass., 1966.

Heise, Lori. "The Global War against Women." excerpted from *World Watch* 2/2 (March–April 1989): 12–21. In *Utne Reader* 36 (November–December 1989), 40–45.

Helland, Janice. "Aztec Imagery in Frida Kahlo's Paintings: Indigenity and Political Commitment." *Woman's Art Journal* 11/2 (Fall 1990/Winter 1991); 8–13.

Herrera, Hayden. *Frida: A Biography of Frida Kahlo.* New York, 1983.

———. "Frida Kahlo's Art." *Artscanada* (October/November 1979).

———. "Frida Kahlo: The Palette, the Pain, and the Painter." *Artforum* 21/7 (March 1983): 60–67.

———. "A Painter's Passion." *House & Garden: The Magazine of Creative Living* 155/8 (August 1983): 98–109.

———. "Portraits of a Marriage." *Connoisseur* (March 1982): 124–128.

———. "Why Frida Kahlo Speaks to the '90s." *New York Times* October 28, 1990: sec. 2/col. 2.

Hoefel, Roseanne L. "Life Portraits in the Surrealist Art of Frida Kahlo and Remedios Varo." *Phoebe: An Interdisciplinary Journal of Feminist Scholarship, Theory, and Aesthetics* 1/2 (1989).

Hoopes, James. *Consciousness in New England: From Puritanism and Ideas to Psychoanalysis and Semiotic.* Baltimore, 1989.

Horkheimer, Max, and Theodor W. Adorno. *Dialectic of Enlightenment.* Trans. John Cummings. New York, 1972.

Irigaray, Luce. *Ce sexe qui n'en est pas un.* Paris, 1977.

————. "Ce Sexe qui n'en est pas un." In *New French Feminisms: An Anthology*. Eds. Elaine Marks and Isabelle de Courtivron. Amherst, 1980.

————. *This Sex Which Is Not One*. Eds. Catherine Porter and Carolyn Burke. Ithaca, 1985.

James, William. *The Varieties of Religious Experience: A Study in Human Nature*. Intro. Martin E. Marty. New York, 1982.

Jameson, Fredric. "Cognitive Mapping." In *Marxism and the Interpretation of Culture*. Ed. and intro. Cary Nelson and Lawrence Grossberg. Urbana, 1988. 347–360.

————. "Foreword" to *The Postmodern Condition: A Report on Knowledge*, by Jean-François Lyotard. Trans. Geoffrey Bennington and Brian Massumi. Vol. 10, *Theory and History of Literature*. Minneapolis, 1984. vii–xxi.

————. "History and Class Consciousness as an Unfinished Project." *Rethinking Marxism* 1/1 (1988). 49–72.

————. *Marxism and Form*. Princeton, 1971.

————. "Notes toward a Marxist Cultural Politics." *Minnesota Review* NS5 (Fall 1975): 35–39.

————. "Periodizing the 60's." in *The 60's without Apology*. Ed. Sohnya Sayres, et al. Minneapolis, 1984. 178–209.

————. *The Political Unconscious*. New York, 1981.

————. "The Politics of Theory: Ideological Positions in the Postmodernism Debate." *New German Critique* 33 (Fall 1984): 53–65.

————. "Postmodernism and Consumer Society." In *The Anti-Aesthetic: Essays on Postmodern Culture*. Ed. Hal Foster. Port Townsend, Wash., 1983. 111–125.

————. "Postmodernism, or The Cultural Logic of Late Capitalism." *New Left Review* 146 (July–August 1984): 53–92.

————. *The Prison House of Language*. Princeton, 1972.

————. "Regarding Postmodernism—A Conversation with Fredric Jameson" (interview with Anders Stephanson). In *Postmodernism/Jameson/Critique*. Ed. Douglas Kellner. Vol. 4, *Postmodern Positions*. Washington, D.C., 1989. 43–74.

————. "Reification and Utopia in Mass Culture." *Social Text* (Winter 1979).

————. "Third-World Literature in the Era of Multinational Capitalism." *Social Text* 15 (Fall 1986).

Jardine, Alice A. *Gynesis: Configurations of Women and Modernity*. Ithaca, 1985.

Jones, Ann Rosalind. "Writing the Body: Toward an Understanding of *l'Écriture féminine*." In *The New Feminist Criticism: Essays on Women, Literature, and Theory*. Ed. Elaine Showalter. N.Y., 1985. 361–377.

Kadar, M. "Behind Every Great Man—Frida Kahlo Letters to Ella Wolfe." *Mosaic: A Journal for the Interdisciplinary Study of Literature* 20/4 (1987).

Kandt-Horn, S. "Sie Dachten, Ich Ware Surrealistin." *Bildende Kunst* 8 (1983).

Kant, Immanuel. *Critique of Pure Reason*. Trans. Norman Kemp Smith. New York, 1965.

———. *Religion within the Limits of Reason Alone*. Trans. with intro. and notes Theodore M. Greene and Hoyt H. Hudson. Intro. Greene and John R. Silber. New York, 1960.

Kaplan, E. Ann. *Postmodernism and Its Discontents: Theories, Practices*. London, 1988.

Kaplan, Janet A. "Remedios Varo: Voyages and Visions." *Woman's Art Journal* 1/2 (1980–81).

———. *Unexpected Journeys: The Art and Life of Remedios Varo*. New York, 1988.

Katz, Richard. *Boiling Energy: Community Healing among the Kalahari Kung*. Cambridge, Mass., 1984.

Kaufman, Gordon D. *An Essay on Theological Method*. Missoula, Mont., 1975.

———. *The Theological Imagination: Constructing the Concept of God*. Philadelphia, 1981.

Kiecolt, K. Jill, and Hart M. Nelsen. "The Structuring of Political Attitudes among Liberal and Conservative Protestants." *Journal for the Scientific Study of Religion* 27/1 (March 1988): 48–59.

Kingston, Maxine Hong. *The Woman Warrior: Memoirs of a Girlhood among Ghosts*. New York, 1976.

Klein, Anne Carolyn. "Finding a Self: Buddhist and Feminist Perspectives." In *Shaping New Vision: Gender and Values in American Culture*. Eds. Clarissa W. Atkinson, Constance H. Buchanan, and Margaret R. Miles. Ann Arbor, 1987. 191–218.

Kozloff, J. "Frida Kahlo." *Women's Studies* 6/1 (1978).

Kristeva, Julia. *Desire in Language: A Semiotic Approach to Literature and Art*. Trans. Thomas Gora, Alice Jardine, and Leon S. Roudiez. New York, 1980.

———. "Oscillation du 'pouvoir' au 'refus.'" In *New French Feminisms: An Anthology*. Eds. Elaine Marks and Isabelle de Courtivron. Amherst, 1980.

———. "Stabat Mater." *Poetics Today* 6/1–2 (1985): 133–152.

LaCapra, Dominick. *Rethinking Intellectual History: Texts, Contexts, Language*. Ithaca, 1982.

Laclau, Ernesto. "Politics and the Limits of Modernity." In *Universal Abandon? The Politics of Postmodernism*. Ed. Andrew Ross. Minneapolis, 1988. 63–82.

Laclau, Ernesto, and Chantal Mouffe. *Hegemony and Socialist Strategy: Toward a Radical Democratic Politics*. London, 1985.

———. "Post-Marxism without Apologies." *New Left Review* 166 (November/December 1987): 79–106.

Laing, R. D. *The Politics of Experience*. New York, 1967.

Langer, Suzanne K. *Philosophy in a New Key: A Study in the Symbolism of Reason, Rite, and Art*. Cambridge, Mass., 1957.

Larson, Gerald J. "Discourse about 'Religion' in Colonial and Postcolonial

India." Paper presented to the Critical Theory Group at the national American Academy of Religion meeting, Kansas City, November 24, 1992.

Lasch, Christopher. *The Culture of Narcissism: American Life in an Age of Diminishing Expectations*. New York, 1979.

———. *The Minimal Self*. London, 1985.

de Lauretis, Teresa. *Alice Doesn't: Feminism, Semiotics, Cinema*. Bloomington, 1984.

Lauter, Estella. "The Creative Woman and the Female Quest." *Sound* 63 (1980).

Lazarus, Richard S. "A Cognitivist's Reply to Zajonc on Emotion and Cognition." *American Psychologist: Journal of the American Psychological Association* 36/2 (February 1981): 222–223.

Lemert, Charles. "General Social Theory, Irony, Postmodernism." In *Postmodernism and Social Theory*. Eds. S. Seidman and D. Wagner. New York, 1990.

Lomas, D., and R. Howeel. "Medical Imagery in the Art of Frida Kahlo." *British Medical Journal* 299/6715 (1989).

Lorde, Audre. *Sister Outsider: Essays and Speeches*. Freedom, Calif.: 1984.

Lukacs, Georg. *The Destruction of Reason*. London, 1980.

Lyotard, Jean-François. *The Different: Phrases in Dispute*. Trans. Georges Van Den Abbeele. Minneapolis, 1988.

———. *Driftworks*. New York, 1984.

———. With Jean-Loup Thebaud. *Just Gaming*. Minneapolis, 1985.

———. *The Lyotard Reader*. Ed. Andrew Benjamin. London and Cambridge, Mass., 1989.

———. *The Inhuman: Reflections on Time*. Trans. Geoffrey Bennington and Rachel Bowlby. Stanford, 1991.

———. *The Postmodern Condition: A Report on Knowledge*. Trans. Geoffrey Bennington and Brian Massumi. Foreword Fredric Jameson. Vol. 10, *Theory and History in Literature*. Minneapolis, 1984.

Marcuse, Herbert. *Counterrevolution and Revolt*. Boston, 1972.

———. *One-Dimensional Man*. Boston, 1964.

Marks, Elaine. "Women and Literature in France." *Signs: Journal of Women in Culture and Society* 3/4 (Summer 1978): 832–842.

Marks, Elaine, and Isabelle de Courtivron, eds. *New French Feminisms: An Anthology*. Amherst, 1980.

Marshall, Paule. *Praisesong for the Widow*. New York, 1983.

Marx, Karl. "Contribution to the Critique of Hegel's Philosophy of Right." In *Karl Marx and Friedrich Engels on Religion*. Ed. Reinhold Niebuhr. New York, 1964. 41–58.

McHale, Brian. *Postmodernist Fiction*. New York, 1987.

McLuhan, Marshall. *Understanding Media*. New York, 1964.

Mellor, Mary. "Eco-feminism and Eco-socialism: Dilemmas of Essentialism and Materialism." *Capitalism, Nature, Socialism: A Journal of Socialist Ecology* 3/2 (10 June 1992): 43–62.

Middleton, David L. *Toni Morrison: An Annotated Bibliography*. Garland Reference Library of the Humanities. Vol. 767. New York, 1987.

Miles, Margaret R. *Carnal Knowing: Female Nakedness and Religious Meaning in the Christian West*. Boston, 1989.

Miller, James. *The Passion of Michel Foucault*. New York, 1993.

Mills, C. Wright. *The Sociological Imagination*. New York, 1959.

Mitchell, W. J. T. *Iconology: Image, Text, Ideology*. Chicago, 1986.

Moi, Toril. *Sexual/Textual Politics: Feminist Literary Theory*. London, 1985.

Morrison, C. L. "Shadow Heroines: A Post-Freudian Look." *Format* 1/4 (1978).

Morrison, Toni. *Beloved*. New York, 1987.

———. *The Bluest Eye*. New York, 1970.

———. *Playing in the Dark: Whiteness and the Literary Imagination*. Cambridge, Mass., 1992.

———. *Jazz*. New York, 1992.

———. *Song of Solomon*. New York, 1977.

———. *Sula*. New York, 1973.

Morton, Nelle. *The Journey Is Home*. Boston, 1985.

Mouffe, Chantal. "Towards a Theoretical Interpretation of 'New Social Movements'." In *Rethinking Marx*. Eds. Sakari Hanninen and Leena Paldan. New York, 1984.

———. "Radical Democracy: Modern or Postmodern?" Trans. Paul Holdengraber. In *Universal Abandon?: The Politics of Postmodernism*. Ed. Andrew Ross. Minneapolis, 1988. 31–45.

Mulvey, Laura, and Peter Wollen. "Frida Kahlo and Tina Modotti." In *Frida Kahlo and Tina Modotti*. London. Whitechapel Art Gallery, 1982. 7–27.

Munro, C. Lynn. "The Tattooed Heart and the Serpentine Eye: Morrison's Choice of an Epigraph for *Sula*." *Black American Literature Forum* 18/4 (Winter 1984): 150–154.

Nesmer, Cindy. "Stereotypes and Women Artists." *Feminist Art Journal* (April 1972).

Newcomb, Horace M. "On the Dialogic Aspects of Mass Communication." *Critical Studies in Mass Communication* 1/1 (March 1984): 34–50.

Newman, Michael. "The Ribbon around the Bomb." *Art in America* 71/4 (April 1983): 160–169.

Niebuhr, H. Richard. *Radical Monotheism and Western Culture*. New York, 1960.

———. *The Responsible Self: An Essay in Christian Moral Philosophy*. Eds. James Gustafson and Richard R. Niebuhr. Intro. Gustafson. New York, 1963.

———. *Christ and Culture*. New York, 1951.

Niebuhr, Richard R. *Experiential Religion*. New York, 1972.

O'Connor, Francis V. "The Psycho-Dynamics of the Frontal Self-Portrait." *Psychoanalytic Perspectives on Art* 7/1 (1985): 169–221. Ed. Mary Mathews Gedo.

Orenstein, G. "Frida Kahlo: Painting for Miracles." *Feminist Art Journal* 2/3 (1973).

————. "Women of Surrealism."*Feminist Art Journal* 2/2 (1973).

Ortner, Sherry B. "Is Female to Male as Nature Is to Culture?" In *Woman, Culture, and Society.* Eds. Michelle Zimbalist Rosaldo and Louise Lamphere. Stanford, 1974. 67–87.

Otto, Rudolph. *The Idea of the Holy.* London, 1969.

Owens, Craig. "The Discourse of Others: Feminists and Postmodernism." In *The Anti-Aesthetic: Essays on Postmodern Culture.* Ed. Hal Foster. Port Townsend, Wash., 1983. 57–82.

Parker, Robert L. "Diego Rivera, Frida Kahlo, y Carlos Chavez—colaboración, desilusión y retribución." *Heterofonia* 19/1 (January–March 1987): 6–29.

Partnoy, Alicia. *The Little School: Tales of Disappearance and Survival in Argentina.* Trans. Partnoy with Lois Athey and Sandra Braunstein. Pittsburgh, 1986.

Peirce, Charles Sanders. *Collected Papers of Charles Sanders Peirce.* Vols. I–VI Ed. Charles S. Hartshorne and Paul Weiss. Vols. VII–VIII ed. Arthur Burke. Cambridge, Mass., 1931–1958.

Pernoud, Emmanuel. "Une Autobiographie Mystique: La Peinture de Frida Kahlo." *Gazette des Beaux-arts,* 6th series 101 (January 1983): 43–48.

Plaskow, Judith. "The Coming of Lilith: Toward a Feminist Theology of Liberation." In *Womanspirit Rising: A Feminist Reader in Religion.* Eds. Carol P. Christ and Plaskow. San Francisco, 1979. 198–209.

————. *Sex, Sin and Grace: Women's Experience and the Theologies of Reinhold Niebuhr and Paul Tillich.* New York, 1980.

Pollock, Griselda. *Vision and Difference: Femininity, Feminism, and the Histories of Art.* London, 1988.

Proudfoot, Wayne. *Religious Experience.* Berkeley, 1985.

Pynchon, Thomas. *The Crying of Lot 49.* New York, 1966.

Raschke, Carl A. "Fire and Roses: Toward Authentic Post-Modern Religious Thinking." *Journal of the American Academy of Religion* 58/4 (Winter 1990): 671–689.

Riley, Denise. "Does Sex Have a History?" In *New Formations* (Spring 1987): 38–40.

————. *War in the Nursery: Theories of the Child and Mother.* London, 1983.

Rivera, Diego, with Gladys March. *My Art, My Life: An Autobiography.* New York, 1960.

Rodriguez-Prampolini, Ida. *El Surrealismo y el Arte Fantástico de Mexico.* Universidad Nacional Autonoma de Mexico. Instituto de investigaciones esteticas. Mexico City, 1983.

————. "Remedios Varo and Frida Kahlo: Two Mexican Painters." In *Surrealisme Peripherique.* Ed. Luis de Moura Sobral. Montreal, 1984.

Rose, Phyllis. *Writing of Women: Essays in a Renaissance.* Middletown, Conn., 1985.

Ross, Mary Ellen. "The Ethical Limitations of Autonomy: A Critique of the Moral Vision of Psychological Man." In *Embodied Love: Sensuality and Relationship as Feminist Values*. Eds. Paula M. Cooey, Sharon A. Farmer, and Ross. San Francisco, 1987. 151–168.

Ross, Mary Ellen, and Cheryl Lynn Ross. "Mother, Infants, and the Psychoanalytic Study of Ritual." *Signs: Journal of Women in Culture and Society* 9/11 (1983): 26–39.

Ruether, Rosemary Radford. *Sexism and God-Talk: Toward a Feminist Theology*. Boston, 1983.

————. *Women-Church: Theology and Practice of Feminist Liturgical Communities*. San Francisco, 1985.

Saiving, Valerie. "The Human Situation: A Feminine View." In *Womanspirit Rising: A Feminist Reader in Religion*. Eds. Carol P. Christ and Judith Plaskow. San Francisco, 1979. 25–42.

Sands, Kathleen M. "Uses of the Thea(o)logian: Sex and Theodicy in Religious Feminism." *Journal of Feminist Studies in Religion* 8/1 (Spring 1992): 7–33.

Scarry, Elaine. *The Body in Pain: The Making and Unmaking of the World*. New York, 1985.

Schachter, Stanley. *Emotion, Obesity, and Crime*. New York, 1971.

Schechter, Stanley, and Jerome E. Singer. "Cognitive, Social, and Physiological Determinants of Emotional State." *Psychological Review* 5/69 (September 1962): 379–399.

Schleiermacher, Friedrich. *The Christian Faith*. Eds. H. R. Mackintosh and J. S. Stewart. Intro. Richard R. Niebuhr. 2 vols. New York, 1963.

————. *On Religion: Speeches to Its Cultured Despisers*. Trans. John Oman. Intro. Rudolf Otto. New York, 1958.

Schurmann, Reiner. "On Constituting Oneself as an Anarchistic Subject." *Praxis International* 6/3 (1986).

Shaver, Kelly G. *An Introduction to Attribution Processes*. Cambridge, Mass., 1975.

Sheets-Johnstone, Maxine, ed. *Giving the Body Its Due*. Albany, 1992.

Showalter, Elaine, ed. *The New Feminist Criticism: Essays on Women, Literature, and Theory*. New York, 1985.

Silverman, Kaja. "*Histoire d'O:* The Construction of a Female Subject." In *Pleasure and Danger: Exploring Female Sexuality*. Ed. Carole S. Vance. Boston, 1984. 320–349.

Smith, Huston. "Postmodernism and the Study of Religion." *Journal of the American Academy of Religion* 58/4 (1990), 653–670.

Smith, Jonathan Z. *Map Is Not Territory*. Leiden, Netherlands, 1978.

Smith, Wilfred Cantwell. *Faith and Belief*. Princeton, 1979.

Spurrier, Jeff. "The High Priestess of Mexican Art Is Turning Her Home in Mexico. . . ." *Connoisseur* 220 (1990).

Starhawk. "Witchcraft and Women's Culture." In *Womanspirit Rising: A*

Feminist Reader in Religion. Eds. Carol P. Christ and Judith Plaskow. San Francisco, 1979. 259–268.

Stoltenberg, John. *Refusing to Be a Man: Essays on Sex and Justice.* New York, 1989.

Storr, Robert. "Frida Kahlo: Self-Portrait with Hair Cut Short." *Art Press* 113 (1987).

Streng, Frederick J. *Emptiness: A Study in Religious Meaning.* Nashville, 1967.

Suleiman, Susan Rubin. "(Re)Writing the Body: The Politics and Poetics of Female Eroticism." *Poetics Today: International Journal for Theory and Analysis of Literature and Communication* 6/1–2 (1985): 43–65.

Sullivan, Edward J. "Frida Kahlo in New York." *Arts Magazine* 57 (March 1983): 90–92.

Sullivan, Lawrence E. "Body Works: Knowledge of the Body in the Study of Religion." *History of Religion* 30/1 (August 1990): 86–99.

Tate, Claudia. "Toni Morrison." In *Black Women Writers at Work.* Ed. Tate. New York, 1983. 117–131.

Taussig, Michael T. *The Devil and Commodity Fetishism in South America.* Chapel Hill, 1980.

———. *Shamanism, Colonialism, and the Wild Man: A Study in Terror and Healing.* Chicago, 1987.

Tendzin, Osel. *Buddha in the Palm of Your Hand.* Boston, 1982.

Tillich, Paul. *Systematic Theology.* 3 vols. Chicago, 1967.

Troeltsch, Ernst. *The Social Teaching of the Christian Churches.* Trans. Olive Wyon. 2 vols. Chicago, 1981.

Turner, Victor, and Edith Turner. *Image and Pilgrimage in Christian Culture.* New York, 1978.

Vance, Carole S., ed. *Pleasure and Danger: Exploring Female Sexuality.* Boston, 1984.

Veltrusky, Jiri. "Some Aspects of the Pictorial Sign (1973)." In *The Semiotics of Art.* Eds. Ladislav Matejka and Irwin R. Titunik. Cambridge, Mass., 1976. 245–264.

Walker, Alice. *In Search of Our Mothers' Gardens: Womanist Prose.* New York, 1983.

Washbourn, Penelope. *Becoming Woman: The Quest for Wholeness in Female Experience.* New York, 1977.

Wehr, Demaris. "Uses and Abuses of Jung's Psychology for Women: Animus." *Anima* 12/1 (Fall 1985): 13–22.

Welch, Sharon D. *A Feminist Ethic of Risk.* Minneapolis, 1990.

Whitehead, Alfred North. *Process and Reality: An Essay in Cosmology.* Ed. David Ray Griffin and Donald W. Sherburne. Corrected edition. New York, 1978.

———. *Religion in the Making.* New York, 1954.

Williams, Dolores S. "Black Women's Literature and the Task of Feminist Theology." In *Immaculate and Powerful: The Female Image in Sacred Image and Social Reality*. Eds. Clarissa W. Atkinson, Constance H. Buchanan, and Margaret R. Miles. Boston, 1985. 88–110.

Willis, Susan. "Eruptions of Funk: Historicizing Toni Morrison." *Black American Literature Forum* 16/1 (Spring 1982): 34–42.

Wolfe, Bertram D. *The Fabulous Life of Diego Rivera*. New York, 1963.

———. "Rise of Another Rivera." *Vogue* November 1, 1938.

Woolf, Virginia. *A Room of One's Own*. London, 1929.

Yau, John. "The Phoenix of the Self." *Artforum* 27/8 (April 1989): 145–151.

Zajonc, R. B. "Feeling and Thinking: Preferences Need No Inferences." *American Psychologist: Journal of the American Psychological Association* 35/2 (February 1980): 151–175.

Zamora, Martha. *The Brush of Anguish*. San Francisco, 1990.

Exhibition Catalogues

Art of the Fantastic: Latin America, 1920–1987. Eds. Holliday T. Day and Hollister Sturges. Indianapolis: Indianapolis Museum of Art, 1987.

Frida Kahlo and Tina Modotti. Essays ed. M. Francis. Conts.: M. Casanovas, P. Neruda, L. Mulvey, P. Wollen, T. Modotti, D. Rivera, C. Beals, A. Breton, A. Gomez Arias. Spons. Visiting Arts Unit and the British Council. London: Whitechapel Art Gallery, 1982.

Science in Surrealism: The Art of Remedios Varo. Eds. Peter Engel and Charlotte Stokes. 1986.

Splendors of Mexico: Thirty Centuries of Mexican Art. San Antonio: San Antonio Museum of Art, 1991.

Treasures of Mexico from the Mexican National Museums. Spons. Armand Hammer Foundation. 1978.

Index

Absolutism, 15
Abuse. *See* Human rights abuse; Pain and pleasure; Suffering; Violence
Academic study. *See* Scholarship
Age, gender difference and, 114
Agency. *See* Subjectivity
Alcoff, Linda, 134n.5, 136n.21
Ambiguity
   of body, 7, 9, 42, 61–62, 63–64, 90, 111, 119
   of Kahlo, 98–99, 100, 101
Ambivalence toward body, 7, 42
Amnesty International, 4, 8, 41, 57–58
Androcentrism, 22, 31, 52
Androgyny, 27, 132n.10, 148n.3–49n.3
Anthropology, theological, of Morrison, 80–83
Artifact. *See also* Body, as sign
   body as, 90, 94, 119
   subject as artifact of thought, 83–85
Atheism
   of Kahlo, 95, 96, 98, 108
   of Partnoy, 4
   religious symbol use and, 4, 96
Augustine, Saint, 67, 140n.7
Authority. *See* Epistemological status; Experience, authority of; Religious experience, authority of
Autoeroticism. *See* Jouissance

Barthes, Roland, 53
Battleground, female body as, 3–4, 25, 111. *See also* Weapon
Biblical parables, revelation of extraordinary by, 4
Biblical theology, philosophical theology vs., vii, viii–ix. *See also* Theology
Biology
   imagination vs., 28, 132n.10
   primacy of, 19–25, 28, 29, 134n.3

Birth, in Kahlo's paintings, 105–6
"Bodied" imagining subject. *See* Body, as site
Body. *See also* Emotion; Female body; Gender difference; Pain and Pleasure; Sensation; Sensuality; Sentience
   as abstraction, 132n.3
   ambiguity of, 7, 9, 42, 61–62, 63–64, 90, 111, 119
   ambivalence toward, 7, 42
   as artifact, 90, 94, 119. *See also* Body, as sign
   as battleground, 3–4, 25, 111
   as crucible, 43
   culture-making roles of, 112–21
   defined, 19, 132n.3
   discourse and, 30–31, 37, 49
   emotion and, 30–31, 42, 49
   epistemological status of
      ambiguities in, 7, 9, 61–62, 63–64, 90, 111, 119
      complexity of debates about, 110–11
      moral and religious authority of body, 51–57, 112, 115–19
      nonnormative experiences and, 6–7
      religious faith and practices and, 7
   experience and, 52
   as feminine concept, 21, 26, 52
   gender difference and, 9, 11, 19, 112–14, 132n.10
   gender making and, 90, 94, 95, 107–8
   imagination and, roles of body, 7, 9, 42, 61–62, 63–64, 90, 111, 115, 119
   imagined. *See* Body, as sign
   justice and, 112, 129
   knowledge and, 5–7, 19–20
   language and, 51
   lived. *See* Body, as site